THE GRAHAM INDIAN
MUTINY PAPERS

Detachment at Exercise or in Action.

THE GRAHAM INDIAN

MUTINY PAPERS

Edited and introduced by

A.T. Harrison, with an

historiographical essay

by T.G. Fraser

Public Record Office of Northern Ireland

Belfast 1980

ISBN 0 905691 04 0

CONTENTS

SOURCES OF ILLUSTRATIONS, AND MAP REFERENCES

Illustrations obtained from the Graham papers, photographs and family portraits, xi, xvi, xviii, xlvii, 2, 16, 58, 134, 154.

Charles Ball, *The History of the Indian Mutiny*, 2 vols. (London, n.d., c.1858), xxxv, 39, 45, 81, 83.

London Illustrated News (contemporary issues for 1857-8), 4, 9, 18, 77, 94, 122.

George W. Forrest, *History of the Indian Mutiny*, 3 vols. (Edinburgh, 1904- 12), 101.

India Office Library and Records, xl.

Contemporary prints and engravings, xiii, xiv.

National Army Museum, 49.

Public Record Office of Northern Ireland, 1975 British Empire Exhibition, exhibit photograph, xxix.

Maps, geographical extent of mutiny - xxx, Delhi - xli.

Front cover design based upon a photograph of the statue of John Nicholson in Lisburn town centre.

Frontispiece, sketch from a Bengal Army artillery drill manual, c.1845, P.R.O.N.I., D.1567, Staples Collection.

Back cover, photograph of James Graham's commission as lieutenant in the East Indian Queen's Army, 1857, P.R.O.N.I., Mic. 305.

FOREWORD

In 1974, the annual Wiles lectures at Queen's University, Belfast, were on the subject of the British Empire, and the Public Record Office of Northern Ireland was asked to put on an exhibition illustrating the range of its imperial material. The visiting academics and, indeed, we ourselves, were surprised at the quality and quantity of what was displayed, although on reflection it is not so surprising that the prominent role played by Irishmen, particularly Ulstermen, in ruling, defending and simply peopling the British Empire, should have made P.R.O.N.I. a significant and perhaps a major repository of documentation on imperial history. A catalogue of this exhibition was published in July 1975, and serves as a basic guide to P.R.O.N.I.'s imperial holdings. It is now into its second edition.

During the mounting of the exhibition the papers of the Graham family of Lisburn were examined. This collection had been deposited in the Office in 1957 and the cataloguer who produced the initial catalogue of it had duly noted that it contained a mass of material recording the Grahams' long tradition of involvement in Indian military life. He also noted that the sections of Indian correspondence and diaries included a great wealth of references to the Indian Mutiny of 1857. This Indian Mutiny material impressed the members of staff employed in the mounting of the exhibition, in which it featured prominently. This book is the result of a decision to feature it more fully and in a more enduring form.

A great many individuals and institutions gave assistance during the preparation of the book. First, and most important, I should like to thank Miss Joy Graham, who made the original deposit (to which she has subsequently added) of her family's papers, and who has contributed to this book in many ways. Thanks are also due to Dr T. G. Fraser of the New University of Ulster for his scholarly historiographical essay, which places the Graham Papers in the context of other sources for the history of the Indian Mutiny. Other individuals and institutions who have assisted in the preparation of this book include: Mr P. M. Bottomley; Belfast Central Library, reference and newspaper sections; the Marquess of Dufferin and Ava; the India Office Library and Records, especially Dr Richard Bingle; the Linenhall Library, Belfast, especially Mr J. R. R. Adams; Lisburn Historical Society, especially Mr Trevor Neill; Messrs Macdonald & Jane, and Mr Alexander Llewellyn; Mr Simon Meade; the National Army Museum; and the Queen's University of Belfast Library, especially the government publications department.

B. Trainor
Deputy Keeper of the Records

March 1980

GRAHAM GENEALOGY

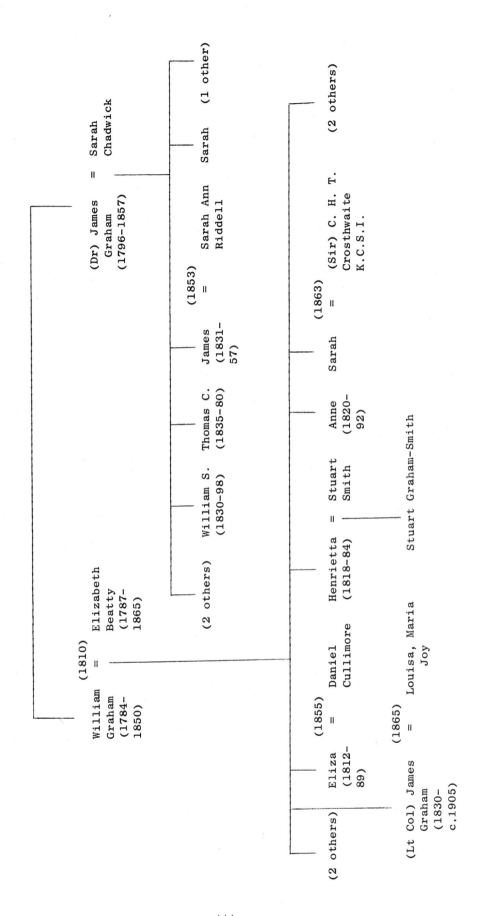

THE GRAHAM FAMILY, JOHN NICHOLSON, AND THE ULSTER-INDIAN CONNECTION

INTRODUCTION

Superficially there seems to be little common ground between Ulster and Indian affairs in 1857. When the topic is examined in detail however a large degree of interaction between the two societies becomes evident. Throughout the history of British India (both pre and post mutiny) Ulstermen were prominent in the affairs of the subcontinent. Ulster was the birthplace of many nabobs, soldiers and administrators who sought their fortunes or made their careers on Indian soil, and many of the collections of family papers on deposit in P.R.O.N.I. contain official, commercial or personal papers of ancestors who served in India in a military or civil capacity, or were involved in Indian trade. The Ulster-Indian connection was crowned in the second half of the 19th century, when two Ulstermen (Sir John Lawrence and Lord Dufferin[1]) held the rank of Governor General. Many Ulster families thus felt personally involved in Indian affairs, and they must have read the mutiny battle reports and casualty lists in the Ulster newspapers with concern. The concern of the editors of these newspapers was, however, of a different kind, as each tried to fit the mutiny into his paper's political stance, which in turn reflected the sectarian bias of his readership.[2]

The reason for the high degree of Ulster involvement in India - which was probably greater than Ulster's proportion of the British population warranted - was that India provided a career outlet for the younger sons of gentry and professional families, who could find few prospects within the limited economy.[3] (Probably for the same reason Anglo-Irishmen and Scotsmen played a disproportionate part in imperial affairs: English society, especially in the relatively prosperous south-east, had the resources to provide for a higher percentage of its gentry and middle class youth than the peripheral and basically rural economies of Ireland and Scotland.) The Graham family originated in Scotland and settled in Ireland some time in the 17th century. By the early 18th century the family was established in the vicinity of Lisburn, then a small market and manufacturing town nine miles south-west of Belfast, and by the turn of the century they owned considerable property in Lisburn town and in the nearby townland of Lisnastrain. The Grahams were one of a group of Lisburn families with a tradition of Indian service; at the time of the mutiny the family had five members in the East India Company's army.[4]

1. _Lord Dufferin's papers including those relating to his Indian viceroyalty are deposited in P.R.O.N.I., reference number D.1071. Some papers have been retained by the Dufferin family and these have been microfilmed, reference number Mic. 22._

2. _This theme is discussed in greater detail in appendix A._

3. _Such a career outlet was of great importance in the pre-birthcontrol age when large middle class families were the norm._

4. _Dr James Graham (1796-1857), entered the East India Company Army as an assistant surgeon in 1820. In 1857 he was serving as superintending military surgeon at Sialkot._

William Stuart Graham (1830-98), entered the East India Company 2nd regiment of light cavalry in 1849.

Large family groups like the Grahams were common to the British community of mid-19th century India. Aventurous and ambitious young men seeking a career, or bored by the prospect of a life of routine employment in Britain and lured by the romance of the east,[5] carved out careers in the military and administrative structures of British India. The sons of such men emulated their fathers and served in India, and their sisters married into other Anglo-Indian families. Family members in Britain used the example and the patronage of relations in India as the means of exporting their surplus off-spring to the subcontinent. Dr Graham was the adventurous young man who laid the foundations of the Graham family's Indian activities. He qualified as a doctor in 1819 and, in 1820, when 23 years of age took up an appointment as an assistant surgeon in the Company's army. Two of his sons died in childhood, but the three who reached manhood, William, James and Tom, all pursued Indian military careers. They were born in India but were educated in Ulster, probably at the Royal School, Dungannon (Co. Tyrone), along with their cousin James. Dr Graham helped his nephew establish himself in India, and James Graham looked upon his uncle as a patron and a trusted adviser well versed in Indian affairs.

The social mechanics of British involvement in India will be familiar to demographers who have studied general patterns of migration, but Anglo-Indian migration exhibited certain idyiosyncratic features, stemming from the fact that most Britons stayed in India only for their

(No. 4 contd): James Graham (1831-57), entered the East India Company 14th regiment of light cavalry in 1849.

Thomas Chadwick Graham (1835-80), entered the East India Company 10th regiment of light cavalry in c.1855.

James Graham (1830-c.1905), entered the East India Company 14th regiment of native infantry in 1850.

The above military details were obtained from the East India Company cadet papers and army lists held by the India Office Library and Records, London.

5. A letter dated 29 August 1861 from Robert Meade (second son of the third Earl of Clanwilliam), a junior official in the Foreign Office, to Lord Dufferin, discussing the careers open to a young man, illustrates this point.

'... If he has good health why should he not try for one of the Civil Service of India appointments? I should certainly have gone in for that had I enjoyed stronger health. That is the only really good career open to a man nowadays that I can see. ...

The upshot of the whole is if your friend is stupid, heavy and humdrum let him bury himself in a government office - he will [?draggle] out his life with as you say a moderate competence and nothing to excite him or disturb the even tenour of his ways. If I had to begin over again I confess between us two I would rather break stones. ...'

P.R.O.N.I. Mic. 22, Dufferin and Ava Correspondence, Reel 6, Vol. XIII.

working lives. They saw their
eventual retirement at 'home' in
Britain as a reward for long
years spent in the trying
environment of the subcontinent.
This form of temporary migration
led to the Anglo-Indian family
being in a permanent state of
limbo, never completely at home
in either Indian or British
society, as if the experience
of the one blighted their
enjoyment of the other. After
years spent longing for
retirement in Britain, away
from the heat, dust, monsoons
and general discomfiture of
India, the old colonel and his
memsahib generally spent their
last years lamenting the cold
and damp of the British
climate, and the poor quality
of British domestic servants
compared to the great army of
Indians who once attended to
their every whim. Many 'old
India hands', bewildered and
searching for the sense of
order and discipline they had

Dr Graham as a young man

known in India were archetypal
Colonel Blimps amidst the rapid
social and political change of late
19th and early 20th century
Britain. Yet, while it is
certainly true that the Anglo-
Indian family was motivated by the
twin ambitions of career and money,
many of those who served in India
did so in no small degree because of
an essentially Victorian sense of
Christian duty. This sense of duty
is reflected by the fact that a
great number of them never returned
to enjoy their retirement but fell
victim to the rigours of the Indian
environment, as the now crumbling

*Dr Graham the ageing Victorian
patriarch*

British graveyards of India testify. This was the social milieu within which the Graham family existed.[6]

The Grahams in 1857 were certainly not out of place in the Punjab and northern India, as two of the most important British officials in this area were Ulstermen: Sir John Lawrence, chief commissioner of the Punjab and John Nicholson, deputy commissioner of Peshawar. Both of these men were members of larger family circles serving in India. John Lawrence was one of three brothers in India.[7] Their mother originally came from Co. Donegal (their father was a military man who had a long record of service in India) and they were educated at Foyle College, Londonderry. Sir Henry Lawrence, who was the equal of his brother John as a civil administrator - he was chief commissioner of recently annexed Oudh at the outbreak of the mutiny - died gallantly leading the defence of the British residency at Lucknow, before he had achieved his full potential in Indian government. George Lawrence, although not of the titanic stature of his brothers, had a relatively successful Indian military career, for which he was created a knight commander of the star of India.

There is doubt over John Nicholson's birthplace. Captain L.J. Trotter, Nicholson's biographer, states that he was born in the Grahams' home town of Lisburn, on 11 December 1822.[8] Obituaries which appeared in

6.   *Plain Tales from the Raj* (London, 1975), edited by Charles Allen, and based upon the excellent British Broadcasting Corporation radio series (composed of interviews with former Anglo-Indians) captures well the split personality of Anglo-Indian society: (1977 paperback edition)

> '... England never ceased to beckon. "We thought England the greatest place on earth ... . We were always talking about home and it was a glorious moment when the mail call was sounded. ... On Sunday morning after church parade we met under the trees on the lawn, the band played and it was very pleasant. Then at twelve o'clock the mail from home arrived and everybody would vanish. You would race back to your bungalow and there would be those longed-for letters from home. ... You lived for that letter day. ..."' p. 195.

> 'A minority went [from India] ... "without a thought, without a pang, without a qualm ... delighted to get away and lose India forever." [Others] went with great regret, taking with them "a nostalgia for sights and sounds and smells" of India.' pp.258-259.

> '"While I was in India, England was always that wonderful country that I had known as a child" ... [but many returned] to find that "the England I had always thought of didn't exist any more."' p. 260.

7.   *George and Henry Lawrence were born in Ceylon where their father was stationed during a period of military service. John Lawrence was born in Yorkshire.*

8.   *Lionel J. Trotter (Captain),* The Life of John Nicholson *(London, 1897), p. 4. Details concerning Nicholson's life have been obtained from Trotter, and from Anthony Bishop's 'John Nicholson in the Indian Mutiny',* The Irish Sword, *journal of the Military History Society of Ireland, Vol VIII, winter 1968, No. 33, pp.277-87.*

Sir Henry Lawrence

Sir John Lawrence

the *Belfast Newsletter* and the *Belfast Daily Mercury*, state that he was born at Virgemont, Dublin, on that date.[9] *The Dictionary of National Biography* records that Nicholson was born in Dublin, on 11 December 1821.[10] His father was a doctor in Dublin, and all sources agree that Nicholson spent most of the first nine years of his life in that city, and then on his father's death his mother (now with seven children) took up residence with relatives in Lisburn. Nicholson, like the Grahams, was educated at the Royal School, Dungannon. He was a moderate scholar and, if not particularly noted for academic work, he was remembered by schoolboy contemporaries for his love of games and schoolboy fights. He took delight in the latter, but from all accounts he usually humbled bullies. Nicholson left Dungannon in December 1838 and, as the eldest boy in the family, it was necessary for him to settle quickly on a career.

In February 1839, he entered the East India Company's army via the patronage of his uncle, Sir James Weir Hogg (another Ulsterman), who had made a forture at the Indian bar, and who, in December 1839, became a director of the Company, (in 1846 he was appointed Company Chairman). His influence in early 1839 was sufficient to secure for his nephew a direct-entry military cadetship. This obviated for the young Nicholson the usual

9.   *Belfast Newsletter 14 November 1857 (reprinted from the Times)*; *Belfast Daily Mercury 14 November 1857*.

10.   *Dictionary of National Biography Vol XIX (Oxford, 1917), pp.462-6.*

cadet attendance at the Company's military college at Addiscombe. He, therefore, sailed direct to India and took up an appointment with the 41st regiment of native infantry. In 1841, he was serving with the 27th regiment of native infantry during one of the periodic wars which plagued British India's relations with the turbulent state of Afghanistan. Nicholson was a member of the garrison at Ghazni - besieged from November 1841 until March 1842, when it was finally forced to surrender - spending the period March to September as a prisoner of the Afghan forces. In September he was rescued by a column under the command of General Pollock, and after the partial destruction of Kabul as a punitive measure, Nicholson took part in the British withdrawal from Afghanistan. On 1 November, at the Afghanistan entrance to the Khyber pass, he met his brother Alexander, who had also joined the Company's army, and, newly arrived in India, had been posted to Pollock's column. Three days later, while riding rearguard for the withdrawing forces, Nicholson discovered Alexander murdered and stripped naked by local tribesmen. In June 1849, another brother, William, serving with the Bombay army, died in mysterious circumstances after either a fall, or an attack by unknown assailants.

Until the outbreak of the mutiny Nicholson held a variety of posts in northern India, both military and civil, and by his ability obtained a succession of promotions until his appointment as deputy commissioner of Peshawar, in November 1856. He served with distinction during the Sikh wars of the 1840s, and due to his powerful personality and reckless courage was even deified by a Hindu teacher as an incarnation of Brahma. A sect of 'Nikalsainis' grew up, much to Nicholson's Christian embarrassment, and, despite harsh treatment at the hands of their god (Nicholson had them whipped and imprisoned to deter them from worshipping him), the sect continued until his death, when some of its leaders committed suicide to be with their master, while others emulated him by accepting Christianity.[11] In 1852, Nicholson was posted to the district of Bannu, which occupied an area slightly smaller than

John Nicholson

Wales, and was bounded by the river Indus and the Afghan frontier. Bannu was renowned as a wild mountainous area peopled by lawless and reportedly untameable tribesmen, but by resolute and dynamic rule Nicholson subdued the area, and forced the local population to live in accordance with his and the Company's law. [12]

Nicholson's crucial role in the suppression of the mutiny is described in section 4 of this introduction, but there remains a strange coincidence in his injury and death to be unfolded (which recalls the death of Alexander). When Nicholson lay dying in the field hospital at Delhi, his brother Charles was brought in from the battle also seriously wounded, and, amidst all the confusion, was placed in an adjacent bed. Charles had an arm amputated and recovered despite the risk of infection under the crude clinical conditions of a mid 19th century field hospital. Out of the four Nicholson brothers who served in India two died and one was maimed without earning more than a passing reference in the annals of Indian history; but John Nicholson who in death '... vanished like a meteor from the scene of his gloriously brief career ...' [13] left a much more enduring mark.

The Grahams, as shown by their letters, knew the Lawrence brothers, and were conversant with their townsman Nicholson's activities. Nicholson, and John and Henry Lawrence, were men of stature who influenced the course of history. Their careers have provided material for the biographer and the historical novelist, and no history of the mutiny is complete without reference to them and their deeds. The Grahams were made of humbler clay. They were passengers, in the events of 1857, playing their roles within a framework in which the Lawrence brothers and Nicholson were determining factors. Indeed Dr Graham's death can be attributed to the policy instioned by Nicholson and John Lawrence of stripping the Punjab of British and loyal Punjabi forces preparatory to the assault on Delhi.[14] Dr Graham's death during the Sialkot rising was a personal tragedy for his family, but only one of many similar tragedies enacted throughout Anglo-Indian society at the time. Nicholson's death at Delhi was however an historic event with numerous repercussions. It removed from the mutiny scene a prominent military leader who had been the main-spring of the British fight to retain control of the Punjab and capture Delhi. If Nicholson had lived, his effect on the post-Delhi stage of military

11.   *The memorial tablet in Lisburn parish church dedicated to Nicholson depicts the storming of Delhi, but Nicholson does not appear on the mural. The traditional explanation is that the 'Nikalsaini' episode had been reported in Lisburn, and had embarrassed the family. Nicholson's mother thus felt it politic to delete any 'idolatrous' portrayal of her son.*

A more modern twist to the 'Nikalsaini' affair was related by the late Brigadier Perry, who wrote that when the British statues were being removed from Delhi in the 1950s he passed the statue of Nicholson just before its demolition. '... A large number of police and workmen were gathered round the statue ... [and Perry] ... asked the Superintendent of Police why they needed armed men there. The man admitted rather sheepishly that "Jan Nikalsayn" had been a very "zubberdust" [fierce] man, and they could not be sure that his spirit would not return to mete out justice to those who disturbed his rest.'

Journal of the British Association for Cemeteries in South Asia (London), Vol. 1. September 1977, No. 1.

12.   *Bannu, originally pacified by Herbert Edwardes, had returned to some of its old ways on his transfer to Jullunder as deputy commissioner. Nicholson finally brought Bannu to heel.*

13.   *Trotter, perface, p.v.*

14.   *See p. xxxv below.*

operations would have been great and, as it was, his death helped provide the British with the inspiration to continue the fight until their rule of India was once more secure. Similarly, as already hinted[15], the death of Henry Lawrence at Lucknow ended the career of a potential governor general of India. In comparison, the most noteworthy 'historical' action of the Grahams during the mutiny was the suicide of Dr Graham's son James during the siege of Lucknow. It is certainly their one act still noted by historians, as it had a '... depressing effect on the whole garrison[16]. ...'

The tomb of James Graham (1831-1857) in Lucknow

        In retrospect the Grahams are thus unimportant as individuals, but their very ordinariness endows them with an historical relevance as typical representatives of Anglo-Indian society during its greatest period of crisis in 1857-8. As Dr Fraser points out this is what makes the letters and papers accumulated by the Grahams during the mutiny valid as documentary source material for historians.[17] But, as well as extending the range of source material for mutiny historians, the Graham papers provide a fascinating view of the complex web of family tradition, patronage, career structure, ambition and financial motivation which governed an Anglo-Indian family's affairs, and which must be of interest to those studying the social organisation of Anglo-India. Dr Fraser also makes the point that transcribed in extenso the Graham papers give the reader a realisation of the human dimension during the mutiny.[18] This point is of importance, as

15.   *p.xii above*

16.   *Surendra Nath Sen, Eighteen Fifty-Seven (Calcutta, 1957), p.216. Christopher Hibbert, The Great Mutiny (London, 1978), p. 241, states that 'Captain [sic] Graham ... shot himself in his bed', during a fit of insanity produced by privation and suffering.*

17.   *p. lv below*

18.   *p. lvii below*

the men of whose affairs historians write (be they the great men of political or military history or the statistical animalcule of social history) were men who ate, drank, laughed, loved, argued and had distinctive personal characteristics.

Thus, Dr Graham emerges from his letters as a pragmatic and somewhat cynical 'old India hand', with firm opinions on all topics, especially the ruthless extirpation of all mutineers. Two of his sons, William and Tom, are portrayed as brave young men caught up in the heady madness of war. William the spendthrift, the schemer, and the lovable rogue of the family, displayed all the bravado of youth in the face of death:

> 'Delhi gone fhut at last, and I was there and had a little to-do in the business. ... But thank God I got all serene out of it, not without one or two nasty patches. One ball through my pugry, and the other a spent ball hit me on the heel. I was riding a 1400 rupee horse which I was in such a state about, I had not time to think of myself. ...'[19]

It is interesting to note that William - perhaps after the sobering effects of the mutiny - retired in the early 1860s, settled down, and even became a justice of the peace on the Isle of Wight. Dr Graham's other son James, the Lucknow suicide, appears from the family correspondence to have been a melancholic, anti-social individual, whose end was in keeping with his personality. There are some references in the correspondence to a quarrel between James and his father, stemming from James's marriage to Sarah Ann Riddell, whom Dr Graham considered beneath the family's social class. Strangely his sister Sarah, who had inherited the resolute character of her father, was the only member of the family with a good word to say for her 'favourite brother' James.[20]

Perhaps, in retrospect, the most important member of the family was Dr Graham's nephew James, for to him we owe the preservation of the documents which form the basis of this publication. An avid family historian and genealogist, in his retirement he organised his papers, and collected and organised the papers of the other members of the family, and carried out a vast amount of genealogical research into the family's origins. Graham, as evidenced by his homeward letters, and by letters he received from his superiors in the commissariat, was a cautious hardworking soldier, and after the mutiny he gained steady promotion, until in 1879, he retired due to ill health with the rank of lieutenant colonel. In retirement Graham settled in Wimbledon and became a pillar of the local community. True to his Ulster Protestant origins and his imperial service, Graham, now an 'old India hand' was a supporter of the Conservative-Unionist cause during the late 19th and early 20th centuries.[21]

19.   *P.R.O.N.I. D.812/14/152 William S. Graham to Daniel Cullimore, 27 September 1857.*

20.   *P.R.O.N.I. D.812/14/170 Sarah C. Graham to Anne Graham, 2 February 1858.*

21.   *Personal details about members of the Graham family mentioned above were obtained from genealogical and personal papers in P.R.O.N.I. D. 812 and P.R.O.N.I. Mic.305. The Indian Mutiny papers which are transcribed in this*

B

Graham's original ordering of his family papers has been preserved as far as possible in this publication, due to the fact that he had the papers arranged in bound volumes (occasionally out of chronological order). For the convenience of researchers wishing to consult the papers in P.R.O.N.I. it has been decided to retain this sometimes inconsistent chronology, in order that the sequential referencing of the documents within the bound volumes is not upset. In the half a dozen or so cases where letters are misplaced chronologically, explanatory notes make this clear to readers.

In the transcriptions of the Graham correspondence and diary modifications of the original punctuation and modernizations of Indian place names have been kept to a minimum, and have only been implemented to aid the reader's understanding of the text. Modern Indian place names have been used elsewhere in the publication.

James Graham (1830-c.1905)

(No. 21 contd): publication only form a small portion of the Graham family papers on deposit in P.R.O.N.I. The remainder of the Graham papers include: long runs of correspondence (some of them from family members serving in India in less troubled times); estate papers; business papers; genealogical papers; and the general trivia collected by a middle class family. The latter is composed of dinner invitations and menus, club and organisation papers (e.g. masonic certificates) etc, which although, unimportant individually, reflect the society in which the family moved in Britain and in India. Three volumes of photographs (retained by the family) have been copied by P.R.O.N.I. and the copies given the reference number T.3263. Many of these photographs were taken by family members in India, and some have been used as illustrations in this publication.

Introduction

THE SIGNIFICANCE OF THE INDIAN MUTINY

It is a general misconception that Britain between the battle of Waterloo in 1815 and the outbreak of the Boer War in 1899 experienced a period of external peace, broken only by the mid century crisis of the Crimean War. The Crimean War was the only 'great power' war Britain fought between the Napoleonic Wars and the First World War, but between 1815 and 1914 Britain was engaged in a series of imperial conflicts[22] of which the most serious, in retrospect (and certainly to Victorians), were the Indian Mutiny campaigns of 1857-9.

The news of the Indian Mutiny, coming so soon after the near disaster of the Crimean War, shocked British public opinion out of its mid century rut of middle class complacency. The Great Exhibition of 1851 had epitomized the confidence of Britain's new industrial society, and it was a basic tenet of this age that there were no limits to scientific, technological and material progress. Another cornerstone of the age's philosophy was that development in these rational spheres of science and industry was paralleled by inevitable evolution in the moral and spiritual fields. It seemed to many that a new prosperous age of peace and security was dawning, and that the benefits of industrial civilization both economic and ethical would soon spread across the globe. Prometheus indeed seemed to be unbound, and the age to be one of improvement.[23] The outbreak of the Crimean War had exploded some of these illusions. The pacific tenor of British public opinion was converted, under the influence of the *Times*, into a bellicose clamour for war. Military conflict was clearly still a force which existed to ravage mankind, and with which the foremost industrial society in the world still had to reckon. Subsequent events on the Black Sea peninsula, however, did not support the view that that society was possessed of any innate superiority in such a conflict. British troops suffered conditions just as appalling as those faced by the soldiers of the other powers involved, and it also became evident that the imbecility of British generals equalled anything exhibited by the high commands of France, Turkey or Russia.

22. *Louis Creswicke, South Africa and the Transvaal War Volume VI (London, c.1902), p. 207 '... The present war is the fortieth war that has taken place during the reign of Queen Victoria. In 1854 there was the Crimea; in 1838, 1849, and 1878 came wars against Afghanistan; four wars against China in the years 1841, 1849, 1856, and 1860; two against the Sikhs in 1845 and 1848; three against the Kaffirs in 1846, 1854, and 1877, three against Burma 1850, 1852, and 1885; nine in India, in 1857, 1860, 1863, 1864, 1868, 1869, 1890, 1895, and 1897; three in Ashantee, 1864, 1873, and 1896; a war against Abyssinia, 1867; a war against Persia, 1852; a war against the Zulus, 1878; a war against the Basutos, 1878; a war in Egypt, 1882; three in the Soudan, 1894, 1896, and 1899; a war with Zanzibar, 1890; a war against the Matabele, 1894; and finally two wars against the Transvaal, 1881 and 1899-1900. ...'*

23. *David S. Landes, The Unbound Prometheus (Cambridge,1969), subtitled 'Technological Change and Industrial Development in Western Europe from 1750 to the present'.*

Asa Briggs, The Age of Improvement 1783-1867 (London, 1959). A general history of British development under the influence of the industrial revolution.

The Indian Mutiny was another hammer-blow which helped to shatter the smugness with which the 1850s had opened.[24] If the Crimean War proved that war had not been banished, then the Indian Mutiny showed that British civilization was not graciously accepted throughout Britain's expanding empire. By mutinying in 1857 the Indian sepoy and the various sections of Indian society who joined the rebellion slapped the face of Britain's confident society. Britain's civilizing imperial mission had been called into question, and a violent reaction resulted in British society. Numerous demands were made, usually in the language of the Old Testament, for swift and bloody revenge. Racialism brutalized and dehumanized the struggle, both on the ground in India, and in the minds of the British public. This trend was strengthened by the (generally fictitious) reports which circulated of sepoy rape and torture of British women and children. Victorian society venerated the matron and her brood of angelic cherubs, and the dusky brutes who violated them were thought to deserve no mercy and generally received none. The Indian Mutiny was remarkable amongst Britain's Victorian wars in that it achieved a degree of totality for the protagonists which was not equalled until the 20th century. This was due to the fact that in many areas affected by the mutiny the British were not just fighting for a simple military victory but for their very survival. There was no possibility of honourable surrender to a gallant and chivalrous foe. The mutineer was in the same predicament. He had committed the greatest crime in the military legal code, and in Indian terms had been disloyal to his salt. The only alternative to victory for both sides was death.

With the inherent savagery of this situation as a backcloth, the story of the mutiny unfolded for the British public like a melodrama, containing as it did many of the elements and characters of that particular dramatic genre so beloved by Victorians. It was seen as a direct clash between good and evil, a view strengthened by the crude equations of colour and morality which most Britons made. The crisis threw up heroes on the British side like Nicholson who performed deeds of courage and daring (and bloody retribution). It also provided Indian villains like the Nana Sahib who in British eyes became the very personification of evil, once the details of the Kanpur massacre became known. The passage of time and the cold eye of historical research have both modified the simplistic starkness of this analysis and reduced heroes and villains alike to men caught in the whirlpool of intense and hectic times. The naive imperialist morality of Victorian society sought to place the blame for the mutiny on an Indian conspiracy. The consensus view which has evolved in the 120 years since the event now sees the mutiny as the result of the complex interaction of westernizing progressive forces, introduced into India by British rule, and the traditional patterns of Indian society. Many of the ideas and trends which stemmed from the British presence proved alien and destructive to the established mores and conventions of India, and this led to a reaction within many sections of Indian society which became disaffected from British rule as they watched the demise of cherished religious or social philosophies and practices, and the undermining of vested interests which were reliant on the maintenance of the status quo. Thus the greased

24.   *J. G. Farrell,* The Siege of Krishnapur *(London,1973). This historical novel of the Indian Mutiny has as one of its main themes the effect of the mutiny upon British middle class confidence, and its shattering of the 1851 Great Exhibition spirit.*

cartridge issue only provided the impetus of revolt - a focus for all the conservative fears of the East India Company's native army, which was one of India's most hidebound centres of traditionalism. When the 3rd native cavalry, the 11th native infantry and the 20th native infantry regiments mutinied at Meerut on Sunday 10th May 1857, they lit fuses which quickly spread mutiny and revolt across northern India.

Thereafter the military development of the mutiny followed a pattern which is quite logical in retrospect. After the initial period of crisis and upheaval the British forces and loyal native troops consolidated their strength, and weeded out any disloyal sepoys within their immediate vicinity. The mutineers if they escaped defeat made for those areas under rebel control. Delhi was paramount amongst these centres and it became the focus of military activity. It was the great symbol of victory or defeat for both sides due to its history, tradition and days of bygone glory. By seizing Delhi the mutineers attempted to adopt the mantle of India's former rulers the Mughals, via the figurehead of the doting confused Bahadur Shah, who although heir to the titles of '... Badshah (emperor) and Ghazi (holy warrior) ...,'[25] had before the mutiny been immersed in the trivia, pointless intrigue and debauchery of an effete court. Once Delhi was again in British hands a great wave of relief swept Anglo-Indian and British society. The *Times* opened its editorial which reported the storming of Delhi with the simple sentence, 'Delhi has fallen. ...'[26] After the long months of suspense these three sober words of print summarized the general public release from anxiety which this news produced. With Delhi secured by British force of arms the mutiny had failed.

In fact the rebellion had had no chance of success. From the start the odds were heavily against the mutineers. The mutiny made a direct challenge to British power, and despite early successes it was destined to failure once Britain had marshalled her resources to meet the threat to her Indian possessions. British rule of India, which was to last for another 90 years, was essential to Britain's status as an imperial power, and this gave her forces a sense of unity and purpose. The rebel forces lacked such cohesion of aim, and the chimera of a Mughal restoration did not provide it, they were a tenuous alliance of diverse conservative groups, each of which had joined the rebellion through a specific grievance against British rule. Thus the causation of the mutiny did little to create unity on the rebel side. The mutiny was not a nationalist war of independence. It was not '... independence for which the heroes of 1857 fought. ...'[27], but for a series of localized issues and aspirations. The mutiny was nationalist only in the sense that it was by its very nature a conflict between Indian and British forces, and such conflicts are inevitable when an imperial power rules the destinies of subject peoples. India had come under British sway due to the fragmentation created by the decline of Mughal power in the 18th century. British rule had imposed unity upon

25. *Sen*, p. 68.

26. *The Times*, 27 October 1857.

27. *Sen*, p. 418. *In the original context of this quote Sen suggests that the mutiny was the embryonic stirring of the struggle for an independent India.*

India and transformed the subcontinent, which had rapidly been degenerating into a purely geographical expression, into a cohesive political and administrative unit. National independence was a post-1789 European concept which was only slowly gaining ground in Europe itself, as witnessed by the failure of the 1848 revolutions. It was certainly not a political ideal which was applicable to the situation of mid-19th century India. Indian society with all its inherent divisions including the great religious divide was not the vehicle or setting for a war of national independence in 1857. It was not until 1885 that India developed an all India nationalist political movement, and it was much later that Indian nationalists progressed from requests for moderate political reforms and increased Indian involvement in the subcontinent's government, to clear and unequivocal demands for swaraj.

The mutiny had started as a spontaneous revolt, and if it possessed any uniformity of pattern this lay in the impromptu nature of the outbreaks in the initial phase. As the mutiny became a reality the divisions within the insurgents' ranks became apparent. There had been no general conspiracy to eject the British from India. If such a consipracy had really existed then there should have been some pre-planned military and administrative blueprint ready to be implemented by the rebels. The area under rebel control was never a homogeneous unit, and there was no coherent overall plan directing events on the rebel side, - it was always a loose amorphous collection of regional rebel groupings in which local leaders and power groups decided on local policies. There was no attempt to establish a centralized state. After the fall of Delhi the mutiny was crushed in a series of military campaigns which lasted until 1859. During these campaigns the British armies and their native allies isolated the various component units of the rebel forces and crushed them one by one. This *modus operandi* in itself shows how disunited the mutineer forces really were.[28] The fact that Britain, especially after the confirmation of her power and authority by the victory at Delhi, could rely on the loyalty of large sections of the Indian population also disproves the war of independence thesis.

The mutiny led to careful examination of the military and governmental structures of British India; in these spheres it had highlighted many glaring deficiencies which were recognised as contributary factors to the rising, and as handicaps to its efficient suppression. These realizations led to major reforms and reorganizations. The most important of these was the abolition of the East India Company, that anachronistic facade of British rule.

Perhaps however the most important effects of the mutiny were subtle and long term. It produced profound effects in the relations between Indians and Britons in India, and on relations between British India and the princely states. It also provided certain historical and political lessons which were of crucial importance for the development of Indian nationalism, and thus for the very relationship between Britain and India. The relevance of the mutiny's impact in these areas of development is more fully discussed in the last section of this introduction.

28. *The disunity of the mutineer forces is highlighted by the fact that the main histories of the mutiny treat the centres of rebel control and the campaigns to defeat them as a separate topics, with specific chapters or sections devoted to each. The historiography of the mutiny does little to enforce the view that the mutiny was a unified war of national independence.*

Introduction

THE CAUSES

Unlike many of his countrymen, Sir John Lawrence, the chief commissioner of the Punjab during the mutiny, did not view the revolt as a treacherous conspiracy against British rule. In a letter written by his secretary to the governor general's secretary on the topic of the trial of Bahadur Shah, Lawrence's views on the causation of the mutiny are presented most lucidly and concisely.[29] They can be summarized as follows: the mutiny began as a spontaneous revolt initiated by the issue of the greased cartridge; the greased cartridge affair strengthened an already existing feeling of deep discontent which prevailed in the East India Company's sepoy army; when the successes of the Meerut and Delhi mutineers became known, sepoy regiments throughout northern India rose in hopeful emulation; various long-discontented and disaffected groups within Indian society joined forces with their uniformed countrymen, but the rebellion never became general even in the areas of rebel control, as the fatalistic peasantry viewed the upheaval and subsequent return of British rule as they would natural disasters. Lawrence's view of the causation and early period of the mutiny was amongst the most accurate of contemporary assessments, but he placed too much emphasis upon the greased cartridge, and too much blame upon Muslim ambition. He also underestimated the general feeling of discontent in traditional India.

To place Lawrence's views in their proper context the longstanding and subtle causes of the mutiny must be examined, and their slow maturity traced until 1857. During the 18th century, when Britain was engaged on the conquest of India and the commercial exploitation of this new eastern sphere of influence, those Britons involved in Indian affairs were too busy carving out military careers and fortunes to consider the deeper implications posed by British rule of India. Britain thus assumed responsibility for India's government without any definite sense of purpose or direction in the subcontinent's administration. By the 1830s British intellectuals, evangelicals, politicians and social reformers had become acutely concerned that British rule of India was not based on any philosophical or moral principles but on a series of political expedients. This realisation (which in many groups especially those of a religious nature became almost a sense of guilt) resulted in a series of reforms which attempted to westernize various aspects of Indian administration, law and education.[30] Macaulay in one of the most influential statements of the new attitude towards India made the following comment on the need for western education.

> '... To sum up ... I think it clear that we are not fettered by the Act of Parliament of 1813; that we are not fettered by any pledge, expressed or implied [to use government grants for the upkeep of traditional Indian educational establishments]; that we are free to employ our funds as we choose, that we ought to employ them in teaching what it is best worth knowing, that English is better worth knowing than Sanscrit or Arabic; that the natives are desirous to be taught English, and are not desirous to be taught Sanscrit or Arabic;

29.   *See appendix B.*

30.   *G. D. Bearce, British Attitudes Towards India 1784-1858 (Oxford, 1966), pp. 153-241.*

that neither as the languages of law nor as the languages of religion, have Sanscrit and Arabic any peculiar claim to our engagement; that it is possible to make the natives of this country thoroughly good English scholars, and that to this end our efforts ought to be directed. ...'[31]

The reasoning behind such a viewpoint was that all traditional Indian administrative, political and social structures were anachronisms which should be swept away and replaced by structures based on progressive western precedents. The reforms instituted during this period in India were thus based upon utilitarian cultural arrogance.

British public opinion was also alienated from India's religions by reports of such practices as suttee which were carried on in the name of religion. Indian religion naturally offended the sensibilities of British Christian morality when Hinduism was discussed in such emotive and western orientated terms as in the following quotation:

'... What can we think of the advocates and abettors of a religion which lends its sanction to such a barbarous rite as that of human sacrifice [the writer is here discussing the Hindu custom of suttee]? It is in truth a strange anomaly in the moral organization of man, that extremes should be so apt to meet - that some of the best qualities of the human heart [religious sentiments], by being forced to an unnatural extension, should so often gradually advance towards deformity until they partake of those very qualities which are diametrically opposed to them. When they approach almost to a point of contact, the good frequently imbibes the taint of the evil, until they finally merge in one. The fastidious mercy of the Hindoo, which is carried to such a pitch of extravagance, save in observing the ordinances of his sanguinary ritual, is so microscopic, if I may be allowed the term, that he would shrink from destroying the most noxious reptile, or even the minutest animalcule which floats in the mote of a sunbeam, were he conscious of extinguishing animal life; and yet there is not a more cold-hearted villain alive than your merciful Hindoo. He would smile at the death-pang of a stranger to his idols; he would exult at the most horrible torture that could be inflicted upon one who denied the supremacy of Brahma, the judgements of Siva, and the avatars [incarnations] of Veeshno. He is only the most civilized of savages. ...'[32]

With the introduction of western modes of education, administration and the suppression of suttee and thuggee, traditional India was visibly coming under attack by forces introduced into India by British rule, and by the machinery of government itself.

During the early period of British rule, Britons employed in India were not so antagonistic towards traditional India. These men were prepared to adopt and countenance Indian customs. Many of them, far from home and with no contact with British female society, took Indian mistresses

---

31.   *Christine E. Dobbin, Basic Documents in the Development of Modern India and Pakistan 1835-1947 (London, 1970), pp. 15-18, quotes at length Macaulay's minute: The Necessity of English Education, 2 February 1835.*

32.   *The Oriental Annual 1834 (London, 1833), pp. 98-99.*

and thus assimilated Indian ideas and conventions. Under the influence of the utilitarian and Christian evangelical movements, this situation altered radically. Britons serving or working in India became alienated from Indian concepts and practices. They began to cut themselves off from Indian social life and to withdraw into Anglo-Indian social circles, which rapidly became replicas of middle class Britain. One of the most important factors aiding this development was the large influx into India of British women who came in search of husbands, and who, when married to Anglo-Indian soldiers or administrators intensified the alienation of Britons and Indians. British women tended to view all things Indian as alien and vaguely evil and they influenced their menfolk in the same direction. Dr Graham in a letter to his nephew James Graham listed the various accomplishments needed by any young lady who came out to India with the annual 'fishing fleet', as one of James's sisters was thinking of doing. This letter shows how sophisticated and bourgeois Anglo-Indian society had become, as Dr Graham advises James to dissuade his sister from wasting her time and money on such a trip, when she evidently lacks the necessary social graces.

> '... Almost all the girls who come to this country tho' but half educated, have a few superficial accomplishments which fit them for the society they are intended for, and they have brass and impudence which gives them conversational powers and with training at home they enter a ballroom as if accustomed to society from their infancy. These qualifications I fear are entirely wanting with Sarah. An easy indifference in manner and movement in society or in a ballroom require some training and experience, and your sister Sarah has had none, and I am persuaded if she could settle at home her happiness would be greater than it ever could be in this country. ...'[33]

Paradoxically as contact between the two societies gradually diminished British missionary attempts to convert Indians from their indigenous creeds to Christianity intensified. This however did not improve relations between the two societies as it was based upon the assumption of British superiority. Missionary activity was largely unsuccessful in that relatively few Indians accepted the Christian faith, but successful in widening the gulf between the British and Indian communities, as it provided evidence of another radical difference between the two cultures. James Graham in a number of letters to his sister places part of the blame for the mutiny on the disruptive influence of missionaries. He accuses them of creating disquiet in the native mind and also of failing to live up to the high ideals they presented to the natives.

> '... Then your Exeter Hall[34] people send out a lot of missionaries who never attempt to convert by setting the people a good example. They merely look after their own pockets, and trying to make as many squabbles as they can amongst both Europeans and natives. Don't believe one word you ever see in a missionary's report. It is all cooked up for the English palate, a mass of lies. I know myself one missionary who is a pork butcher, and instead of saving souls is employed saving bacon. I declare most solemnly that every pice given

---

33.   *P.R.O.N.I., D.812/10/B/2, Dr James Graham, Sialkot, to his nephew James Graham.*

34.   *The evangical centre during the Victorian age. It was situated on the Strand in central London.*

for missionary purposes in this country is a sin, much better to spend your money when you have it, or to give [it] away in alleviating the distress, and converting the miserable outcasts from humanity with which all our large cities at home are filled. The Exeter Hall people have also been doing their best to force education upon a people not ready to receive it, then the people's minds are bothered with everything that can disturb their peace. ...'[35]

Disaffection against British rule was thus developing within traditional India, and a series of government actions alienated certain aristocratic leaders, who later during the mutiny provided the rebel forces with figureheads, and formed power elites. Britain during her conquest of India had not assumed control of all of the subcontinent. She took power in those areas which were of strategic or commercial importance, but if a princely state did not fall into one of these categories then the British administration had been prepared to allow it to retain independence in its internal government as long as it remained loyal to British rule, and did not behave too outrageously in its domestic affairs. This situation changed during the governor generalship of Lord Dalhousie (1847-56) who saw annexation of the princely states not only as a means of extending British power, but also as a means of spreading reform and the benefits of British civilization. Dalhousie was a man with a sense of mission, and his position as governor general meant that he could actively initiate Indian reform. With few constraints on his power he was in effect able to play the part of the enlightened despot. He,

'... did everything in his power to promote popular education; suppressed thuggism; successfully grappled with the crime of dacoity in British India and checked infanticide in the native states, while he improved the controlling machinery in some of the most important departments [of government]. ...'[36]

With such reforming zeal and energy Dalhousie was not the sort of man to assuage the fears of traditional India, as moderation was not a prominent feature of his nature.

'... He was unquestionably a man of a masterful disposition and intolerant of opposition when satisfied that his own view was right. He was tenacious, at times perhaps over-tenacious, in maintaining his own authority, when any attempt was made to interfere in matters which he deemed to lie within his proper province. ...'[37]

Dalhousie's policy of annexation was instituted on a large scale and the following states amongst others were brought under British sway; the Punjab, Satara, Jhansi, Tanjore, Nagpur, Sambalpur and Oudh, and the greatest of these was Oudh. The aristocratic houses of these states who

35.   *P.R.O.N.I., D.812/14/139, 25 June 1857, James Graham, Landour, to his sister Anne Graham.*

36.   *Dictionary of National Biography, Vol XVI (London, 1922 edition), essay on Dalhousie, p. 698.*

37.   *ibid.*

thus lost their *raison d'etre* were not the only Indian factions who were antagonized and upset by this policy. When a state was annexed the reforms which had been instituted in British India were introduced into the newly acquired territory. This heightened the discontent of the annexed state. In British India the reforming westernizing process, although it caused a great deal of disquiet and disruption, was still softened by the long background of British rule and innovation. In the annexed states reforms were instituted by well meaning 'levelling' administrators, who viewed their task as that of dragging the society of the state from the depths of feudalism into the modern age. Reform thus introduced greatly upset the social, religious, economic and political harmony of the annexed states. Certain factions and classes within these states were deeply antagonized, especially the landowners, as British administrators were extremely keen on reforming native systems of land tenure. They viewed indigenous landholding systems in a naive way, with tyrannical landlords and oppressed peasants the basic components of their analysis. The systems they introduced were highly legalistic, and these proved unpopular with peasant and landlord alike. The new systems were inelastic and impersonal and often took little account of such vagaries as bad harvests, whereas the old systems had allowed plenty of scope for the development of human relationships and traditional practices which are so important in a peasant society. Under the old systems there certainly existed grasping oppressive landlords but there also existed landowners prepared to compromise and grant rent reductions on account of crop failures, etc.;

> '... the landlord had been human; he would grant delay if hail had slashed the crop, if locusts or rust or blight had taken their share; he would lend money for a wedding; he would take something on account. But the Government man - you have to pay standing up! No time to sit down and talk it over; no gossip, no bargaining, no allowance for that lawsuit or that long illness. ...'[38]

When Oudh (one of the most prestigious of the princely states) was annexed in 1856 on the pretext of the King of Oudh's misgovernment (despite traditional loyalty and support for the British presence in India), the landowners of this state feared that a reforming administration would introduce measures destructive of their way of life. Their fears were justified, and the new land tenure system introduced here proved alien. A large number of the sepoys of the Bengal Army were recruited in Oudh, and many of these men were small landowners. With this additional grievance the Oudh sepoys played a prominent part in the mutiny.

The princely rulers who were left in control of their states had no peace of mind, as many felt that their states would be next on the list of additions to British territory. For all those conservatively minded Indians frightened by the decline of their established ways of life under the impact of the new ideas and forces introduced into India by British rule, the policy of annexation confirmed that the British rulers were determined to revolutionize Indian society.

---

38.   Philip Mason, *A matter of Honour* (London, 1974), p. 252. *Mason also in this section of his history of the Indian army discusses the activities of the 'levelling' British administrators.*

Introduction

The East India Company army was influenced by all of the fears and discontent which were creating the rift between traditional India and Anglo-India. Many of these general apprehensions were intensified by certain features of military life, and the sepoy had many anxieties which were purely his own. The mercenary soldier had an honourable place in Indian society, within both the Hindu and Muslim communities in which he was part of important social elites, and British attacks upon traditional India threatened his elitism. The British had employed Indian troops since their earliest military involvement in the subcontinent. In this they followed the precedent set by the Mughals who had arrived as invaders and then utilized local military forces to maintain their empire. The morale of the East India Company's sepoy army had been adversely affected by the reverses it had suffered in the wars against Afghanistan, and the Sikhs of the 1840s. During these campaigns the sepoys observed that the British regiments who accompanied them were not invincible, and could suffer defeat at the hands of orientals.

The sepoy army of the East India Company, which was steeped in tradition, had time-honoured concepts of loyalty and duty which governed the relationship between British officers and native troops. Under the impact of the various factors which were dividing Briton and Indian these old-established loyalties were disintegrating. The British officer, who had formerly respected his men's religious beliefs and practices, began to find them offensive. Non-interference with the religious faith of sepoys had always been a central theme of British Indian policy, but the growing influence of evangelical Christianity in Britain itself which lent moral support to Indian missionary activities radically altered this situation. Many officers with evangelical leanings realising the depth of support they could expect from home, disobeyed their orders to refrain from proselytising and were guided by their consciences if not their common sense. Rumours that the British intended to launch a campaign of conversion amongst the sepoys began to circulate within the native army. It was said that army food was being contaminated so that the sepoys would lose caste and then be forced to accept Christianity. One of the most insidious of these rumours was that bone meal was being mixed with the flour supplied to the sepoys. A number of other grievances added to the growing disaffection of the native army. Various traditional bounties paid to the sepoy for service under certain conditions, were removed, and it also appeared as though he would be forced to serve overseas in future British wars. This was a great source of worry to the sepoy, as ocean travel for high-caste Hindus entailed the loss of caste. In the light of these rumours, and fears, the defiling greased cartridge, was only the most serious in a succession of issues, which disconcerted the sepoy mind.

Perhaps the best conclusion of any study of the causes of the mutiny is Bacon's general observation on the nature of *Seditions and Troubles*,

> '... The causes and motives of seditions are, innovation in religion, taxes, alteration of laws and customs, breaking of privileges, general oppression, disbanded soldiers, factions grown desperate; and whatsoever in offending people joineth and knitteth them in a common cause. ...'[39]

39. *Bacon, essay entitled,* Seditions and Troubles, *quoted as a preface to Vol I, Sir John Kaye,* History of the Sepoy War 1857-8 *(London, 1865).*

THE COURSE OF THE MUTINY

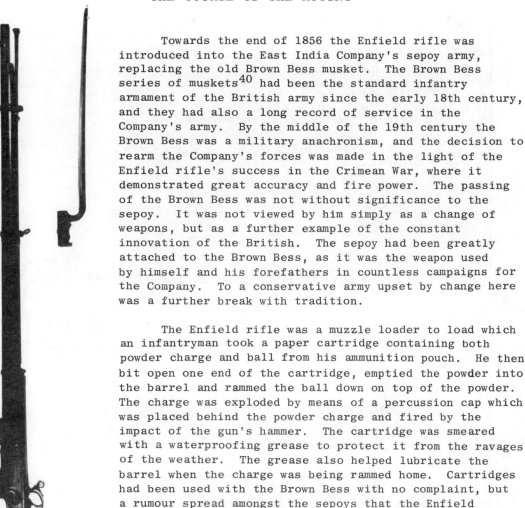

Towards the end of 1856 the Enfield rifle was introduced into the East India Company's sepoy army, replacing the old Brown Bess musket. The Brown Bess series of muskets[40] had been the standard infantry armament of the British army since the early 18th century, and they had also a long record of service in the Company's army. By the middle of the 19th century the Brown Bess was a military anachronism, and the decision to rearm the Company's forces was made in the light of the Enfield rifle's success in the Crimean War, where it demonstrated great accuracy and fire power. The passing of the Brown Bess was not without significance to the sepoy. It was not viewed by him simply as a change of weapons, but as a further example of the constant innovation of the British. The sepoy had been greatly attached to the Brown Bess, as it was the weapon used by himself and his forefathers in countless campaigns for the Company. To a conservative army upset by change here was a further break with tradition.

The Enfield rifle was a muzzle loader to load which an infantryman took a paper cartridge containing both powder charge and ball from his ammunition pouch. He then bit open one end of the cartridge, emptied the powder into the barrel and rammed the ball down on top of the powder. The charge was exploded by means of a percussion cap which was placed behind the powder charge and fired by the impact of the gun's hammer. The cartridge was smeared with a waterproofing grease to protect it from the ravages of the weather. The grease also helped lubricate the barrel when the charge was being rammed home. Cartridges had been used with the Brown Bess with no complaint, but a rumour spread amongst the sepoys that the Enfield cartridge was greased with a mixture of cow and pig fat. Contact with such a concoction would of course have broken the caste of high caste Hindu sepoys, and offended the religious sensibilities of Muslim members of the Company's army. It is believed that the rumour started at the military training depot and munitions centre at Dum Dum in West Bengal, where supplies of cartridges were produced, and selected sepoy detachments trained in Enfield rifle drill. The news of the repugnant cartridges spread rapidly from regiment to regiment through the various cantonments of India, until every sepoy was aware of the new threat to his religion.

A breech loading conversion of the Enfield rifle c.1865

The original cartridges which accompanied the shipment of Enfield rifles from Britain, were undoubtedly coated with a tallow which contained cow and pig fat, and the early batches of cartridges manufactured in India

40.   *The term Brown Bess was a colloquialism for a number of different designs of musket, c.1730-1840.*

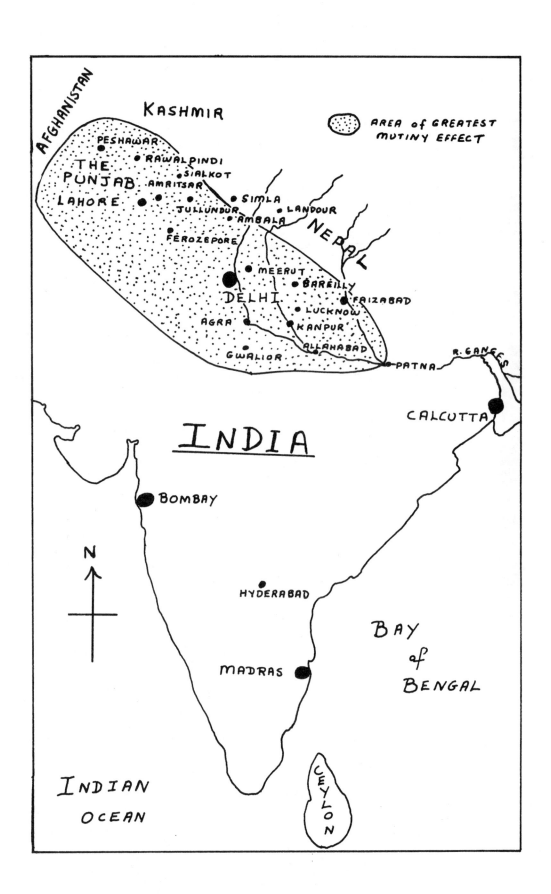

were also probably greased with a similar substance. Despite the growing
rift between the sepoys and their British officers, officers in many
regiments realised their men's misgivings over the new cartridges. On
27 January 1857 a general order was issued that the greased cartridges
stored in the various munitions depots were to be used only by British
troops stationed in India. The sepoy regiments were to grease their own
cartridges with bees-wax or vegetable oil, or some similar inoffensive
material. The damage, however, had been done. The sepoy, Hindu or Muslim,
looked upon the greased cartridge affair as a direct attempt by the
military authorities and the British administration to destroy his religion,
thus forcing him to accept Christianity as his only spiritual alternative.
The order allowing the sepoys to grease their own cartridges was clear
enough to the Company's British officers, who could rationalize the issue
as a typical blunder by the ordnance department, which had failed to make
any allowance for Indian religious scruples. The sepoy in the prevailing
fearful attitude of traditional India did not view things so analytically.
Seeing the episode as an attempt to subvert his faith he regarded the
change in military orders as confirmation of his suspicions; it was a plot,
which had been uncovered. The sepoy also began to suspect that, instead
of the blatantly polluting mixture of cow and pig fat, the cartridges were
now being smeared with some covert agent of defilement which he could not
detect.

Many regiments began to have qualms about using any sort of cartridge
at all, and as the sepoy lines in many stations buzzed with rumour and
seethed with discontent there was talk of refusal to accept the cartridges
greased or not. On 26 February at Berhampur the 19th native infantry pre-
empted an attempt to issue them with a batch of suspect cartridges, by
seizing their arms and preparing to defend themselves. The officers of the
regiment after an attempt to harangue the sepoys into submission made no
effort to force the issue, due to a lack of British troops in the area who
could overawe the sepoys. The sepoys realising the momentous nature of
the step they were about to take stopped short and returned to normal duty.
The regiment was later marched to Barrackpur where British troops were
stationed and here the 19th native infantry suffered the ignominy of
disbandment. The feeling amongst the sepoys generally was at this point
more inclined to disobedience than open mutiny. The Berhampur incident was
however crucial in its effects on other sepoy regiments as the men of the
19th native infantry,

> '... in the eyes of their brother sepoys ... had already become
> heroes and martyrs. In refusing the accursed cartridge they had
> done no wrong. Their only offence was loyalty to their faith and a
> faithless government was on that account going to inflict on them the
> greatest humiliation that a soldier could suffer [disbandment]
> ...'.[41]

The first violent act of the mutiny is generally regarded as the
incident which occurred at Barrackpur on 29 March when Mangal Pande[42] a
sepoy of the 34th native infantry (one of the most disaffected regiments)

41. *Sen, p. 49.*

42. *British troops after the outbreak of the mutiny immortalized Pande
by calling the rebels 'Pandies'.*

under the influence of bhang or opium fired on a number of British officers. Pande was arrested by fellow sepoys after trying to shoot himself and was court-martialled and hanged. Throughout April and May numerous regiments and military stations became infected with the spirit of insubordination. On 13 April a general order was issued giving the sepoys the further concession that in future the cartridge could be opened with the hands and not the teeth. This did little to mollify the sepoys' inflamed feelings. The 34th native infantry were disbanded at Barrackpur on 4 May, and in the early part of the month Sir Henry Lawrence resolutely nipped in the bud an attempt by the 7th Oudh irregular native infantry to stir up trouble at Lucknow. Any one of these, or a host of other incidents had the potential to provide the flashpoint for general mutiny and isurrection. All the factors for rebellion were present at each of these events, but perhaps their combination was wrong, or perhaps one or two officers in each regiment managed to retain enough respect amongst the sepoys to reassure and restrain them from open rebellion. Whatever the reasons these incidents passed peacefully and a fragile normality continued, as the sepoy army remained ostensibly loyal if increasingly sullen.

Mutiny and rebellion could not however be forestalled indefinitely. On 9 May, 85 troopers of the 3rd native cavalry stationed at Meerut had appeared at a punishment parade. On 24 March they had refused to accept a batch of suspect cartridges and the punishment parade was held to impress upon the other native troops at Meerut[43] the serious consequences of such behaviour. The troopers were stripped of their military insignia, fettered hand and foot and then marched off to begin varying terms of imprisonment (5-10 years) to which a court martial had sentenced them. The following day was a Sunday and the British at Meerut settled down to the routine of a typical Indian sabbath. The sepoys, however, were not in the mood for a return to normality, and their lines[44] were the scene of heated debate as men from all three native regiments and their camp followers discussed the fears they held for their religion and traditions, and the fate of their erstwhile colleagues. The remaining troopers of the 3rd native cavalry began to talk about attempting to free their imprisoned brethren, and in the early evening words were transformed into actions when some sowars broke into the civil jail and released their comrades. The remainder of the native troops seized weapons and a general mutiny ensued. The sepoys were aided by their camp followers, and disreputable elements from Meerut and the surrounding countryside. Despite warnings from native officers that a rising was imminent the British had been caught unawares. The night of the 10th and the dark hours of the morning of the 11th were spent by many of the sepoys in an orgy of murder (of British military personnel and civilians) and arson, although small detachments remained loyal out of personal attachment to British officers in whom they had faith. The rioting and violence was extremely dispersed and this made it difficult for the British forces who were disunited and without coherent leadership to come to grips with any mutineer bands. By dawn the mutineers had drifted away towards Delhi, and the British still without effective leaders, counted the cost of the night's mayhem instead of making pursuit. A strong British

43.   *The 11th native infantry, the 20th native infantry, and the remainder of the 3rd native cavalry.*

44.   *The 'sepoy lines' were the lines of huts where the sepoys lived on an Indian military station.*

force was stationed at Meerut and if the mutineers had been pursued and defeated the mutiny might have been contained, and much bloodshed and horror averted.

When the mutineers arrived in Delhi they told of the murders they had committed at Meerut and of the weakness of the British, who had offered little resistance. Their news brought a simmering pot to the boil. The discontent of traditional India had a certain piquancy in Delhi the capital of the old Mughal Empire, where the titular emperor Bahadur Shah resided. Rumours had circulated in the city that 1857, the centenary of the battle of Plassey would see the restoration of Mughal power. There were few British troops in Delhi, but a considerable number of sepoy regiments were stationed here, and soon the Meerut and Delhi sepoys and the city mob were engaged in killing any Britons they could find. Whilst this massacre was taking place some of the mutineers forced their way into Bahadur Shah's presence and asked him to accept leadership of the rebellion. The old man vacillated, as he did not believe the rebels could succeed, and expected that the Meerut force of British troops would soon arrive and take their vengeance. When this did not happen by nightfall the pressures grew too great and Bahadur Shah reluctantly accepted the nominal leadership of the rebellion, for he remained as powerless under the rebel regime as he had done whilst a pensioner of the British. He became a puppet at a court at which his sons, courtiers and rebel military leaders aspired to power. Delhi was the fulcrum of the mutiny, as if the rebels held it they could use its former grandeur and history to justify their war against the British. The British on the other hand had to capture Delhi to prove that they still had both the power and ability to rule India. Rebellion spread quickly from Delhi and Meerut to various towns and areas of Northern India.[45] Sepoy regiments rose and after committing murder and pillage in the neighbourhood of their local cantonment, marched with their bands usually playing tunes the British had taught them to the nearest rebel held area.

British forces were besieged in Agra and Lucknow, and a host of minor stations, many in the great centre of rebellion that developed in the state of Oudh, which had been so rudely treated by the British. Even in these areas support for the rebellion was not complete, as many local landowners and princes waited to see if the Company's star really had fallen before committing themselves.

It was crucial for the British to retain control of the Punjab, as it was strategically placed to the north-west of Delhi, and straddled the frontier with Afghanistan, and it was by no means unlikely that the Afghan tribes would take the opportunity offered by British weakness during the mutiny to attack and plunder northern India. There were a disproportionate number of sepoy regiments stationed in the Punjab, partly to offset the Afghan threat, but also because the British authorities felt that their hold on the homeland of the warlike Sikhs was insecure. The Punjab was a recent annexation to British territory (1849), and the Sikhs had been beaten but not bowed in the hostilities that had preceded annexation. On the eve of the mutiny there were approximately 60,000 Company troops stationed in the Punjab (36,000 sepoys and 24,000 Europeans[46]). The rapid spread of the

45. *See map p. xxx.*

46. *Sen*, p. 327.

C

mutinous contagion from Meerut and Delhi to Oudh and throughout northern and central India placed Sir John Lawrence, chief commissioner of the Punjab, in a dilemma. He quickly grasped the fact that the fate of Delhi was of paramount importance, and he decided that it was his duty to do all in his power to ensure the capture of the city. Lawrence early in the mutiny urged the uncertain commander-in-chief, General Anson, to attack the mutineer forces at Delhi with all speed by asking the rhetorical question:

> '"Reflect on the history of India. Where have we failed, when we acted vigorously? Where have we succeeded, when guided by timid counsels?"'[47]

To aid in the capture of Delhi Lawrence concluded that he had to release British forces from the Punjab to serve with the investing armies surrounding the city. He had however to balance the needs of the Delhi force with the essential requirements of Punjab security (although at one stage he considered withdrawing from the Peshawar frontier area altogether), and in conjunction with his senior Punjab officers[48] Lawrence developed a policy which in the event squared all the corners, but it was a close run thing.

The central theme of this Punjab policy was the ruthless suppression of any outbreaks of mutiny which occurred in the Punjab, and the forestalling of potential mutiny. Mutinous regiments were hunted down and summarily and mercilessly dealt with. During the period May-August 1857 the Punjab scene was dominated by the shadow of the gallows, the sharp report of firing squad rifles and the horrors of 'blowing away' parties.[49] Lawrence and his subordinates took a wide brief when it came to forestalling mutiny, and many regiments who had shown no outward signs of disaffection were disarmed and disbanded along with regiments of obviously doubtful loyalties. To facilitate this end a moveable column[50] was established which

---

47.   *Mason*, p. 283. Alexander Llewellyn, *The Siege of Delhi* (London, 1977), pp. 69-70, quotes Charles Nicholson (brother of the more famous John) as making a similar analysis to Anson in a more jocular manner. '"Clubs are trumps not spades. When in doubt play a big one."' Anson a noted gambler was thus advised to attack forcefully and not to begin a long siege campaign.

48.   Lawrence's main subordinates in the Punjab included: John Nicholson, deputy commissioner of Peshawar, Herbert Edwardes, commissioner of Peshawar, Robert Montgomery (another Ulsterman from Co. Donegal), judicial commissioner of the Punjab, Colonel (later Brigadier) Neville Chamberlain, first commander of the Punjab moveable column. Chamberlain and Nicholson both later served with distinction at Delhi.

49.   The Mughals had introduced into India this form of execution whereby the condemned was tied to the mouth of a cannon and then 'blown away' by the firing of a blank charge of powder. This grisly spectacle was supposed to have a better deterrent effect than hanging or shooting, and was also felt to be less conducive to Hindu reincarnation and to Muslim entry to paradise. Blowing away executions were prevalent during the early period of the mutiny as salutary measures of stern justice, but were later dispensed with for, as John Nicholson reasoned, they were a waste of good powder, see A. Bishop, *The Irish Sword*, No. 33, 1968, p. 283.

50.   A highly mobile force composed of British troops (including officers from disbanded sepoy regiments), civilians (hastily placed under arms) and loyal Indians (largely Punjabis). Chamberlain commanded this force until mid-June 1857 when he was ordered to Delhi. Nicholson was his replacement.

traversed the Punjab by a series of forced marches seizing the initiative against mutinous and 'suspected' regiments. Sepoy regiments in outlying stations realised that the best fate they could expect was the disgrace of disbandment. This realisation fanned any embers of disaffection which existed within such regiments, and they often decided that if they were to be tarred with the brush of disloyalty they might as well earn the obloquy by open rebellion. This is what happened at Sialkot on 9 July. Here the 9th light cavalry were the instigators of the rising, as they had obtained information of the fate of other 'loyal' regiments who had been disbanded. They had also heard that the 14th native infantry had resisted disarmament and had been almost completely wiped out at Jhelam. The sepoys of the 46th native infantry (the other regiment stationed at Sialkot) were largely passive spectators to the mutiny, and they protected many of their officers from injury during the disturbance. Both regiments indeed displayed a general reluctance to go the whole hog and indulge in bloody massacre. The Sialkot mutineers killed only male members of the British community (including Dr Graham[51]), and the murder of a woman and her child during the rising was committed by a low caste flogger from the local jail. At Sialkot the policy of seizing the initiative rebounded upon the British authorities. Here the two sepoy regiments decided to strike the first blow, as with Nicholson on the march with the moveable column they felt they had no alternative than '... to smite or be smitten ...'.[52]

The death of Dr Graham

51. *See appendix C for a transcription of a report from the* Times, *31 August 1857, which describes the Sialkot mutiny and the death of Dr Graham.*

52. Sen, *p. 337.*

Introduction

From Lawrence's viewpoint the policy he followed - despite its injustice to many 'loyal' sepoy regiments, and its inherent danger of forcing such regiments into mutiny - was correct. With every mutinous regiment destroyed, or regiment of suspected loyalty disbanded the security of the Punjab was proportionately increased. Also, he had to impress upon the Sikhs and other martial peoples of the Punjab that the British were not losing their control of India. The Punjabis, especially the Sikhs, harboured a deep hatred for the purbiah sepoys of the Company's army, but Lawrence could not be certain during the early days of the mutiny whether any act of weakness on the British part would result in a general rebellion and attempt to re-establish a Sikh state. His resolute policy however greatly impressed the inhabitants of the Punjab, and they began to offer themselves for service under the British against the mutineers. As the mutiny crisis passed in the Punjab Lawrence was therefore increasingly able to send British and Punjabi forces to strengthen the Delhi besiegers.

Right from the earliest days of the mutiny, when the reinforcements coming from the Punjab had been merely a trickle the British officers from this area had proved to be the most energetic and daring leaders in the British encampment on the ridge at Delhi. Service in the potentially explosive Punjab, with its frontier problems, its volatile and feuding militaristic tribes and peoples had kept the Punjab officers active in both limb and mind, and in this they differed radically from many of their non-Punjabi peers. General Anson died of cholera on 27 May before he could put into effect Lawrence's advice to make a quick attack upon Delhi. Anson's natural inclination had been to marshal his forces carefully (collecting reinforcements in men and materials) before he launched an attack against the stout defensive walls of the city. General Barnard, who succeeded him as commander of the Delhi field force, was also cautious, and uncertain of his own ability. Against his better judgement four plans for an attack were drawn up during his tenure of command. However, the first attack, which was to take place on the night of 12 June was aborted at the last minute because of basic planning errors, and none of the other plans came so close to fruition. Barnard followed Anson's example and died of cholera on 5 July. He was succeeded by General Reed, an aged invalid, who quickly realised his own incapacity and resigned the command on 16 July. Brigadier Archdale Wilson the next commander of the Delhi force showed no more resolution than his predecessors, and things drifted inconclusively through the remainder of July and into early August. On 7 August Nicholson arrived at Delhi in advance of the Punjab moveable column which had been ordered south by Lawrence. Nicholson's effect upon the rather lethargic atmosphere of the Delhi camp was electric. He demanded that concrete plans for an attack be laid, and viewed all counsels of caution as prevarication. The older senior officers at Delhi viewed Nicholson as an arrogant young upstart, and his cold puritanical nature did not help endear him to them. To the lower ranks (British and Punjabi) and to the younger officers Nicholson was a hero, and he rapidly became the leader of the 'action' party who favoured an attack. Nicholson's views in retrospect were becoming more and more valid with every passing day in August, and the arguments for prudence increasingly out of touch with the military realities of the situation. The original argument in favour of a cautious policy had been based on the premise that the larger the rebel force allowed to collect at Delhi the better, as the more rebels defeated here, by a suitably reinforced British force, the fewer would have to be dealt with in troublesome secondary campaigns. By August the rebel force at Delhi had reached its optimum size and divisions within the rebel ranks inside the city increased the chances of a British attack succeeding. Disillusionment also began to take its toll on rebel morale as the religious and patriotic fervour of the early mutiny period subsided and as hoped for Persian and Russian armies did not arrive to support the rebellion. There was also the danger that the British force due to insanitary conditions in camp would be whittled away by the ravages of disease.

Nicholson enhanced his reputation and his influence in the British camp by his impressive victory on 25 August at Najafgarh[53] over a rebel force which was trying to outflank the British on the ridge and attack the advancing British siege train. This victory and the arrival of the siege train on 3 September with approximately 25-30 heavy pieces of artillery, increased British morale, and plans and preparations began to be made for an assault. British engineers[54] made final their work on artillery batteries and forward trenches. The batteries were to concentrate their fire at various points of the city walls in order to create breaches through which the attacking forces could enter the rebel stronghold. A heavy bombardment began on 11 September and by the 13th two breaches had been made. Four attacking columns were to form the basis of the British assault. One column under Nicholson was to attack a breach made near the Kashmir bastion. A second column was to launch an attack via a breach at the water bastion. A third column was ordered to perform the difficult task of pressing their attack after blowing up the intact Kashmir gate, and the fourth column was to attack the area of the Lahore gate. A fifth column was to be held in reserve.[55]

The assault began on the morning of 14 September and after a day of hard fighting the British forces had gained a foothold in the city, but not without cost. Nicholson had been mortally wounded[56] and the column attacking the area of the Lahore gate had suffered heavily. Wilson studying the severe losses sustained by the attackers, and the strongholds still in the hands of the rebels considered withdrawal at the end of the day. He continued to hold this pessimistic viewpoint and on the evening of the 15th the dying Nicholson informed his old Punjab colleague Chamberlain that,

53.   *The battle of Najafgarh is described in a letter from an unidentified writer which is transcribed below in the section of homeward letters (P.R.O.N.I. D.812/14/150).*

54.   *The engineers serving at Delhi were some of the strongest advocates of an 'action' policy. They included: Lieutenant Colonel Richardson Baird Smith, who before Nicholson's arrival at Delhi had been the most influential amongst those calling for an attack on Delhi; Captain Alexander Taylor, for whom Nicholson had a great deal of respect (on his death-bed he made the statement, '"Remember to tell them that Alex Taylor took Delhi."' Llewellyn, p. 137).*

55.   *For details of the geography of the Delhi area see the map on p. xli.*

56.   *Nicholson received a shot which injured his lungs and liver when upbraiding his men for not following his lead and advancing against heavy rebel fire. He died on the evening of 23 September and was buried the following morning near the Kashmir gate.*

'"Thank God! I have strength yet to shoot him [Wilson] if necessary"'.[57]
The struggle to gain the city was long and bloody[58] and it was not
completely in British hands until the 20th. The surrender of Bahadur Shah
on the 21st put the final seal upon the British victory. The campaign
against the Delhi rebels (from 30 May - 20 September) had resulted in
3,837 British casualties[59], (killed, wounded and missing), and during the
final assault on the city 4 Victoria Crosses (the new award for military
valour instituted during the Crimean War) were won.

The capture of Delhi was, as Lawrence had foreseen, the turning point
in the mutiny, and confirmed British power in India. Indians who had
formerly been undecided on which side to cast their lot now committed
themselves to the British cause. The attempted Mughal restoration had been
the only possible banner under which the various disaffected groups in
Indian society could coalesce. During its short existence it had never
achieved this, and on its collapse the disunity of the various rebel factions
became increasingly apparent. If, in retrospect, the real crisis of the
mutiny was passed with the capture of Delhi, it must also be recognised that
the British victory here was only the prelude to protracted campaigns
throughout northern and central India. The see-saw struggle for control
of Lucknow - which was entered three times by British troops before British
control of the city was finally obtained - was the most notable feature of
the post-Delhi military operations. But, campaigns were also fought in
Jhansi, Bihar, Rajputana, Gwalior, the North Western Provinces, and the
remainder of Oudh (i.e. excluding Lucknow). The popular view of the mutiny
is that it was purely an event of 1857, but in fact the struggle lasted
until the early months of 1859[60] when the last remnants of the rebel forces
were pursued to the Himalayan foothills, where they perished squalidly of
disease, exposure and starvation. It is not the job nor the purpose of
this introduction to describe the post-Delhi stage of the mutiny (it has
been ably documented by numerous historians), but, the reader should be
aware of these military operations as they provide the scenario for many of
the letters transcribed in this publication.

57.   *Kaye*, Vol. 2 (1876 edition), p. 657.

58.   *The rebels slowed down the British advance by leaving quantities of
liquor to tempt the attackers. Many British troops after the great
privation of the long siege indulged themselves to the detriment of
military efficiency and discipline.*

59.   *Sen*, p. 108.

60.   *The Indian Mutiny campaigns were slow and ponderous affairs because
of the great distances involved and the backward forms of communication and
transport available to the military commanders. James Graham (1830-c.1905),
a commissariat officer, in his diary, homeward letters, and commissariat
letters (transcribed below) describes the almost feudal logistics of keeping
an army in India fed, clothed and on the move. In 1857 the Indian telegraph
system was still in its infancy, and although it was proposed that
approximately 3,500 miles of railway should be constructed only 300 miles
of track had actually been laid (for details of Indian railway development
at this time see the various reports, memoranda, maps etc contained in the
Parliamentary Papers, Accounts and Papers, 1857, (209 session 2 Vol.XXIX).*

Introduction

The Indian Mutiny campaigns of 1857-9 were remarkable for the savagery displayed by both sides. The reasons for this feature of the struggle were many and complex. Both sides entered the fray feeling betrayed, and men who feel betrayed, are men in whom the passions of violence and hatred all too easily overwhelm their gentler emotions. The sepoy felt betrayed as after years of loyal service he thought the British had made an unwarranted attack upon his faith and traditions. The British sense of betrayal was not diminished by any realisation of responsibility for the mutiny via the blunder of the greased cartridge. The mutiny intensified the ever-present Anglo-Indian community's sense of isolation. Isolated and under attack within an alien population the British in India felt they had no alternative but to take stern measures against the rebels, and the initial outrages committed by the sepoys strengthened the British view that the savagery of the rebels had to be met with an equal (if not greater) retribution. British troops in the early stages of the mutiny went into battle uttering the war-cry 'Remember Mrs Chambers' (a pregnant woman who had been murdered at Meerut), and after the massacre at Kanpur the British entered the fight with the memory of this atrocity to justify their vengeance. As in all wars atrocity bred atrocity, as each side felt morally vindicated in countering bestiality with bestiality.[61] The racialistic nature of the struggle intensified its brutality as the foe was automatically part of a separate racial group who could be viewed as outside the pale of civilization and humanity. The Punjabi and northern Indian troops employed by the British during the mutiny also viewed the struggle as an ethnic one, as to them it was only one more round in the age-old conflict between the peoples of northern and southern India. One brutalizing factor which is often neglected in mutiny studies is the extremely trying conditions under which most of the mutiny campaigns were fought. During the mutiny the troops had to contend with extremes of heat and cold, torrential monsoon rains, the choking dust of the Indian plains and general privation and exposure. The apocalyptic hand of disease was also constantly raised against them. Such men subject to the dumb and fickle brutality of the elements were in no way disposed to mercy.

The mutiny on both sides produced numerous heroes and villains and quite often these two personality traits were found within the one character. Nicholson, although undoubtably possessed of indomitable courage was beyond the ken of ordinary men with his fanatic zeal in carrying out the work of the angels of vengeance and death. He was like the demi-god heroes of classical antiquity with his icy impassivity. He viewed life with the eye of an eagle rather than that of a man, and the fact that he often wept

61. *Nicholson took a typically tough attitude when it came to the punishment of rebels. His was the law of Deuteronomy rather than that of the Sermon on the Mount.*

'"... Let us propose a bill for the flaying alive, impalement or burning of the murderers of the women and children at Delhi. The idea of simply hanging the perpetrators of such atrocities is maddening .... We are told in the Bible that stripes shall be meted out according to faults, and if a hanging was sufficient for such wretches, it is too severe for ordinary mutineers. If I had them in my power today, and I knew that I were to die tomorrow, I would inflict the most excruciating tortures I could think of on them with a perfectly easy conscience." ...' Kaye, Vol. 2, p. 401 (4th edition, London, 1878).

Execution of rebels

in his tent after ordering summary executions only adds to the mystery of his personality. Hodson was certainly a hero and villain combined, and he has recently been dubbed '... no less a hero because he was also a cad ...'.[62] However with his reckless bravery and eye for the main chance Hodson is a much more understandable character than Nicholson. It is impossible to judge such men from our present moral standpoint but we should be aware of both their admirable and reprehensible features. The mutiny was perhaps the greatest internal crisis the British Empire had to face, and during its course heroism and fortitude were inextricably mixed with a hedonistic blood lust, although, even during its most inhumane phases, some Britons and Indians managed to resist their baser instincts and displayed acts of kindness and protection (often at great personal risk) to those they should have considered their inveterate foes.

62. *Llewellyn, p. 169. Major William S. R. Hodson played an important part in the fighting at Delhi in September 1857, capturing and summarily shooting three of the imperial princes, after accepting Bahadur Shah's surrender. Hodson was accused by some of his contemporaries of embezzlement from official military finances, and of using the mutiny for personal gain by looting on a freelance basis. Although looting was an accepted part of British military activity during the mutiny it was supposed to be strictly controlled within an administrative structure which ensured that the spoils of war were divided for the proportionate benefit of all ranks. Hodson was exonerated at the time but the stain on his character still remains.*

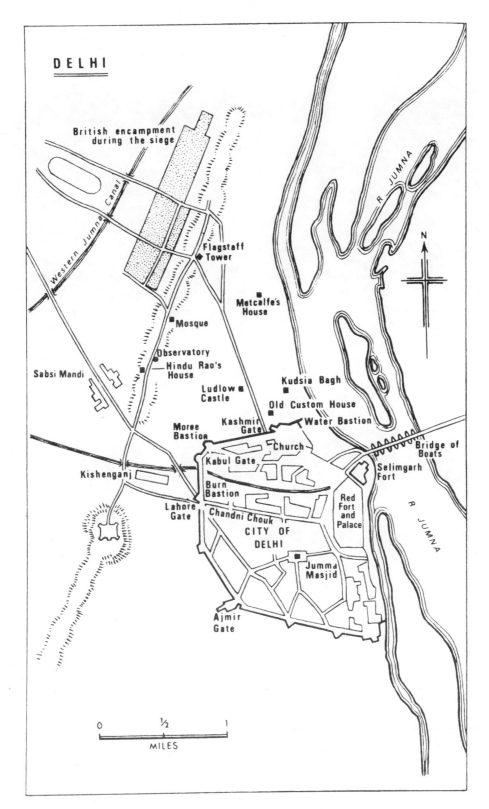

DELHI

British encampment
during the siege

Western Jumna Canal

Flagstaff
Tower

Metcalfe's
House

Mosque

Observatory
Hindu Rao's
House

Sabsi Mandi

Ludlow
Castle

Kudsia Bagh

Old Custom House

Moree
Bastion

Kashmir
Gate

Water Bastion

R. JUMNA

N

Church

Kabul Gate

Bridge of
Boats

Kishenganj

Burn
Bastion

Selimgarh
Fort

Lahore
Gate

Chandni Chouk

Red
Fort
and
Palace

R. JUMNA

CITY OF
DELHI

Jumma
Masjid

Ajmir
Gate

0   ½   1

MILES

Delhi at the time of the siege

The map overleaf was obtained from, Alexander Llewellyn, *The Siege of Delhi* (London, 1977), p.32, and it is reproduced by kind permission of Mr Llewellyn and his publishers MacDonald and Jane's, London.

Introduction

THE EFFECTS

Long before the last group of mutineers had been defeated, the East India Company structure of Indian government had been replaced by the direct assumption of Indian rule by the British crown and parliament.

> '1. The Government of the territories now in the possession or under the Government of the East India Company, and all powers in relation to Government vested in or exercised by the said Company in trust for Her Majesty, shall cease to be vested in and exercised by the said Company; and all territories in the possession or under the government of the said Company, and all rights vested or which if this act had not been passed might have been exercised by the said Company in relation to any territories, shall become vested in Her Majesty, and be exercised in her name, and for the purpose of this Act India shall mean the territories vested in Her Majesty as aforesaid, and all territories which may become vested in Her Majesty by virtue of any such rights as aforesaid. ...'[63]

The East India Company framework of Indian government was anachronistic by the middle of the 19th century, and the mutiny only pointed this out in stark relief. The East India Company administration, created originally to serve British mercantile interests in India, had throughout its history been subject to ever increasing government intervention and control. In 1833 the Company had ceased to be a trading concern, and in 1853 it finally lost all its power of patronage and became a purely administrative body. The Government of India Act of 1858 was the final stage in the relationship between the British government and the Company; it was the constitutional recognition of what was rapidly becoming a *fait accompli*. If the mutiny had been averted the East India Company administration of India could have continued for perhaps another decade or so, but it is unlikely that it could have survived much longer. Without the mutiny to sweep it away it would probably have fallen victim to the great reforming zeal of Gladstone's first ministry.

The 1858 Government of India Act established a Council of India in London to replace the old Company body, the Board of Control. The President of the Board of Control was replaced by a Secretary of State for India who was a member of the cabinet. Westminister was now the paramount power in Indian affairs.

Concomitant with the Government of India Act was a proclamation issued in Queen Victoria's name addressed to the princes, chiefs and peoples of India in which the Queen and the British government promised to respect all existing treaties made between the East India Company and the princes. Indians were also promised religious toleration and the maintenance of the '... ancient rights, usages and customs of India. ...'[64] This proclamation was tacit recognition that the major cause of the mutiny had been the alienation of conservative India from British rule, and it was an attempt to stabilize the situation and rally the influential classes of India and the

---

63. *Parliamentary Papers, Bill to transfer the government of India from the East India Company to Her Majesty the Queen, 1857-58, 41, ii, p. 287.*

64. Cited, *Dobbin*, pp. 18-19.

peasantry behind the British administration. A loyal princely class would maintain order and security in India's independent states, and the peasantry who made up the bulk of India's population could frustrate the spread of rebellion by either active loyalty to the British, or passivity. The mutiny had been a traditionalist revolt and the British reaction to it was to try and establish a conservative settlement of Indian society.

When the British government assumed direct control of Indian government and ended Company rule, the Company's army also came under direct crown control. The new Indian army still retained independence from the British army, but the mutiny created great changes as the military authorities tried to reorganize the Indian military structure to prevent a recurrence of the bloody events of 1857. The Indian army was henceforth to consist of native troops only, with Britons serving as officers. The old East India Company army had contained a small though significant number of British rank and file men. These troops were amalgamated into the British army as the 101st and 106th regiments of foot. The British soldiers affected by this change-over staged their own 'mutiny' as they considered that the issue had been decided by their superiors without any degree of consultation, or consideration of the common soldier's feelings. These 'white mutineers' also felt that as they had freely enlisted in the East India Company's army they were entitled to an enlistment bounty when they changed masters. This minor outbreak of discontent petered out as the British troops being completely isolated in an alien population could not emulate the sepoys and actually rebel. The term mutiny was given to this affair by a sensationalist press fed on the melodrama of the sepoy rising. The transition from East India Company army to the Queen's Indian army also engendered a great deal of concern amongst the British officers affected, and James Graham's home-ward correspondence reflects this concern as he constantly refers to the difference the change will make to his salary, chances of promotion and other conditions of service.

The sepoy mutiny also convinced the military authorities that the number of British army regiments stationed in India should be greatly increased, and the number of native regiments reduced so that the native army would be counterbalanced in any future rising. Britain could not have held India without a native army, as maintaining a purely British army in India would have been prohibitively expensive and logistically impossible; it would also have been a sign that she was holding India by military power alone without either the consent or acquiescence of India's peoples.[65] Before the mutiny there had been approximately 40,000 British troops in India, and approximately 350,000 sepoys; a ratio of roughly 9 to 1. After the experience of the mutiny it was felt that this ratio should be reduced to 3 to 1, and during the years up to the First World war the ratio was assessed at just over 2 to 1. As the mutiny had been predominantly an affair of the Bengal section of the East India Company army and the north of India, British troops were concentrated in this area to ensure the good behaviour of the Bengal presidency native army. The post-mutiny ratio of British to Indian troops was therefore not constant throughout the subcontinent, but varied regionally according to the trust the British felt they could place

---

65. *This was the situation after the 2nd World War when the Indian Army, which had just played an important part in the defeat of the Japanese, could no longer be relied upon by the British due to the spread of nationalist sympathies. This realisation accelerated the end of British rule in 1947.*

in the constituent parts of the native army, and in the diverse peoples which made up India's population.[66]

It also became military policy to mix the various races, creeds and tribes of India within the regiments of the new army, as it was felt that the danger of mutiny was greatest in homogeneous regiments. The mutineers had made great use of artillery in the mutiny so the Indian army as a further safeguard was stripped of its artillery regiments. The Indian soldier had henceforth to rely upon British army artillery regiments to provide him with artillery support.

Indian Muslims, because of the attempt to revive the Mughal dynasty during the mutiny, were held by the British to be more responsible for the rising than their Hindu countrymen. Muslim society therefore fell from official favour for a period of approximately 30 years after the mutiny. During this time Muslim society was extremely introverted as Muslims generally cut themselves off from contact with Western ideas and institutions. Hindu society however utilized Western educational institutions and Hindus sought employment in the lower levels of the British administration. Hindu society thus became more advanced than its Muslim counterpart. Hindus began to adopt western nationalist and political ideas and in 1885 the first all - India Congress meeting was held. It was from its inception a largely Hindu body, and communalist politics once born proved difficult to overcome. Muslim society at about the same time began to stir from its post mutiny introversion, under the influence of Syed Ahmad Khan, but the development gap caused by the mutiny had driven a wedge between the two peoples, and here perhaps can be found some of the origins of the Hindu-Muslim political split of the 20th century, and ultimately of the partition of the sub-continent in 1947.[67]

The Company's army had been largely composed of Muslims and high caste Hindus often of Brahmin status. This had been especially true in the Bengal division, and the experience of the mutiny produced a prejudice against these groups on the part of those responsible for the formation of the new Indian army. This prejudice was a natural one in the circumstances, and was one expressed by most Anglo-Indians quite early on in the mutiny.

> '... The present sepoys will rue in sackcloth and ashes. To them the only field of employment will be closed forever, and they will see stepping into their shoes, the, by them detested, Sikhs and Ghoorkas. They will from the easiest and best paid employment in India, lapse into mere tillers of the soil, and earn a mere existence with labour which after their life of comparative ease will be worse than the treadmill.
>
> The old men who looked forward to drawing their pensions, and passing their remaining years as small lords in their native villages, will now find that they also will have to work hard for their very bread ... .'[68]

---

66. *The military statistics given above were obtained from Mason, pp. 318-319.*

67. *B. N. Pandey, The Break-up of British India (London, 1969), pp. 56-57, discusses the role of the mutiny in the growth of Muslim separatism.*

68. *P.R.O.N.I., D.812/14/139, 25 June 1857, James Graham, Landour, to his sister Anne Graham.*

The prejudices against the traditional military classes who had served in the Company army became an established part of Indian army policy for the remainder of the 19th century. The theory was advanced that the old sepoy classes had lost the necessary vigour and military skills of the warrior, and that to maintain Indian security the British had to tap new sources of military manpower. This post-mutiny critique of India's military situation completely belied the fact that the traditional sepoy classes who had conquered and held India for the British had during the mutiny fought hard against their masters, and had demonstrated how well they had learnt the martial arts taught to them. The sepoys had lacked effective leadership and an overall military plan but they had fought bravely for their cause and it was a myth that the traditional sepoy classes and castes had lost their martial abilities. The real reason for the shift in recruitment policy was the British lack of trust in the pre-mutiny military classes. This is apparent when one considers that the martial classes who manned the new Indian army came from those groups in Indian society who had sided with the British in the mutiny: the Sikhs, the Gurkhas and various other tribes and races from the northern hills of India whom the British idealized as archetypal Indian warriors. Lord Roberts the most famous of the Indian army commanders-in-chief of the late 19th century, and Kipling (who immortalized Roberts as 'Bobs' the general beloved of British and Indian soldiers alike) were perhaps the most public adherents of the martial classes theory.

This theory was part of a retreat from reality by the British in India. The mutiny had pointed out the inherent conflicts which existed in British India, and which exist in any imperial situation where the interests and aspirations of a subject people and those of an imperial power inevitably diverge. This conflict had affected only a relatively small proportion of India's vast population. From the mutiny onwards British soldiers and administrators in India, and the British public, tried to escape from the reality that Indians were increasingly becoming opposed to British rule. The British tried to ignore this fact by concentrating their attentions on the loyal military classes of northern India. As nationalist India developed in strength and political importance and expanded from its original power-base in Bengal, so the British idealized concept of British India continually shrank. The British wanted to believe in a simplistic Indian society composed of loyal peasants, soldiers and princes in which they fulfilled the position of paternalistic guardians, and they eulogized the virtues of northern India. This was especially true of the Punjab where the Sikhs and the martial Muslim and Hindu hill tribes seemingly retained a simple faith in British rule,[69] which was largely based on personal loyalty to the regional administrator and to the officers and traditions of the local Indian army regiment. Late 19th century Anglo-Indian literature's concentration on the Punjab was a symptom of this escape mentality.

> '... The emphasis on the Punjab meant that the image of India in
> fiction was limited. This is certainly not the most typical area
> of India, but in the literature of the period it is made to appear
> as the whole of the country. In this area the solutions to problems
> were largely those in which the army could play the major role. ...
> It was in the Northwest that the British were doing that which

69. *Even the idyllic picture the British had of the Punjab was shattered in the early 20th century by the rise of revolutionary groups such as the Sikh Ghadr party.*

Native officers of an Indian regiment in the new post-mutiny British Indian army.

seemed best to express the ideals of late nineteenth-century
imperialism as they defended the borders of civilization from the
primitive Pathans and the always dangerous Russians while bringing
material improvements to the local peasants. ... Not only were the
Punjab and surrounding areas unique in terms of the British, but
they were equally unique on the Indian side. Here, in one of the
few Muslim majority areas, the war-like Sikhs play an abnormally
large role. Hindu society, which in most areas is dominant, here is
of less significance ... . There also would be far fewer westernized
Indians found in the Punjab than in those areas of India with which
the British had had longer contact. ...' [70]

The mutiny had created a great deal of bitterness in relations between
Anglo-Indians and Indians, although certain groups such as the martial
classes were exempted by the British from this ill-feeling. The bitterness
between Briton and Indian lessened with the passage of time, but the mutiny
left an uneasy doubt in British minds. The precedent for rebellion existed
and the British in India, always an isolated alien minority, were forced by
the mutiny to realise just how alien and how isolated. James Graham
described the change in the relationship between Indian and Briton in the
following way.

'... India though in outward appearance getting round to its old
appearance is much changed, and I think ladies are well out of it.
The link is broken which bound the natives to us. Now we may
always expect little disturbances, which will not annoy bachelors,
but will give many an anxious moment to those encumbered with wives
and families. Mind you I do not mean to say that there will be any
more mutinies or disturbances, but I mean that formerly we used to
settle down into a quiet home (as much as India can be a home), now
we will always be soldiers in camp.' [71]

Graham's attitude, expressed during the heat of the mutiny, was
typical of the views of many Anglo-Indians at the time, and this siege
mentality continued until the end of British rule. It was not always
evident during normal times but the Anglo-Indian community (especially the
'planter' and commercial classes) was subject to sporadic bouts of
xenophobia. In 1883 during the Viceroyalty of Lord Ripon there occurred
one such outburst. Lord Ripon tried to introduce a legal measure, the
Criminal Procedure Bill[72] which extended the power of Indian magistrates,
and gave them the right to try Europeans. This proposal provoked the wrath
of Anglo-India and brought back memories of the mutiny. Racial tension
reached fever pitch and relations between Indian and Anglo-Indian society
were at their worst since the immediate post-mutiny years. Ripon under
virulent Anglo-Indian attack introduced a watered-down version of the Bill

---

70.   *Allen J. Greenberger, The British Image of India, subtitled 'a study
in the literature of imperialism' (London,1969), pp. 36-37.*

71.   *P.R.O.N.I., D.812/14/196, 26 August 1858, James Graham, Landour, to
his sister Anne Graham.*

72.   *Commonly called the Ilbert Bill after Courtney Ilbert (who was later
knighted) the legal member of the Viceroy's Council who was the moving
spirit behind the measure.*

which maintained the principle if not the reality of the original proposal. The experience of the mutiny also provided the reactionary elements of Anglo-Indian society with an anti-reformist rationale. The mutiny had been caused by the alienation of conservative India by British policies which threatened to destroy the traditional framework of Indian society. Therefore the die-hards of Anglo-India argued that reforms if introduced too quickly (some doubted the wisdom of any reform at all) would create discontent and perhaps a repetition of the holocaust of 1857. Indian nationalists, a small section of Indian society in the late 19th century, were represented as an alien group who with their western education had no relevance to Indian conditions or development.

Col. G. B. Malleson concluded his history of the Indian Mutiny in 1891 with the following reactionary plea:

'... More than thirty years have elapsed since the Mutiny was crushed, and again we witness a persistent attempt to force Western ideas upon an Eastern people. The demands made by the new-fangled Congresses for the introduction into India of representative institutions is a demand coming from the noisy and unwarlike races which hope to profit by the general corruption which such a system would engender. To the manly races of India, to the forty millions of Muhammadans, to the Sikhs of the Punjab, to the warlike tribes on the frontier, to the Rohilas of Rohilkhand, to the Rajputs and Jats of Rajputana and Central India, such a system is utterly abhorrent. It is advocated by ... adventurers and crochet-mongers ... started by the noisy Bengalis a race which under Muhammadan rule, was content to crouch and serve, it is encouraged by a class in this country [English radicals], ignorant for the most part of the real people of India, whilst professing to be in their absolute confidence. ... I would impress upon the rulers of India the necessity, whilst there is yet time, of profiting by the experience of the Mutiny. I would implore them to decline to yield to an agitation which is not countenanced by the real people of India. I entreat them to realise that the Western system of representation is hateful to the Eastern races which inhabit the continent of India; that it is foreign to their traditions, their habits, their modes of thought. ... Our Western institutions, not an absolute success in Europe, are based upon principles with which they have no sympathy. ... Sovereigns and nobles, merchants and traders, landlords and tenants prefer the tried even-handed justice of their European overlord to a justice which would be the outcome of popular elections. India is inhabited not by one race alone, but by many races ... subdivided into many castes. ... The attempt to give representation to mere numbers would then, before long provoke religious jealousies and antipathies which would inevitably find a solution in blood. A rising caused by such an innovation on prevailing customs would be infinitely more dangerous than the mutiny of 1857. Concession to noisy agitation on the part of the ruling power would place the lives, the fortunes, and the interests of the loyal classes of India at the mercy of the noisiest, most corrupt, and most despised race in India. Against such concession - the inevitable forerunner of another rising ... I, intimately associated on the most friendly terms, for thirty five years, with the manlier races of India, make here on their behalf, my earnest protests.'[73]

73. *G. B. Malleson, The Indian Mutiny (London, 1891), pp. 412-413.*

D

Malleson's diatribe against the nascent forces of Indian nationalism, and the continuing trend (however diluted) of westernizing reformist British administration, shows how deeply the mutiny experience effected the Anglo-Indian mentality, and his thinking displays a mish-mash of reactionary views in which the martial classes theory is prominent. The martial classes idea had become a sacred tenet of Anglo-Indian conservatism, and Anglo-Indian society became more and more introverted, and less able or prepared to face up to the problems posed by the development of Indian nationalism. Contact between the two societies diminished although the British in India liked to believe in the special relationship between themselves and the martial classes. They had however cut themselves off from the mainstream of Indian development. Britain had introduced western concepts to India, but after the experience of the mutiny British India tried to ignore the results of the forces so unleashed.

Kipling, the literary apologist for late 19th century Anglo-India, grasped many of the essentials of the situation. His view expressed in many of his poems and short stories is that with the martial classes the British could achieve a bond of loyalty and comradeship. This bond was an instinctive one of the blood and not the intellect. He largely ignored the western educated Indian in his writings because, such a character had little place in his analysis.[74] This attitude to the politically aware classes of educated Indians is typical of Anglo-India after the mutiny. The Anglo-Indian considered it impossible for Indians to assimilate western ideas completely. They could obtain a shallow veneer of western ideas without absorbing the basic profundities of western culture. Kipling understood that the process worked both ways, and in one of his short stories *The Man Who Would be King* he illustrates the impossibility of the British ever being able to totally understand Indian society and culture. The plot of this tale is simply the story of two British adventurers who conquer the fictitious state of Kafiristan somewhere in the Hindu Kush. The story can be viewed as a metaphor illustrating the rise to power of Britain in India. The two adventurers, Carnehan and Dravot, represent the two basic British lines of policy to India. Dravot, who wanted to establish an hereditary dynasty by taking to wife a Queen of one of the royal houses of Kafiristan, and who had vague ideas of modernizing the state represented that section of British administrators who desired to understand and reform India. Carnehan represented the anti-intellectualist British approach to India, with his instinctive desire to make the most of their position by taking the treasure they found in Kafiristan back to India, and there using it to purchase the good life, western style. The people of Kafiristan at first view the two Britons as gods but later discover their humanity because of Dravot's earthly desire to establish a royal line. They react violently to this realisation and Dravot is killed when his former subjects cut the supporting ropes of a bridge across a chasm which he is crossing. The symbolism of this is obvious, Dravot fell into the great gulf which divided Briton and Indian, the gulf he was trying to bridge. Carnehan who survives to bring the story back to India, makes the telling comment to Dravot just before his death, '... There's no accounting for natives. This business is our Fifty Seven ...'. Kipling in this story was putting forward his view

---

74. *Hurry Chunder, Mookerjee, the Bengali Babu espionage agent in* <u>Kim</u>*, is depicted sympathetically by Kipling. However his western education and ambition to become a fellow of the Royal Society, are contrasted with his innate orientalism and superstition. He is in fact the book's clown.*

that British rule of India failed when it tried to be anything more than instinctive; it especially failed when it tried either to intellectually analyse or to reform India.[75] This was the attitude of the British Indian army officer, or the district officer, both of whom could develop direct simple relationships with their Indian charges. Many Anglo-Indians could not however develop such relationships, and they withdrew into ever more tighter and restrictive social circles, such as those described in *A Passage to India*.

Kipling had perhaps hit upon the central truth of the British-Indian relationship; that British and Indian cultural concepts (and by implication political aspirations) were basically incompatible.[76] The rise of Indian nationalism was inevitable if viewed in this light, and Anglo-Indian conservatism was a doomed rearguard action that could hinder but not prevent eventual Indian independence. The mutiny pointed out to Indian nationalists that Britain in the last analysis held India by the sword. It also highlighted the futility of Indian rebellion against the might of the British empire. Indian nationalism during the late 19th and early 20th centuries experienced a period of factionalism between one group who advocated extreme and violent action, and a majority who wanted to obtain their ends by peaceful means. Gandhi realised that Indian nationalism and British imperialism could never achieve a moderate settlement. He saw that a direct conflict between these two forces was inherent in the Indian and British relationship, but understood that the clash when it came had to be peaceful on the Indian side. Thus the civil disobedience campaigns were born. The extremist element of Indian nationalism was given its direct head-on collision with British rule, and the majority group was won away from sterile constitutional paths by Gandhi's traditionalist religious appeal and non-violence. Indian nationalists learnt from the mistakes of the mutiny, by gaining an insight into the nature of the British-Indian relationship, and its realities.

75.   *Reference is made to* The Man who Would be King *in Louis L. Cornell's* Kipling in India, *(New York,1966), which discusses this theme in greater detail, pp. 140-175.*

76.   *Kipling, defender of Anglo-Indian ideals, never made the logical conclusion of his observations - nationalist development to independence.*

HISTORIOGRAPHICAL PERSPECTIVES ON THE
GRAHAM PAPERS

T. G. Fraser

New University of Ulster

HISTORIOGRAPHICAL PERSPECTIVES

The mutiny of 1857 has retained a fascination both for the general reader and the historian of nineteenth century India, but although scarcely a year passes without the publication of some more or less worthwhile volume devoted to it, the appearance of a fresh major source is now a rare event. By publishing *in extenso* the diary and correspondence of the Graham family of Lisburn, Co. Antrim, the Public Record Office of Northern Ireland have made available a major collection of contemporary material, unread for well over a century. The events in which the Grahams were involved, the maintenance of British power in the Punjab, the siege and capture of Delhi, the mutiny at Sialkot, the siege of Lucknow, and the north Indian campaigns of Sir James Outram, were of central importance in the crisis and their observations and attitudes must be of interest to anyone concerned with South Asian and imperial history. Specialists in these disciplines will reach their own conclusions about the information the letters and diary contain, but for those less involved what follows is a brief attempt to place the collection in the context of British writing about the mutiny, particularly by those who lived through it.

The mutiny caught and held the Victorian imagination as few other events. Coming as it did so soon after the dreary squalor and incompetence which W. H. Russell of the *Times* had reported from the Crimea, this is hardly surprising. Moreover, it had all the necessary elements of tragedy, heroic endurance and the ultimate triumph of British manhood to make it appear an epic of Attic proportions. It was little wonder that there was an immediate and continuing demand for first-hand accounts. Eager to capitalise on the recent success of his Crimean diaries, W. H. Russell hastened to India to accompany the campaigns in the Ganges valley, the fruits of which, *My Diary in India in the Year 1858-9,* appeared in two volumes in 1860.[1] But as he did not arrive on the Hooghly until the end of January 1858 when events had passed their crisis, his account lacks the interest and insights of his earlier work, or of his subsequent American Civil War diaries. It is interesting to compare his prestigious, if somewhat irrelevant, volumes with one of the first contemporary accounts, *The Crisis in the Punjab* by Frederick Cooper, published locally in Lahore in 1858 under the pseudonym 'A Punjab Employé'.[2] A modest production clearly never intended for the general British reading public, it is replete with information about the state of the province during the period when its loyalty was still a matter for conjecture, as are Cooper's motives for publishing. More akin to the Graham letters are the *Letters written during the Siege of Delhi* of H. H. Greathed. As former commissioner of Meerut and then political agent at Delhi during the siege, Greathed was better placed than most to analyse contemporary events, but the arduous nature of his duties and his death during the assault on the city robbed historians of all but hasty notes sent to his wife, who published them the following year.[3]

Interest did not end with the publication of these early accounts and in the succeeding decades the most celebrated works of mutiny historiography,

1.   W. H. Russell, *My Diary in India in the Year 1858-9*, 2 vols, (London, 1860).

2.   'A Punjab Employé', (pseud. Frederick Cooper), *The Crisis in the Punjab*, (Lahore, 1858).

3.   H. H. Greathed, *Letters written during the siege of Delhi*, (London, 1858).

Sir George Trevelyan's rather histrionic *Cawnpore* and the stately histories
of Kaye and Malleson, were published.[4] Reminiscences and eye-witness
accounts also continued, ranging from Forbes-Mitchell's *Reminiscences of the
Great Mutiny,* the memoirs of a private soldier in the 93rd Sutherland
Highlanders, to the magisterial *Forty-One Years in India* of Field-Marshall
Lord Roberts, published in 1896 and going through thirty-two editions by the
end of the century.[5] By the early twentieth century the comments of such
ill-assorted observers as Queen Victoria and Karl Marx could be put alongside
the accounts of those closer to the scenes of action.[6] Largely missing from
this impressive historiography were, alas, similar accounts from the side of
the 'mutineers' an omission which time had done little to rectify and which
has ensured an inevitable bias in historical writing.

It was only with the passing of participants or their immediate
families that major collections of contemporary correspondence began to
re-appear: few had done so since the publication of Greathed's letters in
1858. This type of source, with the immediate reactions to events, was of
immense value to historians of the period, but now raises problems of
editorial standards. Among many such collections, four ought to be mentioned.
In 1898 the *Letters from India and China during the years 1854-1858* of
Robert William Danvers were published by his family.[7] Danvers had survived
the mutiny to be killed accidentally in China in 1858. Although he had not
intended his letters to be published, his family had in fact done so in the
press during the course of the mutiny, and the selection they issued in
1898 was admittedly incomplete. Danvers' information now seems unexceptional.
Six years later appeared the *Letters written during the Mutiny and Waziri
Campaigns* of Colonel John Chalmers, which had been 'discovered in an old
box during the reconstruction of the house in which his mother used to live'.
In editing them there was, it was claimed, 'no omission or alteration of any
kind'.[8] No such assertion accompanied the *Letters from Persia and India
1857-1859* of General Sir George Barker, which his widow had discovered among

4.   Sir George Trevelyan, *Cawnpore,* (London, 1865). Sir J. W. Kaye and
Colonel G. B. Malleson, *A History of the Sepoy War in India,* 6 vols, (London
1889-93). Kaye and Malleson originally appeared separately.

5.   W. Forbes-Mitchell, *Reminiscences of the Great Mutiny 1857-59,* (London
1893). Field-Marshal Lord Roberts of Kandahar, *Forty-One Years in India,*
(London, 1897, 32nd edition, 1900).

6.   See A. C. Benson and Viscount Esher (eds), *The Letters of Queen
Victoria,* vol. III, 1854-1861, (London, 1907). Unlike many of her ministers,
the Queen took her Indian responsibilities seriously and followed Indian
affairs with a sympathetic interest. Marx's contemporary analyses were
written for the *New York Daily Tribune* as the events developed. In 1959
his articles were published in Moscow in a convenient collection, *The First
Indian War of Independence 1857-1859.* Indian history interested Marx and
his observations, though they were dependent on the evidence of others,
reflect his formidable analytical powers.

7.   Robert William Danvers, *Letters from India and China during the years
1854-1858,* (London, 1898).

8.   Colonel John Chalmers, *Letters written from India during the Mutiny
and Waziri Campaigns,* (Edinburgh, 1904), preface.

the papers of his mother and sister and published in 1915, the year after his death.[9] The collections of Chalmers and Barker were a welcome addition to knowledge. The former witnessed the developing crisis in the Punjab and came to Kanpur and the relief of Lucknow *via* the siege of Delhi, while Barker reached the same destination from Barrackpore in Bengal. Taken together, they provide a fascinating set of reactions to events in north India. Finally, in 1924 there appeared Lord Roberts' *Letters written during the Indian Mutiny*. These letters constitute an important complement to *Forty-One Years in India*, especially as the emotions of the young lieutenant in the heat of action were often markedly different from those recollected in tranquillity by the Field-Marshal.[10] They nicely illustrate the dangers of reliance on later testimony.

How, then, do the Graham papers stand in relation to these established sources? They differ from them in the obvious respect that they are the correspondence of a family with widespread military and financial interests in India, rather than of an individual, however well placed. As such, they are rich in that overworked *cliché* 'human interest', reminding us that the men and women of 1857 were not Victorian superbeings, but representatives of the middle class whose heroism went along with mundane health problems, family tensions and financial worries. As James Graham's suicide at Lucknow reminds us, not everyone was a potential John Nicholson. Conversely, his widow's account of her sufferings during the siege is as poignant a comment as one could wish on the plight of those forced by events to overcome the most severe trials and deep personal tragedy. More effectively than any of the volumes mentioned above, they enable us to approach the 'feel' of the embattled British community.

Few of those involved in the mutiny had time to speculate at length on its nature and possible causes, but here the Grahams were well placed. During the period of nearly two months between the initial outbreak at Meerut on 10 May and his death on 9 July, Dr James Graham in the deceptive calm of Sialkot, like his nephew in remote Landour, did have the opportunity for such reflection. Like many others, notably Frederick Roberts and Colonel John Chalmers, they felt especially aggrieved against the luckless and inept commander-in-chief, General the Honourable George Anson, 'a man', James Graham wrote from Landour to his sister in Ireland, 'who knew nothing of his profession, felt his own incapacity, and, poor man, it was not his fault but those who sent him'.[11] What is noteworthy here is James Graham's strong prejudice that the principal reason for Anson's appointment had been his 'flunkeyism to Prince Albert', a disposition on his part to blame the army's inadequate high command on the Prince Consort.[12] Other published letters on the early stages of the mutiny lament Anson's performance but few of them are quite as venomous in their castigations of the senior commanders and their royal patron as James Graham's correspondence, though he can hardly have been unique in holding such sentiments.

9.   *General Sir George Digby Barker, ed. Lady Barker, Letters from Persia and India 1857-1859, (London, 1915).*

10.   *Field-Marshal Lord Roberts, Letters written during the Indian Mutiny, (London, 1924).*

11.   *P.R.O.N.I. D.812/14/139 James Graham, Landour, to his sister Anne, Lisburn, 25 June 1857.*

12.   *Ibid.*

He was certainly a young man of lively prejudices. High among the causes of the outbreak he placed the inadequacies of the Christian missionaries, a view with which many modern historians of the mutiny would sympathise.[13] His cousin at Sialkot certainly held the chaplain there in scathing contempt and such anti-clerical views were coming not from Laodicean Englishmen but members of an Ulster Protestant family.[14] Perhaps contemporary observers would have sympathised more readily with James Graham's view that the Muslims were providing the essential dynamic for the mutiny and that the Hindus were merely their dupes.[15] It was an interpretation given some apparent substance by the march of the Meerut mutineers to the former Mughal capital of Delhi, one of the great cities of the Islamic world, and their proclamation of the aged Mughal, Bahadur Shah, as Emperor of Hindustan. British animus against the Muslims was only dispelled later in the century when Sir Syed Ahmad Khan and Sir William Hunter argued persuasively that their position had been misrepresented.[16]

Where the Graham papers are most in accord with other such collections are in their feelings of outrage, revenge and shattered certainties. All those who witnessed the scene of the Kanpur massacre, or heard its details, shared such sentiments.[17] Moreover, the family suffered badly in the mutiny, losing two adults and two infants. From the beginning their letters voiced the naked racial fears of a small community facing the prospect of annihilation. 'Lawrence and his officers have established a reign of terror in the Punjab which Blacky appreciates', applauded Dr Graham, and his son William, on hearing of his father's death, wrote that he 'would take to cab-driving' rather than 'command Blacks again'.[18] Yet there also went a generous appreciation, by no means common in mutiny correspondence, of the mutineers' fighting skills. For James Graham, 'Though our regiments are mutinous, they were very fine men, and good soldiers', while three days before his death his uncle made the significant admission that 'Blacky never fought so well or showed such energy in our service as he is now doing', a sentiment which would have warmed the heart of V. D. Savarkar, the Indian revolutionary who in 1909 first advanced the theory that the insurgent soldiers had waged a war for their country's liberation.[19]

13.   *Ibid.*

14.   *P.R.O.N.I. D.812/10/B/12 Sarah Graham, Sialkot, to James Graham, Landour, 10 June 1857.*

15.   *P.R.O.N.I. D.812/14/139 James Graham, Landour, to his sister Anne, Lisburn, 25 June 1857.*

16.   *The important works in helping to re-adjust British perspectives on Muslims and the mutiny were Syed Ahmad Khan, An Essay on the Causes of the Indian Revolt, (Calcutta, 1860), and W. W. Hunter, The Indian Mussulmans, (London, 1871). The result was a temporary alliance between the Raj and the Muslims which lasted until just before the outbreak of the First World War.*

17.   *See, for example, Chalmers, writing from Kanpur on 8 February 1858, he noted that he 'came away with feelings of revenge I never felt before'.*

18.   *P.R.O.N.I. D.812/10/B/32 Dr Graham, Sialkot, to James Graham, Landour, 4 July 1857; P.R.O.N.I. D.812/14/144 William Graham, Jullundur, to Daniel Cullimore, New Ross, Co. Wexford, 13 July 1857.*

The Grahams found their heroes in the Punjab, where their fellow Ulstermen, John Lawrence and John Nicholson, were forging an unshakeable alliance with the population as well as destroying the luckless men of the Bengal Army with an Old Testament severity. One of the most important consequences of the mutiny was the transformation of the army into a largely Punjabi force, a process particularly associated with Lord Roberts when he was Commander-in-chief in the 1880s. As a result, the Punjab became the most favoured province of British India, laying the foundations of an agricultural prosperity which now makes it one of the showpieces of Asia. Amongst Dr Graham's first reactions to the outbreak was the belief that 'high caste has had its day, and Sikhs and low caste will now take place'.[20] Undisputed leader of these new Punjabi forces was Nicholson, who is consistently referred to as the one man whose efforts might retrieve the situation. In his second last letter, Dr Graham wrote of him that 'mercy is a word not to found in his vocabulary'.[21] He was correct. For those of us living in the late twentieth century, Nicholson, with his iron courage and pitiless ferocity, may seem uncomfortably close to a type of soldier who has become all too familiar, to be found on the Russian front in the last war or in Algiers in 1957, but to men like Dr Graham, just hours away from death, he was the only possible saviour in a collapsing world. If his family's papers can make us grasp that point, then they have served their historical purpose.

The Graham papers, then, are not unique but they are important and help us nudge a little closer to an understanding of one of the great crises of the nineteenth century. Certainly, their place in mutiny historiography is now as assured as are the events they describe in the history of British imperialism and of the Indian subcontinent. We can only hope that some mohalla in the old city of Delhi contains a similar collection, its significance as yet unrecognized, which will relate as vividly the fortunes of an Indian family in the same upheaval. But perhaps Nicholson and those who followed him did their work too thoroughly.

19.   *P.R.O.N.I. D.812/14/151 James Graham, Landour, to his sister Anne, Lisburn, 14 September 1857; P.R.O.N.I. D.812/10/B/34 Dr Graham, Sialkot, to James Graham, Landour, 6 July 1857. V. D. Savarkar (1883-1966) was for long a storm petrel of Indian politics, opposed alike to British rule and Gandhi's pacifism. His book* The Indian War of Independence of 1857 *was published in Europe in 1909 and immediately banned in India, though some copies were smuggled in and long extracts were printed by revolutionary presses, such as that of the* Ghadr *(Mutiny) party in San Francisco. His thesis naturally appealed to many Indians. It is interesting to compare the judicious verdict of S. N. Sen in* Eighteen Fifty-Seven, *the best modern history which was commissioned by the Government of India to commemorate the mutiny's centenary.*

20.   *P.R.O.N.I. D.812/10/B/2 Dr Graham, Sialkot, to James Graham, Landour, 18 May 1857.*

21.   *P.R.O.N.I. D.812/10/B/35 Dr Graham, Sialkot, to James Graham, Landour, 8 July 1857.*

JAMES GRAHAM'S INDIAN MUTINY DIARY

guns in front and the Infantry Brigades following. There I
saw the first man actually killed. I was with the Rifle
Marshal's Brigade when a horse with native cav: saddle
was seen galloping about and there was a lookout for the
rider. a rifleman brought him down at once from a tree in
which he was hiding with a bullet and as he fell
a bugler took a hatchet out of his belt and gave him
a blow on the head which finished him –
During that day while we were encamped I saw several
men hanged who without trial by the soldiers who had
been taken with arms in their hands – at least I think
they hanged them but I did not wait to see – Our
baggage came across that evening. and as the enemy
got the range as the camels were crossing the bridge
our cheap pony (Spec: Beds) came to great grief! – We
commenced bombarding the city from our side and they
returned it – The Mess Serjeant's leg was taken off in
one of our mess tents. I remember seeing it after it
was cut off, and it was in one of these days that
a young midshipman who was acting as D.C. to Sir Wm
Peel lost his life, having ridden in front of a revolver just
as it was fired his head was blown away.
Time went on for days till the city was cleared our head
Quarters was for a time at the Dilaram Palace – and I
used to cross the Goomtee on an elephant to get what
crockery and other things I could pick up in the Chutter
Munzil. Finally we were in a house I don't exactly
remember where – but I won't forget one circumstance.
Lord Clyde came up to the door, and an Artillery Officer
(McFadden or not I know not). made some remark about
his horses having to stand all day in harness when Lord

Extract from James Graham's mutiny
diary D.812/20 (see p.10 below).

2

May 1857

D.812/20

[The following entry appears to be a contemporary entry made by Graham at the time of the mutiny.]

'... I took a house with Fellowes of the 107th "Childers Lodge" at [rupees ?] 600 for the season. On the 11th of May Fellowes and I determined to go down to the river to bathe and spend the day. It was very hot going down, but the pull up nearly killed both of us. I tried in the villages to get coolies, or buffaloes to pull me up I was so done. I might have forgotten it but for what followed. That night the [? Gharhwal] Havildar (sergeant) of one of my guards came into my room and said his reg[imen]t had marched out of the [? Dhoou], and what was he to do. I said I knew nothing about it and for him to go to the station staff, and went to sleep. Poor fellow he said his guard had no relief for six months !!! The mutiny at Meerut had taken place on Sunday the 9th, and the mutiny and massacre at Delhi on Monday 10th. [*sic*] On one day of the preceding week I had mentioned at the Club [Himalaya Club at Mussoorie] about the 3rd Cav[alry] having refused to use their cartridges which I had heard from Dickey, who had heard from Water[?ford] the Ass[istan]t A[djutant] G[eneral]. I remember being almost flatly contradicted by a man Barchack of the 20th, and the Dr (Craigie) of the 3rd coming to my room to enquire about [it] after I was in bed that night. He went down the following day[1], to be cut up badly as he drove to church on Sunday evening with the vet of his corps who was killed. As I went down the hill on the morning of the 12th I met our Gen[era]l Steele with a face as long as my arm, and I c[oul]d not imagine what was up. I was too soon to hear it. Poor Fellowes was ordered off at once to join his corps at Agra and had a wonderful journey of it.

[At this point in Graham's diary a page heading 23 March 1881 appears. It would seem that Graham wrote the following entry up in 1881 from memory to fill in a gap in his mutiny diary, caused probably by the confusion and intense activity of the actual mutiny period.]

To give an account of the eventful year 1857 would be one of the whole Indian Mutiny. Gen[era]l Dickey came to chum [share house] with me shortly after Fellowes left for the plains. I think he left on the 12th or 13th [May], and Dickey came a few days afterwards. Panic took the Mussoorie people a few days after that, and they all made a rush for Landour (?). Childers Lodge our residence was occupied by two ladies (Mrs afterwards Lady Arch[d]ale Wilson, and Mrs Greathed or French with six children, five of them Mrs Greathed's, and the other, if I remember rightly, a child of Col Hoggs of the Artillery, of which Lady Wilson had charge, and they stayed for about three weeks). I was with Col Le Strange when they arrived and fancy my astonishment at such a houseful. Col Le Strange was an old man who had risen from the ranks I think, or had been years on half pay and belonged to the 70th in which he was a capt[ain], and was shortly after removed as a major gen[era]l. His favourite place of reading

1. *Graham was stationed at Landour, a town on the fringes of the Himalayas. 'Going down' probably meant going to the major town of the area, Mussooree, which was at a lower altitude than Landour, or to places further south.*

A view of the foothills from Landour

despatches he received was in a Mohammedan's shop in the bazaar, and I
would not be the least surprised if he got them to read the letters for him.

I had great anxiety as we were shut off from the stations in the plains as
regards supplies, and there were at least 600 European women and children
at Mussoorie. Our force was about 100 convalescents without arms of any
kind. Fortunately we soon got the muskets of the furlough men of the
[Gharhwal] Reg[imen]t and with these, the convalescent mounted as well as
they could be on bazaar (tats) ponies, were sent off to attack parties of
the mutinied sepoys who were constantly passing through the [? Dhoou].
With great difficulty I got the Colonel to allow me to store wine and
hospital supplies in the prisoners' cells, and the guards unscrewed the
hinges off the doors and went in and drank a considerable part of the port
wine. I got him to allow me to store wheat in an enclosed covered
r[?acquet] court.

We were expecting day by day to hear of the fall of Delhi and much delay
made the heart sick. I remember the people we saw most of were
[? Vaurenea] and Hamilton of the survey, Muquay of invalids who lived with
them. Our near neighbours in Childers (I think) Castle were the Cha[rle]s
Curries, and his nasty brother Robert whom I did not like. We met
generally to hear the news at Horsburgh's near the post office, [with]

Abercrombie of the artillery, Hilton of the 65th and others. Murray [of the] artillery afterwards an intimate friend was up with his wife's people the Shaugnessys. Dickey at times had visitors: Willie MacDougall, and D'Oyley, [? Alvis] of the stud, a civilian, I forgot his name, who was always (25 August 1857) eating paper, and also [his] nephew, poor Trotter of the 45th who died in the house of liver. I remember being so angry with Robert Currie whom we also took in as his brother had no room, that he used to take possession of the chair we had prepared with pillows for Trotter.

In July we heard of the Sealkote Mutiny and the murder of poor uncle, who had carried on a daily correspondence with me since the mutiny broke out. One [of] his last letters did not reach me till several days after his death. W[illia]m came up from Delhi sick, got a med[ical] certificate and went home.[2]

25 September 1857
I had about 1300 rupees with the Delhi Bank when the mutiny took place and of course all the acc[oun]ts were destroyed, but I had no difficulty in getting credit for it again. I heard men at Mussoorie boast that they owed so much, and had got it cleared off by the mutiny. I sent some of the names and accounts myself to the new manager, Mr Hobson late head ass[istan]t in the Meerut Court Office.

29 September 1857
Bought a pair of large horse pistols from Gen[era]l Cox for r[upee]s 50.

20 October 1857
Bought 200 rupees worth of the gov[ernmen]t tea at the Deyrah sale, and I remember sent a present of one box of the best to Mrs Macpherson.

16 November 1857
I was at Rajpoor on this date on some business.

24 November 1857
I left Landour for good and [? aye] this day, breakfasted at Rajpoor hotel, drove part of the way, and dawked (doolie) the rest of the way to Meerut. I remember the country was very unsafe and I did not like it at all.

2. *At this point in the diary contemporary mutiny entries begin again. It would appear Graham filled in blank spaces of his mutiny diary with his later reminiscences. This upsets the chronological order of the diary. In this transcript the chronological order of the entries has been rearranged to put the events described in their logical sequence.*

5

E

26, 27, 28 November 1857   Was at Meerut and stayed with D'Oyley who I remember was not particularly gracious, and then went to Delhi to see it, and [the] Simpsons who were staying with Marteneau who was officiating there in the court. On my return I stayed with the Simpsons.

28 November 1857   Bought at Meerut a grey arab from Mr Billings for r[upee]s 600. This carried me all through the campaign, and I afterwards sold him to Cox of the artillery at Bareilly.

3 December 1857   Heard of the arrival in Calcutta of a pair of Colt revolvers which I had ordered from England, one of them for Gen[era]l Dickey as a present. They did not leave Calcutta till sometime in Jan[uar]y. Was still at Meerut.

[At this point Graham's mutiny reminiscences begin again. There is a certain overlap with contemporary entries for November above.]

November 1857   About the end of Nov[ember] I was ordered down to Meerut from [which] I was to take down a convoy of stores from that place and Delhi to Cawnpoor. Simpson the Meerut a[cting] c[ommissary] gen[era]l was at Delhi, and I, after staying a couple of days with D'Oyley (now Sir Charles), went there also, and stayed in a temp[orar]y dawk bungalow in the [? Chandiary Chote³], returning to Meerut with the Simpsons. I left Meerut with my convoy⁴, and the Delhi part joined us direct. They consisted of 279 carts with 14,550 bullocks, 150 elephants, 1,419 camels, 2,500 doolie bearers, 2,000 other camp followers, *viz* bheasties, sweepers, and servants of all sorts, 3,040 quilts, 4,318 blankets, 100 cwts [of] ghee, 1,438 soojee, 106 rice, 70 salt, 3,500 wheat, 600 malt, 3,153 ottali, 20 sugar. The miscellaneous servants were for the troops just arrived from Europe. I remember the Rifle Brigade asked me for a "confectioner".

At Bewar we met a brigade under Gen[era]l Sir R. Walpole with which Mylne was court officer, and made over to them a lot of transport and servants, sending more to Fattehghur with them for the troops who had marched up the road with the c[ommander]-in-c[hief]. I went on with the remainder to Cawnpoor under an escort from [Prince of ?] *Wales's* horse. Sir Tho[ma]s Seaton commanded the brigade of escort from Delhi. We halted for some days at Allyghur, when he went out and had a fight. I think some of the

---

3.   *A main thoroughfare in Delhi. The modern spelling is Chandni Chouk.*

4.   *'See* Times *article of 27 Jan[uary] 1858' [Graham's note].*

carabineers and lancers were killed. Here Fellowes joined us again, and I
made Newmarch's acquaintance. Found Christopher at Cawnpoor hard at work
sitting in a bed covered with [? boils]. He was much pleased with the way
I made over charge. He had O. A. Graham as an assis[tan]t !!! I found
Armstrong here with his one leg cut off, and the other badly wounded. He
said I saved his life. The second one I was supposed to have saved in that
month. On leaving Meerut we made up a small mess. There was Fitzgerald,
Hogg my assis[tan]t, J. Forsyth then of the med[ical] dep[artmen]t, a Dr
named Macaulay, and Fellowes joined us at Allyghur very ill with dysentery.
Forsyth said he would be dead before he reached Cawnpoor if he was allowed
to eat as he was doing, so I took him in hand and sent away his plate when
Doctor Forsyth nodded to me that it would not suit him. He said this saved
his life when we parted, [more ?] about Armstrong afterwards.

Col Congreve q[uarte]r m[aste]r gen[era]l Queen's Troops, Arthur Becher
ditto. In troops Sept[imus ?] Becher, d[eput]y adj[utant] gen[era]l. In
troops all went down with us at first. I remember the state Congreve and
Sept. Becher were in after going to meet the c[ommander]-in-c[hief] at
Fattehghur. Congreve, who was a great "bahadoor" when he commanded the
29th at Dinapoor with us there, was sent away as useless, and cried
bitterly in my tent. A. Becher went home wounded, and Sept. Becher who
had I believe spent all the '57 year at Simlah was passed over in promotion,
and sent down to take charge of the Calcutta office.

I remember the difficulty I had in getting my office tent ready for our
mess dinner. From the time we arrived in camp till it was dark my treasurer
weighed out rupees. I remember well how he could take up the first fifty
exactly in his fat fist. The carts were in double line fifteen miles long,
whipped up close by (a riding master) Capt[ain] Douglas our baggage master,
and well whipped up too if they did not keep together. After the brigade
left us at Bewar we used to encamp in the middle of them, and the old gent
himself would not have got through such a *chevaux de frise*. When we
arrived at Cawnpoor I had some [? beer] remaining; I got a h[ogs]h[ea]d
bottled at Meerut, and the balance I gave to Armstrong, who wanted
stimulants and could not get them at any price. He said I saved his life,
and says so still. I remember well going to sit with him daily during my
short stay, and taking him grapes also.

I cannot recount all the incidents of our short march. I remember a huge
Sikh being flogged for looting, and being held out with one arm of a
stalwart Pathan "Yacoob Khan" the havildar of my guard !! Again one
morning as we were leaving camp before daylight, one of my treasure
tumbrils which had no division overturned. All the guard could not right
such a load of silver, so I tied an elephant to the pole, who righted it
indeed, but frightened by the bang of the silver, went off with it at such
a pace that the cart was knocked to pieces, and all the bags burst. We
gathered them up as best we could, and on getting to the next ground found
we had only lost 14. I told dear old FitzGerald about it. He said [to]
report it which I did, and months afterwards came a letter to write it off
to profit and loss, sanctioned by the supreme gov[ernmen]t.

From Cawnpoor I was ordered to Fattehghur by double marches to join the
c[ommander]-in-c[hief]'s force, [January 1858] and immediately on arrival
was sent out to relieve Mylne who had charge of Sir [R.] Walpole's, the

advance column at the Ramganga[5], he being allowed to return to Fattehghur where his brother was with the 82nd. There I first came under fire, riding round the camp with him. We *rode* into a battery where the naval brigade was exchanging shots with the enemy across the river. I suggested we were rather exposing ourselves, and he then told me about the fate of his sisters. His parents had died; he went home in the beginning of '57, sacrificing his appoint[ment], to bring them out to India, even their heavy baggage was despatched. The mutiny broke out, and they proceeded with another brother to Australia. They sighted land, and the ship was never seen nor heard of again. So Mylne said "what was to be was to be".

Found Macdonnell of ours in camp. Sir R. Walpole comm[an]d[er], Barwell brig[adier] major, Tom Casey q[uarte]r m[aste]r gen[era]l, and Warner the o[fficer] c[ommanding] a[ide] d[e] c[amp]. Much bothered with getting things into order, and getting things settled. Got FitzGerald to give serg[ean]t senior again [*sense ?*] who had accompanied the convoy from Delhi. After a few days I was sent for late one night, and told we were to move back to Fattehghur the following morning. We had to take up a raft bridge made of rum casks (kegs) and bring them away with us. From Fattehghur we went off to [the Grand] Trunk Road and I think as far as Cawnpoor, and halfway back again, to protect a convoy of ladies and children coming down from Agra, and to prevent the Nana's brethren and party crossing from Oude. However he did cross, by our police guard sending our boats for them, and I saw seventeen of the said police guard hanging in one tree, if I remember rightly, in consequence.

From letters it would appear [February 1858] we were at Fattehghur in February. Finally we crossed into Oude, and arrived at Lucknow the day before the siege [March 1858] commenced[6]. The day before we had an alarm in camp, and it was most exciting to see the camels and cattle coming in, but it was a false alarm. That night we marched at 9 pm with a long siege train. About halfway, there was a small fort named [*word omitted*], where a guard was placed to allow no country carts with baggage to pass till all the train had gone forward, but as half the shot was on country carts they stopped them too, and all the train. We could not imagine what had happened. It was bitterly cold, and I know I was very glad to get to a fire which some of the camp followers had lighted, and I was disgusted by being again and again dragged forth to interpret, by Gen[era]l Walpole.

On the [6 March 1858] morning of the 6th our division and others crossed the river by a bridge of rum kegs. We were ordered to take no provisions but what we could carry. I took for our staff. I had been with Walpole's on my camel sowars [*sic*], and as I approached the river riding with Sir A. Horsford at the head of his brigade, I heard a voice exclaiming "My God there are elephants". This was Lord Clyde who thought my camelsmen were elephants

---

5.   *River in modern Indian state of Uttar Pradesh. Walpole joined forces with Sir Colin Campbell the commander-in-chief here, during the latter's campaign in the spring of 1858 to clean up the area between Delhi and Oudh of mutineer forces.*

6.   *The attack on the mutineers at Lucknow began on 2 March 1858.*

Nana Sahib

in the dark of the morning. I dived on as fast as I could and heard one of
them shouting to me that a *"man"* had stopped. I did not take the trouble
to go back. I reported myself to Sir James Outram who was commanding. We
drove in some cavalry pickets. It was beautiful to see the troopers in the
open, the cavalry and light guns in front, and the infantry brigades
following. There I saw the first man actually killed. I was with the rifle,
Horsford's brigade, when a horse with native cav[alry] saddle was seen
galloping about, and there was a lookout for the rider. A rifleman brought
him down at once (from a tree in which he was hiding) with a bullet, and as
he fell a bugler took a hatchet out of his belt and gave him a blow on the
head which finished him.

During that day when we were encamped I saw several men hanged, without
trial, by the soldiers, who had been taken with arms in their hands. At
least I think they hanged them, but I did not wait to see [*sic*]. Our baggage
came across that evening, and as the enemy got the range, as the camels were
crossing the bridge, our charpoys (officers beds) came to great grief! We
commenced pounding the city from our side, and they returned it. The mess
sergeant's leg was taken off in one of our mess tents. I remember seeing it
after it was cut off. And it was on one of these days that a young midshipman, who was acting *a[ide] d[e] c[a m p]* to Sir W[illia]m Peel, lost his life:
having ridden in front of a mortar just as it was fired, his head was blown
away. Firing went on for days till the city was cleared. Our head-quarters
was for a time at the [? Dilkusha Kothi] and I used to cross the Gomtee
[river on north eastern side of Lucknow] on an elephant to get what *[word
illegible]* and other things I could pick up in the [? Chattar Manzil].
Finally we were in a house I don't exactly remember where, but I won't forget
one circumstance. Lord Clyde came up to the door, and an artillery officer
(brigadier or act[ing] I know not) made some remark about his horse having to
stand all day in harness, when Lord Clyde pitched into him saying that he had
come to *India* to be made a convenience of, and so had he.

When the enemy were driven out from that part, I paid visits to the Kaiser
Bagh Residency *etc. etc.,* and tried to get loot but failed. I bought some
shawls from Sikh cartsmen who had looted them, which were much admired
afterwards, and finally burnt on their way home with a box full of Louisa's
best things, in the Egyptian Residency in the end of 1868, with an ormolu
set of tea things which Gen[eral] Fordyce gave her, and a lot of other
things, for all of which we got only £42 compensation.

The city may be said to have been fully conquered on the 19 March. On the
night of the 23rd March[7] we got orders to go after some rebels with one
day's provisions. The following day about 1 or 2 pm I was riding with
MacDonnell of ours and asked him to come and have some lunch with me. He
declined as he had promised to go elsewhere. We overtook the enemy about
5 pm. They fled at once leaving fifteen guns, and the cavalry went after
them. In a field of dhal Fred MacDonnell got a ball through his forehead,
and was killed on the spot, and another young cavalry officer got his jaw-
bone shot away, and I believe did not recover. Fred MacDonnell was buried
at Muriaon the next day. That evening at Housa I discovered and got
together about 150 bullocks all of which had what I thought the gov[ernmen]t
(𝄢) mark for Umballah where a *great* number had been purchased the year
before, but in reality they were the King of Oude's inverted fishes ⁑.

---

7.   *This date also appears in the margin.*

When we got them together the troops fell in to march off, and Simpson of
the artillery and I were left to bring them and the captured guns on with
scarcely a single driver. Hodson's Horse[8] got as many more, and I watched
the bridges the next day to see them come in, but I believe they detached
all captured cattle at once towards the Punjab by remote routes.

In the beginning of April Sir Hope Grant's column in my court charge
[? reme] started again, and had a small fight on the 13th April at a
place called Baree. Then the fight was very scattered. A party of their
cavalry went to the rear to attack the baggage, but a company of infantry
gave them one volley and dispersed them. One unfortunate came into the
baggage, and a rifleman in charge of our munition stopped him. He fell
quite close to me, and had on a medal of the 11th irregular cav[alry]. Our
gen[era]l had as staff, Wolsely (now Viscount W[olsely]) as q[uarte]r
m[aste]r gen[era]l, Ansom of lancers as a[ide] d[e] c[amp], and the late
adj[utan]t gen[era]l as q[uarte]r m[aste]r gen[era]l. Gen[era]l Grant was
most kind, his only fault was asking you to dinner too often, and sitting
intolerably late, though he was up always at a very early hour himself, and
spent a long time in forages. I have often seen weary waiting officers
standing outside his camp tent till he had finished. To me he was most
courteous, not only in manner, but in every way. His orders were so
courteously given. I used to get a note from the a[ide] d[e] c[amp]
saying the gen[era]l w[oul]d like to see me at such an hour. Frequently it
was to ask if we c[oul]d stay out longer than was originally intended.
Sometimes it ran us pretty close, but my assis[tan]t Hogg always said,
"Never despair, supplies will come in", and they did, through the enemy.
The camel sowars I mentioned above used to come and go with letters to
Lucknow. On one occasion one of them came into a village with the enemy,
who said they would kill him, but the villagers said, "Not here or we will
pay for it", and he slipped away.

Our next dour was down south to the place where the last of the Cawnpoor
refugees escaped and where Mowbray Thomson and Delafosse got away[9]. We
attacked the enemy at a place called [word illegible] on the 12 May. We
stacked our camp equipage and marched out at 2 pm. The heat was awful. I
believe sixty men had sunstroke and thirty died. I know I drank water at

---

8.   A body of native cavalry composed of Sikhs, Punjabis, frontier
tribesmen, Afridis etc. formed by Lt. W. S. R. Hodson.

9.   Lieutenants Thomson and Delafosse were amongst a small group who
escaped the massacre at Kanpur, in late June 1857. They escaped during
the famous incident of the boats on 27 June, when the mutineers under
promise of safe conduct to the British-held town of Allahabad, allowed the
British residents of Kanpur to embark on boats on the River Ganges.
Whilst the boats were being loaded firing broke out, and many of the
British party slain. Delafosse and Thomson managed to escape with a few
others on a boat which was caught in the mainstream, and carried out of
reach of the mutineers. The survivors of this incident who remained at
Kanpur were later murdered in July.

every well, till I was in great pain. Madras Sappers drew and gave it. We did not do much that day, and bivouacked on the ground. We had a false alarm at night. It was said to have been a snake crossing a Madrassee's face, but there was a good deal of firing, and I believe Major Gibbons of the artillery who had very black hair, and a large white badge on his cap, was knocked down by one of his own men, and shot through the knee. He was returned wounded. He was called Grievance Gibbons as he was always complaining. Ja[me]s Reid was our political officer, and Watson our baggage master.

Our next and fatal fight was at Nawabgunge [? Baraburchee], about twenty miles from Lucknow, where a large party [of] several thousand [of the enemy] were holding the road. We made a double march starting at night. In the morning we went off the road and crossed a stream, by a very temporary passage, over which there was a great difficulty in getting guns. I had thirty elephants with me to pick up stragglers. On the morning of the 13 June about daylight, the fight commenced, and was over about 12 noon. We had very few wounded but lost a great many men of sunstroke. We encamped during the day in a lakh bagh, a garden of ten thousand trees, and I sat all day with a wet towel around my head. We were near the hospital and a great number of men were coming, and brought in with sunstroke. One doctor bled them and every man died of his [? cut]. Many of the others escaped. One reg[imen]t (the 34th) used to dig a sort of bath whenever they got into camp, and plaster every man who got sunstroke with met mud to keep him cool, and found it very efficacious.

All this year we used to march at night, and get in at sunrise. We had a halt for an hour, and I used to lie down alongside my horse, an old white arab, so as not to be ridden over (on a guddellah my camel sowar carried for that purpose) and get what rest I could. We were told to rest ourselves at Nawabgunge [? Baraburchee] and were duly there a month or so, when we got orders to go on to [? Ajoodin], (as the Nepalese who were returning home were afraid of being attacked. Was this not the cause of one of our previous dours? One thing I remember: we found the Nepalese left behind them any smallpox patients they had, simply lying on the ground deserted.) Talking of the Nepalese reminds me that Walsh of ours spent a night in my tent before Lucknow, and left me with the words, "now for a bullet or a brevet". He joined the Nepalese and when he could not get them to go on, slanged them so much as cowards that it was thought better to remove him, as the Nepalese were more there for a political purpose than fighting[10].

Well when we marched for Fyzabad the rains were on, and I remember we lost seven elephants in six days, they simply died from the weight of the wet tents, and once laden never rose. They are such sensitive animals. We had a fight at Durriabad on the way up, and I remember hearing of one circumstance of it; a mounted officer had taken a prisoner, and was leading him alongside of him by tying the man's pugree round his neck. A Sikh sowar galloped past and in doing so applied the edge of his sword to the prisoner's neck. The impetus of the horse took off the head without any further force.

10. *The Maharajah of Nepal Jung Bahadoor wished to have British support in the internal political strife affecting Nepal. His aid to the British during the mutiny was thus an attempt to consolidate his own position, see Sen, p.237.*

We had with us the Rajah of Kapurthala with some guns and men. He was then engaged to an Eurasian, and was asking frequently to send telegrams to his "Missee", whom he afterwards married, and I dined with them at Kapurthala. One day (the Sikhs are very fond of wine and spirits) he sent to me to know if I could let him have any. I replied I had only enough for the hospitals. The messenger came back with the Rajah's most profound compliments, and a request for one bottle of "Ald Tam", Old Tom.

Another incident of the march was [when] Fitzgerald directed a native agent to take mills (hand ones) with him and grind flour as we went along. The thing was an utter impossibility, but the man professed to be doing it. When we got to Fyzabad I asked where it was, that I might inspect, and the truth came out. I said to the man, "I'll take you to the general and have you hanged", when to my astonishment he fainted dead off at my feet. Years after he came to me again looking for employment, and when I reminded him of this circumstance he said, "By the blessing of God, he had a wonderful escape on that circumstance".

On one of our dours, the native officer of a cavalry escort who went out for the protection of the elephants at graze, came and reported that one mahout kept his elephant back, and he could not get him into camp. He did not turn up, the elephant was then lost, but after some weeks the mahout came into camp and said he had been captured by the enemy. In fact he was discovered in camp and taken as a spy and brought to me. I ordered my serg[ean]t (senior) to flog him, and he did so in my presence till he dropped senseless. We never lost another elephant. The said elephant was afterwards recaptured.

At Fyzabad General Grant made me over an old palace on the banks of the Gogra, a glorious house where I lived till April 1859. We had Fischer, a Madras man, as brigadier, and dear old Arthur Drury as major of brigade. During this year I had some dozen of men as assis[tan]ts, all or nearly all my seniors. Wilkinson 10th cav[alry], Graeme 5th n[ative] i[fantry], Macgennis 42nd n[ative] i[fantry], Shaw 37th n[ative] i[fantry], dear old Hogg, Lambert, P. G. Scott, and of these I could get no work out of Shaw, who slept and wrote to his wife, and Lambert as I afterwards found him was a quarrelsome "cantankerous" disagreeable party. I detached him to [*word omitted*], and when there he applied for leave and got it, but I gave the d[eputy] c[ommissary] gen[era]l a hint, and he was dispensed with. I believe in after years he drove his wife mad. During the winter the troops crossed the Gogra, and finished the campaign, but I did not go with them. The bridge was made of boats, floored and connected with bamboos, with anchors of bamboo holding them to their places. There was a small river steamer at the ghaat, which took troops daily to cut out boats for the bridge. I remember hearing a man say (of the 53rd) as they returned from one of these trips, and found the grog at the landing place, "Here comes the grin of the evening". Round shot came frequently across into the compound of the old palace, one of these cut off the branch of a tree close to the house, and one of my native Bengalee writers was so alarmed that he let all his books drop. I asked him what made him do it, and he replied, "We are naturally not brave".[11]

11. *Graham's reminiscences at this point return to an earlier period, due to his examination and summary of his mutiny financial accounts.*

When we were at Landour the dep[ut]y commissioner adopted a system of paper money. I collected the paper and tried to pay off court advances in it, getting the discount ½ [anna ?] in the rupee for the dep[artmen]t, but Keane would not give it, and I had to give in. I got a clearance in full from the Deyrah treasury dated 31 May 1858.

Living in the field in 1858, I had little or no expenses, as I could spend nothing. I see my remittances to the Delhi [Bank] were Dec[ember] 57 r[upee]s 69, Jan[uary] 1858 r[upee]s 396, Feb[ruary] 239.2, March 239.2 (my mil[itar]y pay I suppose) + 178.11.8, April r[upee]s 150+500, May 42/12 and 244/12 + 300, June 458/12 and so on.

Sometime in 1858/59 we presented a memorial to Col Ramsay on his retirement. It was proposed for each to give a month's staff pay. My share would have been 300/- [rupee]s, but it was reduced to ½ and I paid r[upee]s 150/-.

8 March 1858   I had a correspondence with the Mil[itar]y Orphan Fund about Sarah's pension. I was informed that my uncle had never paid the extra donation for the increased and continued pension. I find I first remitted r[upee]s 54/12 the family contribution from 1 Jan[uar]y 1856 to 8 July 1857, which was only acknowledged on the 29 June. This was by mistake credited to the acc[oun]t of Dr J. C. Graham who was murdered at the same time, but this was corrected on 20 November.

After the capture of Lucknow I looted from the prime minister's [of Oudh] house an immense [? palhel] gharree [cart]. It was far too large to take about so I left it at Lucknow. In 1859 I got it repaired and sold it, but got little more than the repairs cost. From the same house I got a picture of a durbar, of the Mohammedan festival of Mohurrum which I have still, and a map of Oude which was stolen from me at Monkstown [Co. Dublin]. In a Nawab's house in Oude which was burnt I got the desk I have still (which I got [repaired ?] at Bareilly), and in it a number of women's silver ornaments, an etui case, eight-bladed knife *etc. etc.*

When I got to Fattehghur in Dec[ember] 1858 I went to see Henry Hamilton Maxwell who was lying wounded in the foot. He had quite forgotten me, but knew me at once when I said that, "Modesty was the sweetest attribute of youth". When in 1849 we were sleeping together in one room in the Shrubbery at Darjeeling, he used as a joke to impress this on me night and morning. The next time I saw him was in the theatre at [? Nymatul] when he said, "The last time I saw you, I had met with an accident. I have met with another since: let me introduce you to Mrs Maxwell" ...'.

[Graham's diary at this point starts entries for 1859. The references to the mutiny end, and the crisis of 1857-8 is passed, and Graham concentrates on the routine work and life-style of an Indian officer.]

INDIAN LETTERS

Letter from William Graham to James Graham,
12 July 1857, D.812/10/B/38 (see p. 44 below).

8 May 1857

D.812/10/B/1

Dr James Graham, Sialkot, to his
nephew, James Graham, Landour.

This letter concentrates on a discussion of
two topics close to Dr Graham's heart; the
finances of the Delhi Bank of which he is a trustee, and his coming leave
which he intends to spend in the hills to escape the worst of the summer
heat. '... Sarah and myself determined some little time ago to spend my two
months privilege leave on the summit of one of our neighbouring mountains,
seventy-eight miles from this station to the north-east of Jumnoo. It is by
far the finest site for a convalescent depot of any yet discovered in India.
At the top of this mountain you have level ground extending sixteen miles,
no thick bush jungle, no thick forest, but wooded like a nobleman's park.
It is from eight to nine thousand feet high with a beautiful puka fountain
which pours out water throughout the year. ...

My leave commences from the 16th instant and we shall escape the hot winds,
the furnace heat of which you know I dislike. ...' Dr Graham also informs
his nephew that his son, William, is also travelling from Kanpur to spend
some leave at this hill station.

Towards the end of the letter there is a very slight reference to the first
stirrings of the mutiny. '... I have nothing new to give you, our sepoys are
quiet and well behaved notwithstanding the rumours you see in the papers to
the contrary. ...' The letter ends with a discussion of the affairs of
friends and relations.

18 May 1857

D.812/10/B/2

Dr James Graham, Sialkot, to his
nephew, James Graham, Landour.

'Many thanks for your letter just received.
Our Europe letters from this all go *via* Agra
and all those sent by last mail have a poor chance of reaching Bombay.

We have had no letters from Delhi or any place lower down the country for
the last five days.

It makes one shudder to think of the treachery and massacres that have taken
place at Meerut and Delhi.

We know nothing of the details, and it is folly to reason on results. Our
sepoys here have shown no signs of open mutiny, but the brig[adier]'s
arrangements have been such that we owe their forbearance more to fear than
love. There can be no doubt the mutinous feeling is universal, but we have
not the means at our command to adopt strong measures, tho' every hour's
delay is submitting to a prolonged disgrace showing and proclaiming to the
whole world the slender hold we have on this mighty empire. If the horizon
clears however past events will result in great good.

As far as accounts have been received we are all safe in the Punjab.
Jhelum has given no trouble yet I believe, and letters received this morning
say the 39th n[ative] i[nfantry], marched out of that station all staunch.
Your old corps therefore is likely to keep its honour and character. At
Lahore the disarmed are trying to escape. At Ferozpore a rupee a head was
offered the villagers to seize the 45th n[ative] i[nfantry], and they have

[? boned] at least 500 of them, and the 57th are laying down their arms. Jones is puzzled as to what to do with so many prisoners. Had the Punjabees got a hint that dead or alive they would receive a reward for all heads brought in (dead or alive) not a man would have escaped! H[er] M[ajesty's] 27th marched in progress to join the moveable column on the 15th from Niashera. Phillore is safe: a dour from Jullunder was just in time. The [? Nusseeree] batt[allio]n from [? Sutog] accompanies the siege train from that place to Delhi. This corps made some difficulty in moving, but has repented of its folly. The 61st at Jullunder has shown a bad spirit, but letters from that place say it was to be polished off!

Goolab Singh is *poz* [possibly ?] dead, but this is not likely I fancy to affect us. What loss the Delhi Bank will sustain I cannot say. Beresford's [the manager of the Delhi Bank] murder is a sad catastrophe for it [the Bank], and if the books and Churcher have all disappeared it is impossible to guess the results. The cash balance was never or seldom above a lak. This has been looted beyond a doubt, but as we had a lak and eighty thousand of a reserve fund, we could rally without much feeling this heavy loss. Perry is a good man and he must come from Lucknow. I hope Churcher has escaped, his name is not amongst those said to be murdered.

The Delhi Bank

How mutable are all human schemes and prospects. I had a letter from Beresford dated the 10th when business was flowing on prosperously and no loss whatever expected from the failure of the London and Eastern Bank, next day he was slaughtered and the city sacked!

On the subject of Sarah's coming out to you, it is I feel a very difficult thing to speak on or decide. Had such been your intentions years ago she ought to have been sent to a good school where both her manners, carriage and education would have been well attended to. She has not had, poor girl, the opportunities given your other sisters. She is I hear remarkably awkward in her movements, and is wanting in those pleasing ways and little accomplishments which we see in this country. Under such circumstances I am afraid your disappointment would be great and her chances of a comfortable settlement but very small. Almost all the girls that come to this country tho' but half educated, have a few superficial accomplishments which fit them for the society they are intended for, and they have brass and impudence which gives them conversational powers and with training at home they enter a ballroom as if accustomed to society from their infancy. These qualifications I fear are entirely wanting with Sarah. An easy indifference in manner and movement in society or in a ballroom require some training and experience, and your sister Sarah has had none, and I am therefore afraid life in this country would have few charms for her, and I am presuaded if she could get settled at home her happiness would be greater than it ever could be in this country.

I have you see ignored expense, knocking about and every other *consideration*. I give such *considerations* no *consideration* for I know your pride and ambition would overcome all such, but it is those very feelings of pride and ambition which I think would be wounded in finding that money would not in any way make amends for the want of early training and that an expensive fit-out, or any other amount of expenditure would not give your sister those graces and little accomplishments which are prized and looked for in this country. I have not my dear James allowed my feelings to withhold my honest views on this important point for your sister is my own flesh and blood, and therefore there should be no concealment or reserve. Nor would I have written as I have done, but on the best information.

William arrived here on the 9th and has been ordered to do duty with the 9th cavalry. Brind thinks it is not possible for him to retrace his steps at present. We are all very kooch, notwithstanding the *hubbub*! What a sensation this will create in England, and what changes must follow. High caste has had its day, and Sikhs and low caste will now take place. The [? Brammins] and others have cut their own throats. Our European regiments must be trebled and you must have an increase to your department.'

19 May 1857

D.*812/10/B/3*

Dr James Graham, Sialkot, to his nephew, James Graham, Landour.

'I have just received yours of the 13th with enclosure for your sister which I shall keep bye me.

Many of those said to be murdered in Delhi have turned up and are now either at Meerut or Amballa and things in the end will not turn out so disastrous as you imagine. A letter from Montgomerie the commissioner at Lahore says the crisis in the Punjab is over; the country to a man in our favour; Sikhs enlisting with eagerness; and the chief commissioner has urged the c[ommander-in-]c[hief] to unite [the] Amballa force with that at Meerut and march on Delhi. The electric telegraph from Meerut to Calcutta all right, and in working order, so there can be little if any commotion lower down.

The guide corps and 4th Sikhs are making forced marches to join the c[ommander-in-]c[hief] and the moveable column is fast approaching Jhelum.

This mutinious cloud depend on it will soon disappear, and will end in good for the country.

If our [Delhi] Bank books are saved we shall rise again without difficulty, our losses (if books are forthcoming) will not absorb our reserve fund. Now I think I have given you enough to comfort your feelings. We are all serene here, and more than a match for any treachery that can be shown. All we want at present in the Punjab is some assurance that our friends and the country below Delhi are not pushed or in danger. This good news is delayed by the Delhi [? row] but it will come to us speedily I have no doubt, and if need be the Punjabees will thrash the Hindostanees whom they despise. Our native reg[imen]ts still true to their colours, and in charge of treasure. Those at Peshawar wanted the 21st n[ative] i[nfantry] to join them. The latter very cooly handed their correspondent's letters to the authorities, and gave their rascally friends a pukka jawab.

The hosp[ita]l at Jullunder burned in open day, but we are strong enough here. Thanks for the home news ...'. Dr Graham ends discussing the affairs of members of the Graham family, and of various friends at home.

21 May 1857

D.812/10/B/4

Dr James Graham, Sialkot, to his nephew, James Graham, Landour.

'H[er] M[ajesty's] 52nd, the whole of the art[iller]y, a squadron of [the] 9th cavalry, and the 35th n[ative] i[nfantry] leave this on the night of the 23rd to join the moveable column at Wuzeerabad.

We shall on their departure only have the 46th n[ative] i[nfantry] and two squadrons of the 9th cav[alr]y at this place. The news from every quarter of the Punjab is cheering; the people are with us and are eager to enlist, and show their zeal by seizing all the deserters they can get hold of.

We have nothing to fear and as good accounts have been received from Meerut, Agra and other places we are decidedly looking up. The taking of Delhi and departure of the c[ommander-in-]c[hief] for that city which you speak of in your letter are not facts, but they will be so soon I trust.

If the English bank books are lost the native ones will I trust be forthcoming. At present no steps can be taken, and in fact nothing authentic is known of the late massacre at Delhi, and it is folly to speculate regarding results. I have today seen letters from Amritzar, and Jullunder giving good accounts of the state of feelings in the native troops at both these stations. One was from the com[mandin]g officer of the 61st n[ative] i[nfantry] declaring the corps had never in any one instance shown anything but the most willing loyalty. What can we believe when we see such contradictions and that too from the best authority.

What we want to hear of is an advance on Delhi by the c[ommander-in-]c[hief], and large force. If the mutineers are slaughtered there as they ought to be, I am persuaded the mutinous cloud which now hangs over us will with all others disperse. The moveable column will be at Wuzeerabad on the 25th, and will I dare say march right on to Amballa.

I had a letter from Sir J[ohn] Lawrence yesterday from Rawal Pindee, but it contained little of importance save the movements I have mentioned, and that he thought it would be well if the ladies here went to Lahore, telling me Sarah could go to his large house there. At present we don't think of moving.'

23 May 1857

D.812/10/B/5

Dr James Graham, Sialkot, to his nephew, James Graham, Landour.

'Punjab all quiet. Letters from Jhelum this morning. Your corps and all there *kooch*.

I could fill a quarto sheet with rumours, but it is no use, *common fame* is in these days but a lying strumpet! The c[ommander-in-]c[hief] has sent off some detachments but is delayed himself for want of carriage.

Reports regarding Delhi differ. The mutineers without organization some say, while others say the contrary, and that they have mounted guns, on the walls and armed themselves from the magazine of small arms which was not blown up.

The 9th n[ative] i[nfantry] at Allyghur have it is said joined the insurgents at Delhi, ditto a company of sappers and hussars. Forty-seven men of the 45th n[ative] i[nfantry] have been seized near Amballa by the Patiala Raja, all of them exhausted.

A message has been received from the gov[ernor] N[orth] W[est] P[rovinces] saying [the] Madras fusiliers, 35th regiment from the Mauritious, and another from Ceylon ordered round and another Eur[opean] reg[imen]t coming up the Indus from Kurrachee, [and a] further two reg[imen]ts and artillery from Persia, and that orders have been given to intercept the China force on its way out. The rajas over the country have refused generally to join the mutineers.

Nusseeree batt[alio]n only helped themselves to three months pay from [? Dukshie] treasury and have returned to duty at Simla where all is now quiet.

This is all good news. Still we have no letters from Calcutta or down country, and the whole of our European force here and the 35th n[ative] i[nfantry] leave us tonight to join the moveable column. William too goes with [a] squadron [of] 9th cav[alr]y. A further batch of Delhi folks (twelve of them) have reached Karnal, and doubtless others will yet turn up, so I trust the traitorous massacre has not been so great as at first supposed. Sarah still with me and kooch.'

F

27 May 1857   Dr James Graham, Sialkot, to his
nephew, James Graham, Landour.

D.812/10/B/6

'I have had no letters from you for the last
three or four days, and we hear that
Saharunpore is threatened by the [? goggurs] which may account for your
apparent silence. Our European troops left us to join the moveable column
two days ago, and we have only two hundred Europeans of H[er] M[ajesty's]
52nd, and 46th n[ative] i[nfantry] now at this station, but all is
quiet. Smith of your corps has committed suicide, ditto Col[onel]
Spottiswood of 55th (late 21st) n[ative] i[nfantry]. The 55th, 58th and
64th n[ative] i[nfantry] in open mutiny. [The] 58th fired into the 10th
irregular cavalry. Law, 3rd in command shot a sepoy but got severely
wounded. Brig[adie]r Cotton with his art[iller]y and cavalry [are] now
hunting the sepoys of these reg[imen]ts down. Only one hundred men of the
55th stood staunch. Nicholson [the] d[istric]t com[missione]r [of] Peshawar
seized an editor of some nat[ive] newspaper who had just issued an
inflammatory letter inciting sepoys to mutiny, tried, condemned and hung him
in one afternoon. Sir J[ohn] Lawrence has approved of this sharp practice,
and telegraphed it down country. This decisive mode of treating mutiny is
what is wanted. Act on their fears and trust not on their forebearance.

Your reg[imen]t [the] 14th n[ative] i[nfantry] all right. The cause of
Smith's or Spottiswood's committing suicide not known. The rascals of the
55th seized their officers it is said as a guarantee for their own safety.
Orders just received; Sealkote force to join H[er] M[ajesty's] 24th foot,
leaving a troop of h[orse] art[iller]y at Wuzeerabad. If Cotton's force
cuts up three nat[ive] regiments it will do us much good, and may keep us
quiet here and elsewhere. Down country news I do not give as it would be
second-hand to you. W[illia]m is with [the] Sealkote force *en route* to
join [the] moveable column. Sarah is with me. She has had an invitation
from Capt[ain] and Mrs Lawrence at Lahore. We have had no down country dak
today.

Just heard that Bowie of the 51st n[ative] i[nfantry] has also committed
suicide. We hope this will find you and all your Landour friends well.'

30 May 1857   Dr James Graham, Sialkot, to his
nephew, James Graham, Landour.

D.812/10/B/7

'I need not give you the c[ommander-in-]
c[hief's] death at Karnal or any other down
country news. Such items must reach you long before my notes can. Now for
up country. The 10th irr[egular] cavalry have shown a doubtful feeling and
one of the nat[ive] officers held back when he should have acted against the
55th, and Nicholson has hung him, also a subadar major of some native corps,
and it is said that one man in every ten of the prisoners at Peshawar are to
expiate their acts on the gallows! N[icholson] is just the man for the
crisis now existing. The Queen's 24th reg[imen]t marching down with the
moveable column had reached Wuzeerabad but has just been ordered back to
Jhelum cause not known, and I hope your regiment has not been misbehaving.
Before closing this I may be able to give you more particulars. ...'

Dr Graham continues discussing the rumoured romance between James Graham's
sister Sarah and her cousin Joe Beatty, which was opposed by Beatty's father.

He then returns to the theme of the mutiny and the repercussions it has had on his financial affairs.

'... I owe the Bank of Bengal some 11,000 r[upee]s and have no money to speculate in Delhi [bank] shares, but tho' the loss may be heavy, equal to our reserve fund [rupees] 1,80,000, it cannot be more, and therefore do not throw away your shares.

I should not be surprised if Beresford and his wife and his children yet turn up. He had many friends amongst the natives to conceal himself and family. If he offered any resistance to the ferocious brutes of course he was slaughtered, then and there. On these matters however it is folly to speculate. If the books and securities be found our loss cannot be irreparable.

Orders just received for all the Europeans, and all our European sick to be sent to Lahore. Sarah will start tomorrow evening with Mrs Graham, and I trust [they will] reach [Lahore ?] in safety. They will stop during the heat of the day at Goojanwalla. It is rumoured that on the arrival of the moveable column at [? Mian Mir] the nat[ive] troops are to be mustered, nat[ive] officers ordered to the front and asked to point out the ringleaders, and that if the latter are not forthcoming thirty guns are to open on the whole body.'

3 June 1857   Dr James Graham, Sialkot, to his
                                nephew, James Graham, Landour.
D.812/10/B/8
                                'Today I have a letter to tell [that] the
                                last of our Europeans left us on Sunday night
and we remain quiet.

The moveable column expected to reach Lahore yesterday, and is not to go further. Sarah is still with me stout in heart, and in good spirits. Lahore is a disgusting place for ladies. They are obliged to go to barracks at 6 pm and are not allowed to leave them until 6 am, and all are in a mortal funk! Dak this moment in gives good news. Brig[adie]r Wilson has *licked* the insurgents at Hindown river, and taken some five pieces of heavy ordnance.

On our side the struggle is only commencing, and we cannot doubt the results. A signal vengence we must have for the brutal massacre at Delhi. Lots of court martials [*sic*] going on at Peshawar, and the 45th n[ative] i[nfantry] have not nearly all been seized. Bombay [troops] (550 of them) expected at Mooltan on the 15th. Others from that presidency to follow in their wake. Hewitt's khansamah was in league with mutineers and was shot by the *aide-de-camp* when carrying off his master's plate. H[ewitt]s being put to one side is a gain, such a fellow was never fit for command, a mere animal.

I am glad you have heard from Tom. He has not deigned to write to any one of us tho' Sarah has written him half a dozen of letters. The 45th [*sic*] murdered Spottiswood's khansamah the day before he shot himself. Full of confidence in the corps he had entreated the authorities not to send troops against Mardan. He thought he had brought the men to a sense of duty, and when he heard of the approach of our troops he retired to his room and blew his brains out.

Grant the c[ommander-in-]c[hief] at Madras it is supposed will come round
to Bengal. Your regiment is behaving well at Jhelum. The crisis may now I
think be considered over, if all goes well for us at Delhi, and if we can
give the rascals a lesson there never to be forgotten, opposition will cease
and tho' almost every corps in the army is tainted the fellows alive to their
own interest will fawn, cringe and show their obsequiousness.'

6 June 1857   Dr James Graham, Sialkot, to his
                                 nephew, James Graham, Landour.
D.812/10/B/9

                                 'Very little to write about, all quiet here.
                                 At Lahore the good folks are in an awful
funk, why or wherefore I don't know.

Goolab Sing and all the native chiefs behaving well.

To speak of Hissar Hansi and Wilson's fights with the insurgents would be
stale to you. Moveable column still at Lahore, and I suspect at Ferozpore,
and [at] that place the mutineer prisoners will receive a severe lesson ere
many days pass. Jones has been ailing. Heath who is now our [? executive]
engineer has had 5000 r[upee]s stolen out of his treasure chest. Sepoys
have had nothing to do with this matter, native treasurer suspected and will
have to pay account.

Sarah serene. Our padre Boyle the greatest of all the horror stricken here.
We have very few ladies except those of the 46th here. Fitzgerald has been
ordered to join the moveable column. Mrs F[itzgerald] and family with Mrs
Heath start for Murree tomorrow night, and F[itzgerald] at the same time for
Lahore. General Gowan has joined and now commands the division. A letter
from W[illia]m just rec[eived], officers of 8th cav[alr]y in a great rage,
believing their men staunch and loyal. Horses drafted into the horse
art[iller]y, and horse batteries. Very few nat[ive] cav[alr]y remain,
dragoons will be the order of the day! Madras fusiliers now near to
Allahabad, and the reg[imen]t from Mauritious in [sic] the river, 84th at
Cawnpore, and the reg[imen]ts returned from Persia will soon be at
Kurrachee. These are all quick movements. Success complete, and signal
vengence at Delhi will end the crisis.

14th n[ative] i[nfantry] and folks at Jhelum all right and nothing of any
importance up country. Owing to some false alarm 35th n[ative] i[nfantry]
marched in Lahore between wings of the 52nd. The latter capped and loaded
and the corps is so pitched that its position is commanded by twelve guns!'

7 June 1857   Dr James Graham, Sialkot, to his
                                 nephew, James Graham, Landour.
D.812/10/B/10

                                 'Yours of the 2nd has just come to hand, and
                                 as I have a few minutes to write before post
goes out I may as well tell you that we are all kooch and quiet here.
Beyond the bulletins of Wilson's success we have nothing very important.
Rumour says his force killed 2,000 of the insurgents in his last action with
them. If this be true their numbers and power I fancy are much diminished,
and they can make but a poor fight of it within the walls of Delhi.
Tomorrow I trust we shall hear the glad tidings of the city being in our

possession, and that a just vengeange for the brutal and gigantic crimes committed is in progress. If a Shahzada was with them so much the better. His presence will facilitate our future acts and policy.

The people at Lahore are in an awful fright. Ladies and gentlemen (or but a few of the latter) ever show themselves. We had a letter from William yesterday. His news would be stale to you. The moveable column remains for the present at Lahore, and I fancy you will ere long hear of some sharp and decisive punishments amongst the mutinous prisoners at Lahore, Ferozpore and Peshawur. Mercy to them is out of the question; firmness and decision, and the fate of our empire all require the last penalty, and die they must. Maudlin humanity and over indulgent sentimental feelings have placed us in our present position. Had we been rigid, stern and unhesitating in our rule our present difficulties would never have shown themselves, but it is folly now to speculate, for change our ways we must. The only good order I have yet seen is that of hanging the authorities, and burning the villages at all places where the electric wire has been cut or injured. Had the 19th and 34th reg[imen]ts received their reward - sharp and short as the cannons roar, we would have had no massacres to chronicle. Humanity and forbearance in this country are put down to fear! Might is right, and when not exercised is put down to pusillanimity. Our timid conciliating orders and policy are a lasting disgrace to our rule and will be so recorded in history.

No I did not write by last mail by the Scinde route, having seen the notice in the *Lahore Chronicle* when it was too late. Our down country and Agra daks are cut off by the marauding villagers. Our last letters from Agra are of the 26th ult[imo]. The officers of the 8th cavalry are greatly disgusted with the breaking up of the corps, ditto those of the 5th at Peshawur. Dragoons will I trust take the place of these regiments. Fitzgerald leaves this to join the moveable column at Lahore. Ladies and babas go to Murree. This station is deserted, nothing but empty houses. It is quite true Sir P[atrick] Grant is ordered round. Chester was the man to propose it. ...

Tom is not with the wing of his corps gone to [? Sirsar]. He has volunteered for Seik levies'.

8 June 1857   Dr James Graham, Sialkot, to his
                                nephew, James Graham, Landour.
D.812/10/B/11

                                'Your of the 3rd just received, and thanks
                                for the news it contains. Sergeant Tucker
of the art[iller]y here received a letter from a sergeant in Brig[adie]r
Wilson's camp dated the 2nd. It confirms almost all the items you gave me.
Wilson's force when it left Meerut consisted of 1,100 Europeans. They were
attacked at 5 pm on Saturday by the insurgents 1,500 strong. After a fight
of an hour and a half the rascals retired. On Sunday they made their
appearance in great force (9,000 strong) and after a fight of five hours
retreated, but were not pursued. Wilson's force being too small to allow
of this. On Sunday the rascals had seven guns. Our h[orse] art[iller]y
opened the ball on Sunday evening, but suffered so much that an eighteen
p[ounde]r was brought up to draw off the fire from them. The eighteen
p[ounde]r was manned by art[iller]y recruits of whom many were sun-struck
the heat being tremendous.

On Saturday we lost thirty-five, on Sunday twenty-six men killed and wounded.

The enemy's horse kept hovering around Wilson. The ammunition of Wilson's force reduced to twenty rounds, but more had arrived from Meerut. Troop lost fourteen horses on Sunday, the carabineers sixteen.

Sergeant MacRae who writes this letter holds a staff app[ointmen]t in the adj[utan]t gen[era]l's office Meerut, and commanded the eighteen p[ounde]r here alluded to. He is a clever clear-headed fellow.

The work of retribution will shortly commence at Peshawur, and elsewhere. At Peshawur nothing but court martials [*sic*], and at Lahore these courts commence today. At the former place Cotton intends to spare none. We are quiet here, no fires or other signs of disaffection. Your corps all right. The h[ea]d q[uarte]r force were to reach Delhi on the 5th, and now all must be there.

I have no time to look over this. So you must take it with all its faults. Wilson's force must ere this have joined the others.'

10 June 1857   Sarah Graham, Sialkot, to her cousin,
                                James Graham, Landour.
D.812/10/B/12

                                'Papa is busy, so bids me give you the news
                                today. William has joined the 16th irregulars
which marched on the night of the 8th from Lahore after a few hours notice *en route* to Jullunder the scene of the recent disturbances, and which place they were to reach in three days, marching upwards of thirty miles a day. Their ultimate destination is thought to be Delhi, but is not as yet known for certain, but [we] will hear from W[illia]m when he gets to Jullunder.

The moveable column was to have left Lahore on [the] evening of [the] 9th, destination not known. The Seiks of the 16th, 26th and 49th n[ative] i[nfantry] reg[imen]ts had their arms given back to them. The 7th, 350 in all are in the fort on duty, and the Seiks of all reg[imen]ts below Rawal Pindee are to be sent to Lahore to join the rest to form a battalion for duty there. When the art[iller]y guns from Hoshiarpore entered Jullunder the native reg[imen]ts it is said got so alarmed on seeing them, that they immediately ran to seize them, but were repulsed by art[iller]y, when so, they wounded several of their officers, and then ran off. Twenty rupees a head and fifty with arms [is] offered for any that are brought back. Brig[adier] Johnston with two hundred Eur[opeans] on elephants and the guns in pursuit of them [*sic*], also an irr[egular] corps under command of Captain *Nicholson*, but Papa thinks he must mean Chamberlain. There was a panic at Rawal Pindee William writes, and the European inhabitants all slept in the church, but [it] is said to have subsided. Capt[ai]n Coke's reg[imen]t all Afreedies and border men were at Lahore and were to go with the column also. It is said the 6th cav[alr]y at Jullunder headed the disturbance. W[illia]m had asked General Gowan to allow him to go and join his reg[imen]t, but was told he had better wait till the road was safe, and if he had started would just have been arriving in Jullunder at the time of the fracas.

I am glad to see by today's *Extra* that so many of the Jhansi and Hissur people escaped after all. We keep quiet here still, altho' one does not feel quite so comfortable now the Europeans have all left us, with the exception

of thirty sick men who could not be moved and a guard of forty for them. I
have not gone to Lahore after all. I was twice on the point of going Papa
thinking it better for me to do so, but the parties with whom I was to have
gone *viz.* Mrs Fitzgerald and Mrs Graham both changed their minds, thinking
we might as well remain until there was some cause for alarm, but nearly all
of the ladies have taken flight, but the accounts of the barrack's life at
Lahore is so dreadful that I feel quite glad I am not there, altho' I had an
invite from Capt[ain] Lawrence, but every lady I believe is obliged to sleep
in the barracks, and after all one is as safe here as there where they seem
to have been in an frightful state of alarm, altho' they have had up to the
present moment such a number of our guns, and only allowed to go to their
houses from 6 am to 6 pm and then alarmed to do so. W[illia]m on arrival
went to [? Mian Mir] but could only see *one* European who was ready armed
for an attack with revolvers *etc.*, so I intend to enjoy the comforts of life
quietly as long as I can, but the best of natives are not now to be trusted.
I think it is lucky for us all that the 46th and not [the] 35th remained
behind, for it was two of their sepoys who were blown from the guns. I am
glad you are all quiet at Landour. The poor padre here sets us all a very
bad example. *He* ought to be ready to die but he is in *such* an excited and
alarmed state. [He] came to call on us the other morning with his leather
belt with two pistols on. [He] went to Lahore under the pretence of
escorting Mrs Baker and [? Bourebier] over, but in truth to try and get
ordered with the moveable column as its chaplain. [He] telegraphed Sir John
Lawrence to know what he was to do, when [*sic*] the reply was *to do as he
liked*. In the mean time [he] had an order from the brig[adie]r *here* to
return immediately, asking him if he was not the chaplain of *Sealkote*.
[He] has now applied for the chaplaincy of Fort William. In fact [he] does
not know what to be at. Padre [? Cave-Browne] too came down with the force,
but has been ordered back to *Peshawar* forthwith. W[illia]m had no horse so
[I] have lent Robin to him and I only hope nothing will happen to him, poor
animal, for I would never get another like him. Captain Fitzgerald left to
join the moveable column two nights ago. Tom does not go to Sirsar with the
wing of [the] 10th. I hope W[illia]m won't get sick from all this exposure,
for the heat must be dreadful in tents. When he wrote it was 120° in tents,
but he was under shelter while at Lahore. No overland letters in yet. We
are all most anxious for the *Delhi* news. This station looks so deserted –
not a buggy or a single individual scarcely to be seen in the evenings,
exception Friday's 46th band night.'

11 June [*sic*] 1857   William S. Graham, Jullundur, to his
                             cousin, James, Graham, Landour. William
                             misdated this letter (probably written
                             on 11 July) when upset by the possible
D.812/10/B/13   death of his father and sister during
                             the Sialkot rising of 9 July.

'Just one line to tell you Sealkote Brigade gone too. Brind mortally wounded,
Bishop, B. M. killed, Balmain of the 9th wounded; they were with some other
Europeans (who not known had got into the fort). Montgomerie had to ride for
his life to Gogranwalla and sent the news on. As you can fancy I am anxious
about Sarah and the old governor – God grant they are to the fore and [I] am
anxious looking out for news. I am *en route* to Delhi, and start tomorrow
night by mail cart and trust I will be in time for [the] storming. I will
send you from Umballah a letter for the governor which keep pat in case
anything happens me, then send it to him. Amongst other things I will strongly
urge it on him to make peace with James, and a handsome ring in memory of Miss
Roberts. In these uncertain dark times should you not receive it, this show
him with love.

12 June 1857   Dr James Graham, Sialkot, to James
                                Graham, Landour.

D.812/10/B/14

                 'At this station and at Jhelum all quiet.
                 At Peshawar nothing but court martials [sic]
and blowing rascals away from guns. Letters just rec[eive]d mention thirty-
seven of the 55th had been sent out of this world in this way, and that
three had been shot by musketry. Very few of this corps remain unpunished,
but a number have had their sentence of death commuted to transportation.
You will have heard of the nat[ive] corps at Jullunder, and Philore, their
attempt to seize the guns, their repulse and their desertion. Their flight
not being ascertained until morning, gave them a long start of our troops
who are now in pursuit of them, but it is generally believed they cannot
escape and that they will be destroyed. W[illia]m volunteered to join the
16th irr[egular] cavalry, and is now with that corps which started from
Lahore to intercept the rascals going by the Hurraki ghat. They were to
make thirty-five and forty mile marches. I don't know what Robin will say
to such stages, but his blood should tell. Tom volunteered to go with
General Courtland's irregulars, but I fancy none of our officers have been
taken for it. The moveable column has gone after the Jullunder villains,
but it must be slow in its movements.

Eleven officers were wounded at Jullunder but none seriously. The nat[ive]
artillery behaved splendidly; no holding back. They first fired when they
rushed on their guns, killed fourteen and wounded it is impossible to say
how many. I have not seen a list of all the wounded but, amongst them were
Bagshaw, Bates, MacMullen and Dunsford. Some of these runaways have got
into the fort at Loodianah in which they are surrounded by the Seikhs, and
last accounts say the latter had some guns and were booming away at them.

No tidings from Delhi yet. When a blow is struck there matters will
improve no doubt. I write in great haste to save the post. Sarah unites
in kind love.'

13 June 1857   Dr James Graham, Sialkot, to his
                                nephew, James Graham, Landour.

D.812/10/B/15

                 'Thanks for your letters of the 7th and 8th
                 and all the news they give. I have letters
to send you on this occasion. The Jullunder and Philore mutineers have I
fear escaped without much cutting up, but you will see in the papers all
about their breaking up. We continue quiet here and not only occupy our own
homes, but take our drivings morning and evening as if the whole country was
serene.

We received yesterday the acc[oun]t of Gen[era]l Barnard's having beaten the
mutineers from the entrenched outposts and driven them into the city of
Delhi; but of the further doings of our force we as yet know nothing, but as
the telegraphic wire to Amballa and Lahore is now complete we shall I trust
have further intelligence soon. [? Wylly] of the 9th cavalry is in arrest
at Lahore. He went to Chamberlain drunk and I fancy nothing can save him.
The moveable column is now halted for orders at Umritzar, its future
destination not known.

Glad shall I be to hear of the safety of Beresford and his family, he is a
good man in every sense, and would at this crisis be invaluable to the Bank.
I have not yet seen anything in *The Friend* or *Mofussill* regarding him, but
our daks are still in arrears. No doubt many will yet turn up, and in Delhi
our gov[ernmen]t and the late European residents have still many well wishers
who would show kindness in any way.

I think your mother is wrong in withholding her assent to Sarah's
accepting Joe Beatty's offer. I am however free to confess that it is
objectionable and I can enter into her feelings, nevertheless your sister
has no chance of another such offer, and I would therefore allow her to
accept it. Miss Pack has I believe £3,000, and her deafness is her only
fault. I hope you will not at this season be obliged to move to the plains.
Of course you send old Nuthall frequent accounts of his babas, and when next
you write tell me all about them; what they are like, and if intelligent
nice-locking children. The mutineers at Delhi fought right well in their
outpost affair. After it numbers have fled in all directions [*text torn*] ... ·
These quailing proclamations from the gov[erno]r of Agra are bad. He is a
white feather and should be removed or told not to issue such trash to be
recorded against us in history. Trifles are significant in these days and
the natives will only bow to a strong and intrepid will. At Lahore they
have been commuting the sentence of death to that of transportation; a bad
policy I think. All right at Jhelum and other stations above this.'

14 June 1857   Dr James Graham, Sialkot, to his
                                nephew, James Graham, Landour.
D.812/10/B/16

                        'Letters from Jhelum rec[eive]d last night
                        express anxiety regarding your reg[imen]t
the 14th. The news comes from Brown the d[istric]t commissioner, but
particulars I have not heard, and cannot I am sorry to say give you. If I
hear ought more of interest you shall of course hear. We are quiet here
and the 46th and [the] wing of cavalry now here have sent a petition to
gov[ernmen]t offering their services against the mutineers, also [the] 70th
at Barrackpore.

With Rawal Pindee on one side, Lahore and the moveable column on the other,
your corps will think over it a little before they commit themselves.
Gen[era]l Reid is calling out for more troops at Delhi, and Jullunder for
the present is to be abandoned and the 8th Queen's go on to join our force
[at Delhi ?].

We have had accounts from Delhi up to [the] 10th all going on well. This
morning we hear we have silenced the mutineers' guns at the Cashmere Gate
and that the rascals are determined to make their last stand at the palace.
The hope of aid from Bareilly and Wusseerabad keep them together. Tom has
not gone with the Seikh horse and is all right at Ferozpore. Jones it is
said is inclined to be too lenient.

At Agra they are in a awful fright; taking everything from their houses,
ladies in [the] fort and officers in barracks. Once the blow is struck at
Delhi all this nervous excitment will cease. Send me a few lines every day
with any [? gleams] you have. I am glad to hear such good accounts of
Nuthall's babas. He will feel your kindness and attention to them, and

write to him frequently regarding them. In this way you make him a warm
friend. William is now with the 16th irr[egular cavalry], he volunteered
to join them, [and] Chamberlain agreed and allowed him to take the loan of
a horse from [the] 9th [cavalry], and with Robin he is getting on well. The
16th [? makes] Jullunder from Lahore in two [marches] and I believe
Loodianah [by ?] the 3rd! This is doing well and they will if allowed to
continue soon be at Delhi. At Jullunder W[illia]m arrived just in time to
see six dak [? peons] hanged. When the row commenced these youths plundered
the Dak Ghur Treasury.'

16 June 1857   Dr James Graham, Sialkot, to his
                                nephew, James Graham, Landour.
D.812/10/B/17

                                'Yours of the 12th just received. Thanks for
                                it. I have had no further particulars
regarding the uneasy feeling in your corps. It may be the result of mere
suspicion. If they go wrong and come this way they will disturb the harmony
of this station. A wing of H[er] M[ajesty's] 61st and art[iller]y from
Ferozpore ordered to Delhi. The Queen's 8th and art[iller]y from Jullunder
go also. The moveable column taking the place of the latter. A letter just
received from William dated Loodianah with the 16th irr[egula]rs. He says
the Jullunder mutineers are off to Delhi moving in excellent order to the
bugle call. Nine more seditious rascals of the 35th Sikh n[ative]
i[nfantry] handed up by the nat[ive] officers for trial.

Chamberlain it is reported is to be our new adj[utant] gen[era]l. All the
officers of the guides were wounded at Delhi. W[illia]m expects our
squadron will remain at Loodianah and that the rest of the body will go on
to Delhi.

Ramsay Nuthall your chief's eldest son, who was a patrol officer in the
Bhramlpore country got to Ferozpore and Tom gives us a curious passage of
arms which occurred between them (they are schoolfellows). I quote from
Tom's letter, "Ramsay Nuthall strange to say made his appearance here on
the night of the fires. He had come in from Bhramlpore and when close to
cantonment he came across a whole lot of the 45th men, who commenced
regular file fire at him as he passed them. I myself being on sentry duty
at the time heard some one gallop in our direction after this firing had
occurred and immediately rode out to challenge the party - who would not
answer! The consequence; I pursued the fellow and being on a good horse
soon overtook the animal and the villain turned out to be my old friend and
schoolfellow Nuthall."'

18 June 1857   Dr James Graham, Sialkot, to his
                                nephew, James Graham, Landour.
D.812/10/B/18

                                'The rumoured strong suspicions regarding
                                the loyalty of your corps have passed away
and letters received from Jhelum yesterday say it is staunch and sending a
petition to gov[ernmen]t offering its service either at Delhi or elsewhere.
This will be very gratifying to you, and has been a great relief to
residents here, who feared any bad or unsettled feeling amongst your men
would end in something untoward here.

All at Peshawar and above this is tranquil, but our anxiety to hear of
progress at Delhi remains, tho' not yet great. I have no news to send you
today. The state of nervous excitment at Lahore continues excessive, and
so anxious are they there to get every European, that all our sick leave
this tonight and go over in two stages, so we have nothing but the hope of
the 46th n[ative] i[nfantry] remaining true to their salt. I had no letter
from you yesterday, and we felt the absence of your bulletin as you generally
give news. If you have leisure therefore send us a line every day with any
scrap you may pick up. I had a letter from Parsons from Aleuorah yesterday;
all right there he thought, but they had to disarm the artillery. I had no
letter from W[illia]m yesterday, and our Calcutta daks and indeed all below
Amballa are nearly a month behind time. The 26th ult[imo] are the latest
dates we have recieved [*sic*].'

19 June 1857   Dr James Graham, Sialkot, to his
                                nephew, James Graham, Landour.
D.812/10/B/19

                                'Nothing since yesterday worthy of special
                                notice. Thanks for yours of the 14th. The
dak from your quarter more regular than others. All right at Jhelum, but I
suspect the civil authorities got a little alarmed about your corps. The
feeling however has passed away, and a small detachment (two comp[anie]s)
has been sent to Rawal Pindee. Here we continue quiet. A sepoy of the 46th
n[ative] i[nfantry] used threatening language to the subadar major yesterday.
He was tried immediately by a native reg[imenta]l c[ourt] martial. It
proved a case of mere black-guardism, and want of temper. The court however
did its duty [and] was quite ready to hang the fellow if occasion required,
and gave him five years with hard labour on the roads, and got rid of the
rascal. We have heard of our success at Delhi on the 13th but no
particulars. Bad look-out that on the 12th. What imbeciles we have got,
caught napping in such times. These sorties tho' attended with loss to
insurgents do not allay their energy.

You will have heard the following items before this reaches you. Sir H.
Somerset [is] to be c[ommander-in-]c[hief] in India until a nomination be
made at home. Sir P[atrick] Grant [is] to be c[ommander-in-]c[hief] in
Bengal for [the] same period. Sir H. Barnard [is] to command [the] Delhi,
field force. Chamberlain [is] to be adj[utan]t gen[era]l and Nicholson to
take his present command of [the] moveable column. A European reg[imen]t
has reached Allyghur *en route* to Delhi. Officers of disbanded or mutinious
corps [are] invited to serve at Delhi, field and staff off[ice]rs [are]
excluded. All [are] to proceed at public expense. 8th Queen's and [a]
wing of 61st go to Delhi.

No letters from W[illia]m. Johnstone the brig[adie]r at Jullunder very
much blamed. All stations above this quiet. I am afraid matters are very
unsettled in Rohilcund, but the news of that quarter will reach you quick.

21 June 1857   Dr James Graham, Sialkot, to his
                                nephew, James Graham, Landour.
D.812/10/B/20

                                'No letter from you for the last two days,
                                probably owing to the irregularity of the
daks. Yesterday we had no news. It had been arranged that our force would

have stormed Delhi on the 13th. The approach however of reinforcements made it prudent to delay the attack. This is perhaps fortunate. The rascals have increased in number, and let us hope the blow may be more terrible. The 14th n[ative] i[nfantry] is all right again, and have volunteered, ditto the 58th at Rawal Pindee. The latter cheered Sir J[ohn] Lawrence when he left their parade. *Entre nous* and strictly private your old friends were shaking, not that the officers would believe it, but are under the impression that the civilians had erroneous information. However some little delay in receipt of pay drafts and pay was to have been the excuse for a row. The d[istric]t c[ommissione]r made the com[mandin]g officer apply for an advance, and two co[mpanie]s ordered to Rawal Pindee, since which time the uneasiness in the corps has ceased. Here you have the whole and true account, but don't say a syllable of it as Gerrard and officers like others have been deceived and believe the whole story got up to the prejudice of their men.

It was supposed they would have come this way for the 46th and cav[alr]y and [then] have gone on to Hoshiarpore for the 33rd. The Ghats were guarded and boats broken up and sunk and all arrangements made to prevent their departure until served as the 55th n[ative] i[nfantry] were.

We continue quiet here. This delay in taking Delhi is bad. Brigadier Johnston it is said showed great want of energy. Had he been active not a man of the Jullunder mutineers would have escaped!

The officers of the mutinious reg[imen]ts are called on to volunteer. Many will not like this. Heroes they are until ordered to the breach! W[illia]m is now at Hoshiarpore with 280 sabres of the 16th irr[egular cavalry] to overawe the 33rd. He is not wanting in pluck and has been sent there by Chamberlain who gave him a horse (the loan) from the 9th cav[alr]y to use while absent from his regiment.

We have no news from down country. No daks from Calcutta. All stations above this quiet. We hope Landour keeps serene. Tom has been out in a raid and is quite well. We have had two or three letters from him of late.'

22 June 1857   William S. Graham, Hoshiarpur,
                          to his cousin, James Graham, Landour.

D.812/10/B/21

                         'Yours of the 14th [has] but come to hand
                         today, and [I] find you are not well
acquainted with matters down country. You say no down country daks in [? weeks]. We have heard of [the] arrival of [the] Chinese expedition with no end of guns on [? Lancaster's dodge] [*sense ?*] all coming up with 1,000 marines, more power to their elbows. We were detached from the moveable column at Lahore and was [*sic*] certain we were on our road to Delhi, but were brought up at Loodianah where we found them in a funk. We settled matters there and have been sent over here to Hooshyarpore I suppose to keep a look out on the 33rd they having showing [*sic*] signs of gagyness. They greeted us by firing their lines, as we entered cantonment, but still their fool of a commandant says he thinks it was accidental. Fancy putting such things down to accident now-a-days. We have but one hundred and fifty sabres here, but think they are good men and true, but who knows now-a-days who is such. I may tell you before I go further that I am with [the] 16th irr[egula]rs now on same footing as the 4th officer in Punjaub reg[imen]ts. Chamberlain gave

it me on applying for it. Have seen lots of hanging, and if we are kicked
out and can get as far as England I can take to Jack Ketch['s] business.
Lots of excitement now-a-days, and if it only would keep a going I would be
a young man when entitled to my furlough. Sad to read of those wretches at
Delhi, but there is a day of reckoning for your Hindoos and Mussalmans.
There is no death bad enough for them. Hanging they dont care a keep about.
You see up in these parts chaps cutting jokes with the hangman when they
have the ropes adjusted on their necks, and the other batches waiting their
turn grinning like good-uns when they see their comrades launched into
eternity ahead of them. Bareilly business bad to. If you know Cawnpore
[? gass] give it me in full as of course my stake likes [sic] in those
quarters. I would be sorry if anything happened [to] the 2nd chaps. After
this is all over I think we will find ourselves dragoons. What a blessing
when fellows get rid of command[in]g such scoundrels. I would sooner take
to cab driving. Fancy [the] 68th begging the officers to get down their
families from the hills the day before they broke out, and swore they would
protect them as well as themselves, they having a plot made at the time to
murder them and their officers. I hear they hung a lot of European
res[iden]ts. Its not a nice style of death is it. Tip us a line and give
us all the news. ...

[P.S.] Tell me all you hear about James. I believe he was all right.'

22 June 1857   Dr James Graham, Sialkot, to his
                                nephew, James Graham, Landour.
D.812/10/B/22

                                'I have sent you a few lines every day for
                                some time past, but no letters being
received from you, I imagine the daks are closed, and neither yours or
mine find their way to their destinations.

Here we are all quiet. The moveable column has not halted at Jullunder but
is returning in this direction. We had a letter from Delhi camp dated the
18th yesterday. The 66th n[ative] i[nfantry] had joined the insurgents on
the 13th but did not get in without heavy loss from us. It was supposed
the Rohilcund mutineers had also joined. The assault was not to take place
until reinforcements came up. This may not be before the 27th or 28th. We
have not only to storm the city but also to protect our position and
batteries outside, and can afford to risk nothing.

Post going out so must conclude.'

23 June 1857   Dr James Graham, Sialkot, to his
                                nephew, James Graham, Landour.
D.812/10/B/23

                                'Private letters from Delhi camp yesterday
                                gave somewhat more cheering accounts:
Gen[era]l Reid did not want more troops; Wilson had recrossed [the] Jumna;
insurgents dispirited and showing no bold front! The assault and
reoccupation of the city cannot be far distant.

A campaign may be necessary in Rohilcund, but Khan Bahadoor Khan will ere
long find his true position on or under the gallows.

We continue quiet here and your corps at Jhelum is serene also. All
stations above this tranquil. The active measures taken [? are] final and
the fate of the 55th have had their effect. Punjab rivers have risen, ghats
looked to, boats not available, and the moveable column ready for a dour
anywhere to polish off any rascals who may show their teeth. Received your
letter of the 18th yesterday. A circular from post m[aste]r gen[era]l,
N[orth] W[est] P[rovinces] received here yesterday directs all letters
intended for Agra, Lucknow and down country to be dispatched *via* Kurrachee
and Bombay. Since [the] 7th no down country daks received. This state of
siege will soon have an ending.

Sarah has had a little fever for the last two days, nothing like ague but a
dry burning heat and thirst - still however stout in heart no frettings,
pinings or high doings like other ladies around us. All art[iller]y
officers on staff employ [are] ordered to join army h[ea]d q[uarte]rs at
Delhi. Heath leaves this to-night and his wife and babas go to [? Murree].

This move takes away all protection from Mrs Fitzgerald and she and the
O'Dowda go to Lahore this evening. The moveable column is now at Jullunder
and is not to cross the Sutlege. Nicholson joined it on the 19th when
Chamberlain started for Delhi. The Queen's 8th and other reinforcements
cannot reach Delhi before the 27th or 28th. Our friends in England know ere
this of our mutinies, an express steamer left Bombay on the 20th ult[im]o.
You will see how Palmerston and buoyant little England will vindicate her
insulted dignity. I trust however ere the influence of their acts can be
available we shall have done something to establish the honor and rights
of John Company.

Write to me every day. Your dak is open regular. Give me all news you can.'

25 June 1857

D.812/10/B/24

Dr James Graham, Sialkot, to his
nephew, James Graham, Landour.

'Thanks for yours of the 20th. Of course
you see the *Lahore Extras* and thus get the
Punjab news.

I have just seen letters from Peshawar and other up country stations, all
right and quiet there. The [two words illegible] and Pandays have had awe
stricken into them. They have cut their own throats too. We are to have poz
[possibly ?] 50,000 native contingent troops and a large increase to our
Europeans in the Punjab. Among the former no poorbias I imagine.

The 14th n[ative] i[nfantry] going on well and the officers have great faith
in them. Jones of the 61st was saved by some of his men. They made him
dress as a Hindoo and act the part of one. He was in the midst of them and
the very men of whom he had formed the highest opinion and thought most
attached were those who cried out, "Where is he, don't let him escape"!

We have rumours here of large reinforcements but where are they to come from
unless we have caught the China expedition? In England they now know of our
difficulties. An express steamer with fresh acc[oun]ts left Bombay on the
20th ult[im]o.

The 46th here continue to give no annoyance, no incendiarism or ought else

to indicate doubtful feeling, but who can tell if they will continue loyal?
Those who are not with us and for us are against us. Prudence and self-
interest may prompt delay and a wish to know how the tide of affairs may
ultimately tend, but any feeling beyond this cannot be calculated on. Not
that we are intrusive aliens or oppressors, for they have not good feelings
enough to be patriotic, but simply because they have been too pampered and
spoiled and allowed to talk of caste and dictate to the gov[ernmen]t, that
a feeling of contempt has grown up amongst them for their officers and
gov[ernmen]t.

Sarah has still some fever, tho' better today, she is still unable to write
or do anything.

Give me a line everyday ...'.

28 June 1857   Dr James Graham, Sialkot, to his
                                nephew, James Graham, Landour.
D.812/10/B/25

                                'I had two notes from you by yesterday's dak,
                                the latest dated 21st. Many thanks for them.
I may be wrong but I think this or tomorrow will decide the fate of Delhi,
and all the mutineers in it. Glad tidings you give of Lucknow, Cawnpore and
Fatteghur being all safe. Cheering too, to hear that the 84th was so near to
Delhi. Letters have been received at Ferozpore from Calcutta dated the 3rd
instant. Up to that date nine European regiments had reached the
presidency. Yesterday we heard that the China force with [? its] art[iller]y
were on their way up [sic], so we can't be pushed to extremities now. I had
a letter from Tom yesterday, he had just returned from a raid to intercept
some rascals crossing at a ghat. All right with him and at Ferozpore. The
head [? imidal] of the magazine was to be hanged. This man had served
gov[ernmen]t for more than thirty years, had the unbounded confidence of
Lewis, was entrusted with the keys of the magazine, brought them at sunset
every night reporting all well. In fact he was the factotum of the magazine
establish[men]t. When the [? amentia] took place he was [not] even suspected,
nor would Lewis believe anything regarding him. He was allowed for days after
the row to retain the keys, and make his report. On his trial he confessed he
had for months past known all that was brewing, and what would take place, but
tho' offered a pardon if he would give the history of the past, he declined.
We shall get to the bottom of this deep hid plot in the end, nevertheless yet,
the history will only be one of treachery and intended massacre.

Rumour here says the 33rd and 35th n[ative] i[nfantry] have been disarmed by
Nicholson. It is but a report but I hope to have letters from W[illia]m
today. All quiet at Jhelum and we continue so here, and at all stations
above this. We are to have in the Punjab I believe 50,000 native levies
(Seiks I suppose) and a great augmentation of our European force.

Sarah is better tho' very weak and without appetite. She sends her love to
you. The moveable column is still at Jullunder and does not cross the
Sutledge. I hope you will not be moved from Meerut, and that you will not
fail to write to Nuthall and show all kindness to his babas. This state of
affairs may expedite Ramsay's return and I wish him back on account of the
Delhi Bank. He would be most useful at this crisis to its re-establishment.
If our books and securities turn up I do not despair. Without these the
result it is difficult to forsee.

The *Lahore Extra* you see so I do not give you its items of news. ...
P.S. I have no time to read my letters over.'

29 June 1857   Dr James Graham, Sialkot, to his
                                nephew, James Graham, Landour.
D.812/10/B/26

                                'Hard work our troops had on the 23rd. An
                                excellent account of the whole days fighting
has been received here, dated Delhi 24th. The rebels chose ground full of
gardens surrounded by high stone walls, and intersected by narrow roads. I
know the place well. During the day we lost four men by *coup de soliel*, and
some seventy killed and wounded. So exhausted were our men, that Europeans
who had just reached camp after a march of twenty-two miles, were ordered
into action! Great want of art[iller]y officers. Tombs and his troop
distinquished themselves, [and] had a great number of horses killed and
wounded, but no men.

Nothing Sir J[ohn] Lawrence says in the way of assault [on Delhi] can take
place before the 1st or 2nd prox[im]o. Our reinforcements from the Punjab
cannot reach [Delhi] before the 28th-29th.

China force not yet arrived, but the other reg[imen]ts on the move up the
country. All quiet here and above this. Who is Capt[ai]n Jackson killed
in last action?

I know not a soul in Cashmere, very few there now. Not more than twenty-
four, and ^{2}/3rds of these ladies! Make no purchases until you can better
see your way. This Delhi Bank affair may make a change in my movements.
Sarah is free from fever, but very weak and no appetite.

Jullunder is deserted only one co[mpany] of 8th there. You see the 33rd and
35th disarmed, a bad lot, and I believe not to be trusted. Nicholson will
serve them out if occasion be [necessary ?].

Our rains have commenced, and change pleasant, but they will not add to the
comfort of our gallant fellows at Delhi.'

29 June 1857   Dr James Graham, Sialkot, to his
                                nephew, James Graham, Landour.
D.812/10/B/27

                                'A few words will tell you all I have to say
                                today. I have seen also letters from [the]
judge advocate gen[era]l. What he says of the dates when the great assault
is to come off is all humbug. He has been out more than once to my
knowledge. We do not expect the fall of Delhi before the 2nd and shall not
hear of it before the 5th or perhaps 6th. Chamberlain superseded at
Mooltan his seniors; put them to one side and ordered the disarming parade,
saying he would not stand with his arms across to have his own throat and
the throats of his countrymen cut.

Nicholson, too, managed well. The 35th and 33rd thought they were on their
way to Delhi and it is supposed they would have bolted after passing Loodianah.
At Phillore two hours before the 33rd reached that place he disarmed [the]
35th, and on the 33rd coming up after a long forced march when worn out and

fatigued he disarmed them. Each corps after putting down their arms was obliged to put them in carts which were ready for the purpose, and into Phillore magazine all were put in a twinkling. Nicholson's orders to Sandeman com[mandin]g the 33rd were, "If you have carriage so much the better, but with or without it you will two hours after the receipt of this communication have your regiment on its march to meet me." All this time everyone supposed they were bound for Delhi. He did not quail before the rascals but pointing to the guns told them what their fate would be if any act of their's indicated sedition or disloyalty.

We are quiescent here and so are all stations above this. Sarah tho' free from fever is still very weak. I wrote to your sister Anne yesterday.'

30 June 1857   Dr James Graham, Sialkot, to his
                                nephew, James Graham, Landour.
D.812/10/B/28
                                'Tho' I have little to give you in the way of
                                news yet it is something to receive a friend's
sign manual in these days of throat cutting.

I have seen an e[lectric ?] t[elegraphic ?] m[essage ?] from Delhi dated 28th sent here from Lahore express. The rascals continued their attacks on our picquets and had been invariably repulsed with but trifling loss on our side.

Our reinforcements arriving fast and most acceptable they were. Knatchbull's batt[er]y which was disarmed but a few days ago, and now at Lahore is ordered to Delhi. It will be useful mixed up with Europeans. Great want of art[iller]y and art[iller]y officers. Europeans have been working eighteen p[ounde]r batt[e]r[i]es which they did cheerfully and well. 9th n[ative] i[nfantry] had left the rebels, got out of the city pursued by some of the rebel horse. We are making but little progress, tho' our reinforcements getting stronger.

Sarah still very weak and without any appetite or strength. ... P.S. That born idiot Wood should be got rid of. In these times he is not to be trusted.

All quiet here and around this.'

1 July 1857   Dr James Graham, Sialkot, to his
                                nephew, James Graham, Landour.
D.812/10/B/29
                                'Very little today for you. Some
                                combustible materials were found at Jhelum
near the engineers' go-down, placed there for no good purpose, and it was supposed incendiarism was about to commence preparatory to a row more significant, but I am glad to say nothing has occurred, and all remains quiet, and I think you may calculate that with tranquility here and at Rawal Pindee and Noorpore and Umritzar, we have reason to hope there is an end in this quarter to mutinies. However all depends on our success at Delhi. Your note of yesterday was written in *parvo* and gave us lots of news. The Baughput bridge has been broken up, but not until we had received all our military stores, all that was necessary for the assault.

37

G

How are the Rohilcund rebels to cross the Hindun and Jumna? The destruction
of the Baughput bridge has cut them off, and how are our reinforcements to
join our head-quarters from down country? The Jysore contingents were in my
day a set of ragamuffins, but I believe [they] have improved, tho' I should
say not to be depended on.

Sarah keeps free from fever, but very weak. She sends kind love to you.

The moveable column comes back to Lahore.'

2 July 1857   Dr James Graham, Sialkot, to his
                               nephew, James Graham, Landour.

D.812/10/B/30

                       'It is hard to say what may be news to you,
                       and I fear what I do write is stale and flat
to you. I told you the 10th irr[egular] c[avalr]y had been disbanded. It
appears they affected to charge the 55th when pursued by Chamberlain. They
did so but when in the midst of the rebels never struck, killed or wounded
a single man of them! Hence they have been disbanded, their horses, arms,
accoutrements and all the money on their persons confiscated by gov[ernmen]t.
They leave penniless, and this is a kind of punishment they will feel and
understand. Hard fighting at Delhi on the 27th. It lasted four hours. They
came out to take our advanced batt[erie]s, returned well beaten, with a loss
of seven hundred killed and wounded. Our Europeans got amongst a lot of them
that had taken shelter in some old houses - put them all "out" with the
bayonet. This is the first time they have felt the cold steel. They did not
fight as well as usual. Our reinforcements among [which the] 29th n[ative]
i[nfantry] stand fast it is said. Nothing said of [the] 8th irr[egular]
cav[alr]y. Some sepoys in camp, a co[mpany] of 3rd and some of the 61st,
they are looked on with great suspicion, and Europeans would like to get rid
of them. Their small arm ammunition is failing. All our men were killed by
slugs made from the e[lectric] t[elegraph] wire. This news may be depended
on. It came from the best authority in camp. Report has it that the
g[overnor] g[enera]l is opposed at present to an assault and urges simply a
continuation of shelling.

Sarah is better but very weak. ... [P.S.] An officer of the 10th
irr[egular cavalry] sent a report of the doings of his men in pursuit of the
55th. He declared they had killed four hundred of them !!!

No letter from you yesterday!'

3 July 1857   Dr James Graham, Sialkot, to his
                               nephew, James Graham, Landour.

D.812/10/B/31

                       'Many thanks for your two kind letters of
                       the 27th and 28th, and for all the news they
contain. Your news is most interesting. I think, indeed [I] am sure I get
all your letters, but as yesterday they sometimes reach me two at a time.
No accounts yet of the fall of Delhi, but we are expecting them daily. The
Lahore Chronicle which you see hints that the assault would take place on
the 1st and Chamberlain writes on [the] 29th that he hopes then in the
course of two or three days to hear the good old honest saxon cheer inside
its walls. I hope so or the Gwalior contingent will add much to the force
of the rebels.

Delhi Bank affair bad, and loss must arise, and that too heavy, but I do not take such a gloomy view of its affairs as Simpson and yourself. If Ramsay were in the country he would be most useful, in this our day of trouble.

Hobson I have voted for tho' I know not the man, but Ramsay had the highest opinion of him. I wrote to Mr Murphy on the subject and I know he rec[eive]d my letter as I had a letter from Mr Healy arising out of my vote for Hobson, however he has not replied.

Our eastern and down country news comes *via* Bareilly to Lahore. It is given you in the *L[ahore] Chronicle* sooner than I could send it you. A bad business that at Benares - the 11th Seiks refusing to act. Nicholson continues blowing away deserters. He quails not and makes the native art[iller]y do the work, or die the same death. He is now on his return to Lahore, and it is whispered he will disarm the [? 59th] at Umritzar, but this is mere rumour. He has struck awe by his bold and decided steps. The word is said and death surely follows; no idle threats, and if he were put in command of the moveable column [*sic*] a just vengence would have its course and his very name would strike terror wherever he made his appearance, I mean the column for hunting

Lurid contemporary engraving of a mutiny execution scene, in which the condemned sepoys were 'blown away' from field artillery guns.

down the rascals. All continues quiet here and above this. A letter from Tom yesterday, all well at Ferozpore. W[illia]m has had no reply to his application for guide corps. I don't know why but the people at Lahore were in a state of great nervous excitement. Where are our reserves, I mean those corps from [the] Persian Gulph, Bombay and Madras which we know reached Calcutta weeks ago? In the assault I am only afraid of mines, the explosion of which may occasion great loss as they did in the entrenched camp at Ferozshah. A gallant band that one hundred and eighty Europeans at Benares.

Sarah is better I am thankful to say but very weak, and without appetite.'

4 July 1857	Dr James Graham, Sialkot, to his nephew, James Graham, Landour.
D.812/10/B/32	

'We have letters from Delhi as late as the 30th. No one then knew when the assault would take place. It is just possible that Chamberlain may try and blow open one of the gates. All the reinforcements had reached [? Hurdun] and the Jhansi contingent blamed for giving up the Bhaugfut bridge. Nothing new in this part of the world. All quiet here and above this. The moveable column dodging about and Nicholson hanging deserters. Not a man of them escapes, and he makes the native art[iller]y do the work.

I hope the subadar major and non-commissioned officers of the 69th n[ative] i[nfantry] will be hung at Mooltan. Lawrence and his officers have established a reign of terror in the Punjab which Blacky appreciates!

Sarah keeps free from fever, but still very weak. She sends her kind love to you. We should hear from England by next mail I think. On the 20th of May accounts of mutiny left Bombay. Nothing from the eastward beyond what the *Lahore Chronicle* gives. Ponsonby you see has been set to one side, and I fear the rows at Benares, Lucknow and other places detain our reserves. Grant cannot come up the country without an escort of a regiment at least.

This is a poor return for your letters which are full of news.

14th at Jhelum all right in spite of that madman Wood. What is to become of him? [? Wylly] of the 9th cav[alr]y still in arrest at Lahore for drunkeness. Farquharson the brigadier of Mooltan still here.'

5 July 1857	Dr James Graham, Sialkot, to his nephew, James Graham, Landour.
D.812/10/B/33	

'We have several letters from camp dated the 1st. They give no hint as to what is to be done or when it is probable the assault will be made, only express the hope that something decisive will soon be decided on. The small arms ammunition of the rebels expended. Our advanced picquets caught a fellow picking up caps and bullets. On being questioned [he] confessed he got one anna for the former and two for the latter. Their shells are filled with [? kunkur], and their powder is of their own making and bad. This is all satisfactory. People at Lahore uneasy, why I can't say. Gaitskill and Gray of the art[iller]y have been ordered over there from this, and three co[mpanie]s of H[er] M[ajesty's] 24th with three guns left [Rawal] Pindee

on the 1st for that place. Here and above this we are all serene. Of the
moveable column we don't hear much beyond the blowing away from guns. At
Jhelum all quiet. Brind had a letter (overland) from Gen[era]l Taylor
yesterday clearly hinting that there existed a good deal of anxiety at home
regarding the dread of a mutinous spirit being general in our native army,
and you will have seen what the *Lahore Extra* says on the subject in an
extract taken from the "*Press*".

It is generally believed that Cawnpore is safe. So W[illia]m will not be
the ruined man he supposes! Six horses no bad stud for a sub! He is still
at Hoshearpore, anxious to be off to the guides. Sarah is better but very
weak. She sends kind love to you. Some talk of no pay for three months,
but this I do not believe.

Old Goolab Sing keeps quiet and has sense enough to remain so. The Chumba
Raja fired a salute when he heard of the mutiny. His sun will soon set!
The [? 10th] cavalry are employed (part of them) with two officers to
escort military stores from Ferozpore to Delhi. This will be a test and
trial for the gentlemen. Tom is not of the party. As you see the *Lahore
Extra* I say nothing of what you find in them [*sic*]. Montgomerie is very
guarded in his news.

We know nothing of the whereabouts of the 84th and other regiments coming
up country, save what the [*Lahore*] *Extra* of yesterday gave us of the 64th
and 78th.'

6 July 1857   Dr James Graham, Sialkot, to his
                                 nephew, James Graham, Landour.
D.812/10/B/34
                                 'We have had letters from camp dated the 2nd.
                                 They give detailed accounts of the actions
of the 19th and 20th which were very severe, but as these dates are old I
shall say nothing of them, but pass on to what we were doing on the 1st and
2nd instant.

"Since yesterday" says the writer, "our batteries have given the enemy the
heaviest fire they have yet had. Last night we had destroyed the bastion at
the Lahore Gate [and] dismounted their guns. This morning we found the
whole repaired with sand bags and fresh guns mounted. We are now pitching
into them with shot and shell without ceasing and certainly they keep up a
good fire in return.

They have four batteries besides the guns on the bastions playing on us.
They have used stone shot of late thinking they would do more execution in
splintering.

The rebels have received large reinforcements. On the Meerut side they had
a very large camp yesterday, and we could see large bodies passing. This
morning the tents have disappeared, with these fresh men we shall have
another desperate attempt on our batteries. The c[ompan]y of the 3rd and
other sepoys in camp have been paid up and told to go to their homes which
is just as well, as they were looked at by our men with great horror and
suspicion. General Wheeler having got Europeans have [*sic*] given the
rascals a thrashing at Cawnpore. Col[o]n[el] MacKenzie of the art[iller]y
has just been brought in wounded, but I am glad to say slightly.["] This is a

41

long extract but it will show you that we are hard at work, and it may be
Sebastapol *"Feu denfer"* before the assault, tho' I doubt it. Blacky never
fought so well or showed such energy in our service as he is now doing!

[? Bus] for today. We remain quiet here and I should hope the great crisis
of revolt is over.

Sarah is better but still weak.'

8 July 1857   Dr James Graham, Sialkot, to his
                               nephew, James Graham, Landour.
D.812/10/B/35

                               'No very good news to send you. A private
                               letter just received by us marked *secret*,
says the 14th n[ative] i[nfantry] at Jhelum mutinied this morning at 6 am
(the 7th), particulars not known. In fact we alone have received the news.
Another letter from Goojerat from [the] same person says heavy firing of
art[iller]y at Jhelum has been heard for at least ½ an hour. H[er]
M[ajesty's] 24th (three co[mpanie]s, three guns and some four hundred
Moltanee horse) had left Rawal Pindee for Lahore it was said, but no doubt
Lawrence had his eye on the 14th and they must have reached [Jhelum ?] just
in time to put the rascals down, its hoped. I trust not one of them will be
spared, they have been deceiving their officers who have been indignant that
a suspicion should have been attached to their loyalty. The civil
authorities however have been right, and if the officers and their families
have been spared they have them and no other to thank for their safety.

It is not improbable that this affair will lead to the disarming of all
other native reg[imen]ts in the Punjab. Nicholson and his moveable column
will make a desperate effort to cut these rascals up. Mercy is a word not
to be found in his vocabulary!

You will be in a great state of suspense to hear further regarding this
affair, and you may rest assured as far as we can you will have full
particulars.

The dak has come in from Jhelum which in part proves they have not got out
of the station. An e[lectric] t[elegraph] communicated the facts stated.
Cripps has gone to Wuzeerabad with two hundred police to cut up stragglers.
They cannot escape I think, our rivers are so full. The 46th here, the 59th
at Umritzar and 4th at Noorpoor and Kangra appear all right. I have told
you in my last letters that there would be no assault on Delhi until some of
the Eur[opea]n corps from below would [reach it ?]. The death of Barnard is
a merciful event. Reed, I know well, but he will be in the hands of
Chamberlain, from whom great things are expected.

We have letters of the 5th from Delhi, but nothing in them worth repeating.
Sarah is better with some little appetite. My home plans are unsettled. At
present I feel it impossible to decide on what I shall do. The chances for
and against going are equal showing the mutability of all human schemes!
This will not go off until tomorrow morning the 9th, and I shall keep it
open to ought I may hear further.

I have nothing more to add to this.'

9 July 1857   Dr James Graham, Sialkot, to his
                               nephew, James Graham, Landour.

D.812/10/B/36

                               'Yours of the 3rd just rec[eive]d today. I
                               have no news. We have the news of an
e[lectric] t[elegraph] of the 5th from Delhi which says Coke attacked a
party outside with a force, and twelve guns and gave them a good dose! All
other accounts refer to Wheeler's coming with two or three European
regiments to co-operate with investing force. Moveable column at Umritzar.
Thermometer 114° in tents. Some references have been made to h[ea]d-
q[uarte]rs regarding Chamberlain and Nicholson's appointments, complaining
of the supercession. The answer was "If you have any objection to serve
under them, you may take leave of absence for an indefinite period". I have
not heard from W[illia]m for two days, and he usually writes every day.

I do not think the assault will be made until the reinforcements coming up
arrive, and it is very provoking we cannot hear of their where-abouts.'

9 July 1857   [Misdated ?]   Dr James Graham, Sialkot, to his
                               nephew, James Graham, Landour.

D.812/10/B/37

                               'Your news received two days ago regarding
                               Gwalior and Jhansi confirmed by today's
Lahore Chronicle.

It is very sad to think of all the brutal murders which we now see daily
recorded! I write to you always in doubt thinking all my news will be stale
to you, but if so you must make allowances. I have good accounts of [? Sevat]
country and the remaining mutineers of the 55th n[ative] i[nfantry]. The
latter were surrounded by Becher's force and could not escape, and Vaughan
had hanged a [? Sevat] chief. Our investing army is getting closer letters
say, and the rebels more cowardly. The moveable column was two days in
crossing the Beeas. How will Knatchbull get on having only his officers
(his men and guns being left at Lahore) with twelve heavy ammunition
wagons? The [? Kummaon] batt[a]l[ion] take eight laks and ammunition from
Phillore so they will be long in reaching [sic]. Seikh art[iller]y being
raised for neighbouring stations, and Seikh horse for investing army.
Bombay fusiliers taking it easy, making but regular marches from Mooltan.
59th all right at Umritzar. A false report that they would be disarmed.
The Calcutta gov[ernmen]t in reply to the question, "Where are the 84th and
the Madras fusiliers", answer, "Somewhere up the country", showing how all
communication is cut off. 37th from Ceylon hourly expected in Calcutta.
The brigadiers at Delhi are Jones (an excellent man but as you know too
nervous), Langford, of him I know nothing, Showers and Grant; these two
latter said to be queer religious fanatics.

We continue quiet here and all stations above us is [sic] the same, and will
I think continue to be so, the rise in the rivers being against any escape
to Delhi or their homes. Your reg[imen]t is behaving well I hear.

It is strange but you still hear timid fools recommend mercy and leniency
for our mutineers. They must be driven to desperation! This is cowardice.
The fellow who talks so only shows the white feather, and ought to suffer
the penalty affixed to it. Depend on it if the terrible urgency of our
affairs does not receive a just retribution, the native regiments who have

mutinied will think we are afraid of them, or that in our eyes they have committed no crime,and [they will ?] seek an early opportunity of again having the pleasure of murdering the sahib log and their wives and families.

Bus Khyr for today. ... [P.S.] Lieut[enant]s Locke, Blair and Yorke wounded on the 30th. First and last very dangerously. News from Cawnpore tho' not full particulars - Sir H. Wheeler managed to hold his own by hard fighting and has now reinforcements of Europeans.

The rascals came out to erect a batt[er]y to enfilade ours and caught it.'

12 July 1857

D.812/10/B/38

William S. Graham, Jullundur, to his cousin, James Graham, Landour.

'Just one line to tell you it is reported in the *Lahore [Extra/Chronicle ?]* of today that my poor father is amongst the murdered at Sealkote. Is not this dreadful news, and nothing certain known about Sarah, God grant that she is amongst those that have got into the fort. I am in a dreadful state about her and have telegraphed up to Blackall at Gogeranwallah to send and find out, and to let me know at once. This sad news has made me alter my plans, and if Sarah is alive I will at once start upwards. I will send her home by Mooltan. I trust she has not fallen into their hands as death I think [is] preferable, knowing what wretches they are.

I know nothing of the poor old governor's affairs and if I mistake not you know more, and if his papers and all are not recovered (as I hear they looted everything) I fear little will be forthcoming. Give me your advice, and knowing what a father we have lost I know you will feel for us in our grief. He sacrificed himself for us for he had no business coming out here again, but he had noble ideas regarding the duties of a father, they were too much so, address me to Jullunder. ... [P.S.] I am writing to Anne.'

27 July 1857

D.812/10/B/39

William S. Graham, Sialkot, to his cousin, James Graham, Landour.

'Many thanks old fellow for your last two kind letters. It is indeed kind of you speaking of our poor father in the affectionate terms you do. I know you loved him, and few there were in India who had so many friends. Young and old here lament his loss. Everyone has some tale, of his kindness or what he was to great and small, to tell us,which is a kind thing to us all, who now when he is no more fully appreciate him. His life he sacrificed for us, and [I] am sure one with so many noble and honest qualtities and whose every thought was honor, is now a partaker in a better world. Tell me *one* parent in India like him, none like him in any way. I have found his will and last codicil of 53. There was another unsigned, cutting James of[f from] everything, but I am just as glad as we all are that things are as they are. If Delhi Bank had been all right he would have had five lacs or thereabouts. I sent you my letter to Parsons to read, since then I find I am an executor as all his sons will be once they arrive at twenty-five years old. This I am glad at as it prevents inquisitive people gratifying their curiosity. He divides all into thirty parts; James and I 16½ each, Tom 4, Sarah 7 and Phoebe 4, but its a rum will, not but that its based on good sense, and all for our good and believe me we appreciate it.

44

To show you how glad the world are [*sic*] to oblige his memory I had a letter from Dick Lawrence yesterday asking me if I would like to join Golab Sing's force of 3,000 strong of infan[tr]y, 250 cav[alr]y and six guns, native officers to com[man]d their own men, and the few Europeans to be appointed to make themselves generally useful, and if I would take the appoin[tmen]t my pay would be r[upee]s 600 a month (fancy if the old gov[erno]r was but here to see this would he be not happy). Dick L[awrence] is to be made brig[adie]r gen[era]l and comm[an]d, and of course I have accepted. We are to be at Jullunder on [the] 4th of the month and join the force there. Luck is it not, we will be at Delhi about ten days afterwards. I volunteered for Nicholson's force and got out but a few hours later, unfortunately [not] in time to have the gov[erno]r's coachman and mate [? Benni] shot *[sense ?]*. His [? Mussalchee] was hung here, he having rode out to Wuzeerabad for information for the mutineers as regarding the strength of H[er] M[ajesty's] 24th art[iller]y *etc. etc.* His military career was a short one, and was polished off on his return. Only two servants stuck true [? Causomat and Dirsie]. All jewels *etc.* looted. House awfully destroyed, and everything nearly broken. Let me thank you my dear fellow for your kind offer of money to send Sarah home. Until things are settled, namely the Delhi Bank transactions, one knows not what they can call their own [*sic*], and perhaps if Sarah did go home now it might only be to come out again. Tell me what you think of that bank's affairs, and if you think they can come down on trustees or directors *etc.* Deeds I should say all destroyed. Address me to Jullunder.'

Nicholson's attack on the Sialkot mutineers

[Mid-May ?] 1857   Thomas C. Graham, [? Ferozepur], to
                    his cousin, James Graham, Landour.

D.812/10/B/40

'I have just seen your letter to
[Brigadier ?] Innes in which you tell him to
make me write to you. It is all a bang about our having cut up the 45th,
there are now about two hundred and fifty of them here, who have come back
and given themselves up. The rest with a portion of the 57th took their
departure the day after they had burnt our houses. A squadron of our
regiment which is thank God *staunch to the backbone* together with two guns
went after these fellows, but they had got two or three hours start, and
having separated on the road, we in consequence missed them. There are
however about nine hundred of them in the gaol here, the villagers having
pukharooed a lot, and brought them in. Everything is all quiet here now.
We are in camp up here by the barracks which are just next door to the old
fort where all the ladies, powder and [guns^{12}] are carefully stowed away,
and now I fancy we are only waiting for the c[ommander]-in-c[hief's]
hikkum meaning "order" as to whether we are to continue remaining in camp
or not. What a dreadful affair that was at Delhi. Have you had any news
from Mooltan. I hope your reg[imen]t is all serene. Write and tell me
what news you have.'

20 August 1857   William S. Graham, Jullundur, to his
                    cousin, James Graham, Landour.

D.812/10/B/41

'Our force has arrived at last and we are I
hear to make all haste to the imperial city
and [I] [? trust] we will be in time to have a share in the [? walking] into
Pandy. The poor old 2nd gone to a man I fear. James [? Vehart] having been
killed with Tudor Tucker of [the] 8th cav[alr]y at Fatteyghur. I suppose he
was trying to get down. I am the only one of the old lot to the fore, and
many is the good fellow gone. We must have vengeance and of no ordinary
description. I had a letter from the Bank of Bengal yesterday, it was
addressed to the old governor. The half year's dividend was declared at
eleven per cent. This is not bad. His dividend was 3,840 [rupees ?] for [the]
half year. I have written to both these banks namely Bombay and Bengal for
a statement of their acc[ount]s, and if I find anything not out at interest
I will have it put into this new six per [cent] loan for the present.

There is great uneasiness felt at Lahore about Lucknow. When you hear
anything of James let us hear. I trust he is all right. I want you to write
me a copy of [a] letter that I should write about Sarah, and tell me who I am
to address it to.

We had a letter from Anne last mail - no news. I hope to start with [the]
force in a couple of days, so address me to Loodianah, ... [P.S.] I have told
the sec[retarie]s of [the] banks to address me to your care. I will tell you
where to forward me to [*sic*]. I wrote to Miss Roberts last mail and if the
old gov[erno]r will come down handsome I hope still to be spliced to her.'

12. *Deleted in original text.*

24 August 1857   William S. Graham, Jullunder, to
James Graham, Landour.

D.812/10/B/42

          'You know me too well to look upon me as a
dun, I am infernally hard up having had to
lay in a regular new set of things, having only brought up three changes of
everything when I left Cawnpore. If you can have an order for 80 [? diks]
awaiting my arrival at Umballah, I will feel very much obliged to you, but
don't inconvenience yourself. I am starting for Delhi with some twenty
Seikhs. Address me to await arrival. [Dick ?] Lawrence is not a general,
a simple captain.

We start from this on Tuesday. Sir John [Lawrence] is here and reviews the
force tomorrow.

This suspense about Lucknow is bad. I trust Havelock will not be too late.
There is uneasiness felt at Lahore regarding the fate of Lucknow. You see
the 10th have gone at last. Its a blessing, but the brutes could not go
without murdering before starting.

We will be in lots of time for Delhi business. Mew is with me, he has got
the adj[utanc]y of a new Punjaub inf[antr]y reg[imen]t at Mooltan; as good
a fellow as ever, and deeply laments the loss of his many friends in the
second. No news.'

27 August 1857   William S. Graham, Ludhiana, to his
cousin, James Graham, Landour.

D.812/10/B/43

          'Many thanks for your kind note addressed to
me here and [I] will follow your advice as
regards Sarah's getting into the fund. Her health was never better than it
is now both mentally and physically. She wrote to me yesterday on the same
subject telling me that the same was reported at Simla much to her disgust.
I told her to cheer up and not mind ill rumour. We heard last night that
Lucknow has been taken and oceans of niggers polished off. Gen[era]l Neill
also wrote to say that 15,000 men, women and children had had their
desert[s] from British bayonets at Cawnpore. This is awful retribution
but we [? refunded] it. We have got off with the force at last, and I have
never seen more soldier-like looking fellows with any natives before [sic].
They are much superior to the [? Patiala] or [? Kapurthalia] forces.
We start tonight and get into Umballah in four days, and by going at that
pace we are in hopes we will be in time to see the fun. Rouse up old Dickey
and get him to put me into the stud. No man takes greater interest in
horse flesh than your humble servant so get him to nominate me to go to
[? Ampalia] to help in purchasing horses. Government will have to do something of this sort after things settle down. Just bring my name prominently
forward to him, and tell him [of] my fondness of the noble dumb Hannimal
the Os [sic].

Anne's letter was on what you mentioned. I did not answer it thinking that
my advice would have little weight, but if you wish I will write and can
conscientiously recommend it.

Is Simpson or any of the other shareholders exerting themselves about the
Delhi Bank affair. Tell me if you have heard what they mean to do about
it. ...

[P.S.] I find I have left out the most important part of my letter. You were kind enough in case of Sarah's wanting to go home to lend us something for that purpose until we can get my poor father's affairs settled. Sarah wrote to me yesterday and is awfully anxious to start, and promised me she might make arrangements to start before the month is over. Now if you can let us have r[upee]s 3,000 at interest of course in case anything should happen, one or other the three of us will sign a promissory note for the amount. If you can do this I will feel much obliged.

11 September 1857

D.812/10/B/44

William S. Graham, Delhi, to his cousin, James Graham,

'It was expected the attack would have been made today, but I fear there is no chance of it for some days at any rate. We have two of our advance batteries open and the old [? Moree] Bastion we have knocked to bits, but they show wonderful pluck and still fight their guns in it [*sic*]. I hear it is a Seikh who commands it, and he must be a very fine fellow. I heard from one of Nicholson's friends that he is in communication with the above party, and I [think ?] the Seikhs who are inside once the attack is made are ready to hold any part of the city for us we like to name. I can't vouch for the truth of this, but report says so. Everything is kept uncommonly dark, and at Lahore and other places outsiders receive much better news of what is going on that we who are on the spot do. We will have some thirty guns or so now open on them before evening, and a mortar battery of ten two inch how[i]tzers which ought to warm our friends up a trifle.

Lots of sickness in camp, but its wonderful what our Europeans stand. The rose-buds go down to trench duty, and are very kooch I swear, they kill no end of fellows. Johny Pandie's days are wearing short. Ni[cho]lson issued an order the other day entreating our Europeans when they get in [inside Delhi] not to forget they were Christians, and spare women and children, but no quarter to any one else. Prize agents have been appointed, and we are all looking forward for the great event. It will be hot work the street fighting, but [? *two words illegible*] won't wait long once we are in the walls.'

Sarah you will be glad to hear has started. [Sir] John Lawrence got my poor father's pay so that is all right, not but what we are deeply obliged to you all the same for your kind offer of assistance. Tom took her as far as Mooltan. She goes from that with Mrs Younghusband of [the] 35th [*sic*]. Here it is continual firing night and day and the inf[antr]y fire sounds just like the irregular hammering you hear in a dockyard when caulking ships. What English news had you by last mail?'

20 September 1857

D.812/10/B/45

William S. Graham, Camp Delhi, to his cousin, James Graham.

'Delhi is at last ours, but not [until ?] after seven days hard fighting, and after dreadful losses; sixty-seven officers killed [and] wounded, and I hear some 1,200 rank and file. You can fancy how we were polished off. I told you in my last the part we took in the attack on 14th, and the poor rose-buds got an infernal licking and lots polished off. I was with one hundred of Lawrence's police, and had twenty men and twenty-six horses killed and

*Both sides of an
Indian Mutiny
service medal with
clasps for Delhi
and Lucknow
campaigns*

wounded. Some five hundred of us got in the clutches of some 4,000 Pandies
and did they not pitch it into us like bricks. When you are writing to
Simpson tell him to write to the paymaster of divisions not to give up the
letters of form signed by parties taking out loans from Delhi's banks,
telling them when to cut into, and to what date such cuttings were to go on,
as there are a lot of undisciplined young sons, who are anxious to get these
as they know they are proof against them, and fancy the shareholders of
[the] Delhi Bank have no longer any claim against them. I will tell you one,
Caulfield of the 9th cav[alr]y, who I knew *entre nous* to be an undisciplined
young hound. Don't forget to make Simpson do this. There was none of the
bank papers found, the place being a mass of ruins. I am indeed glad to
hear of Sarah's [James Graham's sister] marriage and I think it a good
match. Joe [Beatty] is steady and she will make him a good wife. Poor
Nicholson is dying. I cannot tell you what a fellow he is. His loss like
Mackeson's and Sir H[enry] Lawrence's is a dreadful calamity, especially in
such times. His poor mother I pity for, well may she be proud of such a son.
I have had symptoms of cholera and our two d[octo]rs insist upon my going
for [a] change as this is so rife at present. Yesterday Greathed of [the]
c[ivil ?] s[ervice ?] died and Metcalfe of [the] c[ivil ?] s[ervice ?] not
expected to live. Now that Delhi is gone I think it likely I may go, so
address your next [to] Umballah. If you were going to remain at Landour I
might come your way.

Tell Simpson if they get a copy of these forms from each paymaster it will
enable the sec[reta]ry to trace loans.'

24 September 1857

D.812/10/B/46

William S. Graham, 'Hotel Umballah',
Ambala, to his cousin, James Graham.

'Just received yours with Delhi Bank information which is good as far as it goes, but how
Mr Sec[reta]ry flatters himself that because he has a list of twenty lacs of
rupees of loans he is sure of getting them, is more than I think. You know
as well as I do what Indian ideas and morals are, and what a number of
loose fish were indebted to banks.

I am afraid myself it is more difficult than it is imagined, and if we get
fifty per cent of what is paid up in shares we will be lucky, and I will bet
you a quiet five G.M. [*sense ?*] we don't get this. If what you say *is true*
it will make me very comfortable and make some five lacs of rupees of the
poor old governor's for distribution amongst his family, of which I get 6½
[shares] it all being divided into thirty shares. This will make my share
about £13,000 and this by the time I am thirty-four six years hence would be
a good £20,000, and then please God cut the whole thing. I am very seedy
with diarrhoea, and am not allowed to leave my bed today which is a bore as
I wanted to be in Delhi within the ten days. I am indeed sorry that such a
thing has even been mooted as an uncovenanted commis[saria]t, but of course
you fellows now in it would have the option of joining it, and it would still
be on the old footing of pay which of course you would do, and no doubt get
the b[reve]t rank of capt[ai]n before leaving the army, which you are now by
the bye entitled to, and which it never struck me to now I have never
myself given you but will be more careful for the future. I told you I think
that Lawrence's police, one hundred of them I had out on the day of [the]
attack, behaved well, but had a severe loss of twenty-nine horses and twenty-
two men killed and wounded out of this small party. I had one or two awful
[? patches], but thank God [got] out of it all serene. I wrote yesterday to
Mr Hobson and asked him to write and tell me what had been decided on for the
future management of the bank and whether if was to be wound up or otherwise.
What news from England! Chalmer's brother who is at home is to be married to
Miss Marshal, his cousin, a girl with lots of coin and a swell at singing,
and a great friend of Miss Roberts. *Adieu* in haste.'

1 October 1857

D.812/10/B/47

William S. Graham, 'Umballah Hotel',
Ambala, to his cousin, James Graham.

'Just rec[eive]d your last, and nothing would
I like better than coming up to Mussoorie. I
have written today to Balfour the d[octo]r here telling him everything is
over at Delhi, and hoping he will grant me an extra month, but I don't think
there is a chance of it, although I have been in bed four days out of the
seven I have been here, but that confounded colour sticks to me all the
same. I tell you two birds to tell the sec[retar]y of [the] Delhi [Bank]
to keep sharp [? muster on],Caulfield and Dixon of [the] 9th cav[alr]y, the
former more especially, and to find from [the] pay office at Lahore what he
has paid in instal[men]ts *etc*, and to look sharp after him, but for God['s]
sake don't mention my name. I hope the sec[retar]y won't be guddah enough;
to let them suppose his suspicions have been raised against them in any way.
It is not the men believe me my dear James who have the names of being the
blackest sheep that are so. The bank, I think you will find, will find them
the most honorable and open of their constituients. I am infernally hard up,
what with having to lay in a complete supply of everything. We each get

r[upee]s 5000 (our poor mother's fortune) cash, but I don't see the
slightest chance of my father's estate being settled for another two years.
Lucknow heard from on the 19th, had just run short of [? corn], but has
enough for five days more, expected relief on or about today the 1st [of]
Oct[obe]r. ...

[P.S.] Do you know how many lacs of floating deposits were supposed to be
in the bank? I wish my good old [? boss] had made you an exe[cuto]r
instead of Parsons or Fordyce. I think y[ou]r head sense better, and [you]
more a man of business, and you and I w[oul]d have arranged things better.
I don't look forward with any pleasure in being one, for James, once he gets
his finger in the pie, will be suspicious and full of fancies, and his wife
is a knowing old gal and will be meddling, but I will take care that my poor
father's wishes be carried out to the letter. One thing I feel is, my
father at our own deaths not having given us the willing away of our shares,
for I am a rum fellow and [for ?] any one to get my share but those I liked,
makes me cogitate much over my future plans, and makes me think more
earnestly of setting up in child manufacturing on my own hook. Tom or
Sarah I w[oul]d give my last sixpence to, but *entre nous* I w[oul]d not to
James, and as things go now, and I have no children nor Tom either, it goes
there. I dislike the thoughts of my share being thrown away on his [? gals]
and would much sooner see Tom get it. I have written my last proposition to
Miss R[obert]s. My future plans lie with her, and her answer.'

30 November 1857   Mrs Sarah Ann Graham, (wife of James
                               Graham of Lucknow), Kanpur, to James
D.812/10/B/48   Graham.

                               'I received your kind letter on the 13th
                               Oct[obe]r addressed to my poor James. It was
kindly brought by Capt[ai]n McBean of the commissariat when troops came to
our relief. How I wish it had come a little sooner it might have been a
great comfort to James to have known that his father had forgiven him. You
must have heard by this time that he shot himself on the 5th of Sept[embe]r.
Dear Boy he was not to blame in the least. In that awful affair at
[? Chinhat] he got a sunstroke which brought on an apoplectic fit, and
after that his mind was totally deranged, he knew it, and told me that if
he was not care taken of [*sic*], he would put an end to himself. I told all
this to the doctor and begged of him to take care of James, but he only
laughed at me and said that if I doubted him it would make him worse. Now
I cannot help feeling that he has been sacrificed through entire neglect.
I was not able to leave my bed from an attack of cholera and other diseases
and little Sarah was very ill, every moment I thought would be her last, but
I am thankful to say she has been spared. Little Fanny, James's favourite
child died three days before him. I know he felt her death deeply. I had a
little baby who was born on the 23rd of August, she died on the 19th of
Oct[obe]r. Were I to tell you of all we here endured during that horrid
siege you would hardly believe that human nature was equal to it. When I
think of the past I feel frantic and wish the earth would open and swallow
me. I cannot help repining, still something tells me it is wrong. We have
got this far all right, I am happy today but I must own I feel far from
comfortable. Cawnpore is now attacked by the Gwalior rebels. They are
setting fire to every place they come near. The c[ommander]-in-c[hief] has
just ordered the ladies and wounded to start tonight, and an attack on the
city is to be made tomorrow. I sincerely wish we were all safe at Allahabad.
We travel in hackneys and the jolting is frightful. I wrote to Sarah [her

sister-in-law] by the last mail. Someone told me she was in England.
William's and Tom's whereabouts I have not been able to find out. When you
write to them give them my love. I shall be very glad to hear from you,
address your letter to Findlay's. I intend going home as I can get an
outfit, I have nothing but what I wear, and James had no debts but what his
pay will cover. I can't tell you how wretched I feel.'

25   ?   1857   William S. Graham, [? Hymen Cottage],
                                   to his cousin, James Graham.
D.812/10/B/49

                          'Thanks for the note which I return. The more
                          I see of Anne's letters the more of her good
sensible ways and ideas come to light. I will write home next mail myself.
When in Meerut go to Hobson and tell him that my father had 250 shares or
2.25000 rupees worth. I mentioned this in my notes to him, but he never took
any notice of it. In haste no news.'

22 January 1858   Mrs Sarah Ann Graham, Danapore, to
                                  James Graham.
D.812/10/B/50

                          'I received your very kind letter at Benares,
                          and was not very well or I would have
answered it there. I am on board the steamer "Lady [? Thackwell]" *en-route*
to Calcutta, and hope to arrive there in a few days. Many thanks for all
your kindness. I do not want any money, or would ask you for it. I have
had 100 r[upee]s from the relief fund, and I have no doubt I will get more
when we arrive in Calcutta. Since we left Cawnpore everything has been
promised for us, and on the whole people are very kind. I am ungrateful I
know, I can't help it, for when I most needed kindness it was not shown me.
I would indeed have been very glad to have seen you at Cawnpore. We
suffered great discomfort. At the same time I am very thankful that we were
so mercifully preserved. I was one of the three ladies who were obliged to
remain till night the other side of the river, and nearly the whole time we
were under fire. The bridge of boats was so crowded with hackneys that we
could not get over it.

I am glad William has gone home for I do not think he is happy in this
country, and the short time he has to live may as well be spent comfortably.
How fortunate he was to have taken the two months leave in Sealkote. I
wrote to him before I left Allahabad. Mr Manderson sent a little chit to
James a short time before they capitulated, and wished him to say good bye
to William if he ever saw him again. He said that they were quite resigned
to their fate and hoped that their sacrifice would be the means of saving us,
which it undoubtably was. I have only had one letter from William since the
siege and that was from Landour. Dr Graham has been most liberal towards me
considering I had no right whatever to any of his money. I am very thankful
for all he has done, at the same time I *would* rather that it had been left to
my little Sarah, I think James would have liked it better. Poor Boy! I can
hardly believe that I am never to see him again.

If you have the time to spare will you try and find Mr Capper of the civil
service. He is one of our Lucknow party and is I hear at Cawnpore. I had
a treasury draft for 141 r[upee]s which James got before he left Secrora to
send to Captain Wyld. At his death I gave it to Capt[ai]n Boilian, as he

was manager of James's affairs, and he gave it to Mr Capper who promised to give me cash for it, but has never done so. So will you kindly look after it for me. I do not know him and would rather have nothing to say to it [sic]. If you get the money send it to Capt[ai]n Wyld. He lent me that sum before I left Umballa. I think he is at Lahore. I know Capt[ai]n Davidson's cousin very well, she is on board this steamer. Her husband died during the siege. He became delerious like poor James, and threw himself off a high verandah in the hospital, which was the cause of his death. What painful associations are connected with that horrid siege. The scenes I have witnessed haunt me and I sometimes think I shall never recover the feeling.

I now regret that I did not go down from Allahabad, for we are continually sticking on the sands, and may still be some time before we reach Calcutta. I fear all the best steamers will have left *via* the Cape, and I am not strong enough to bear the fatigue overland. Write and let me know where a letter will find you, and I will let you know when I am likely to leave this country. Little Sarah quite enjoys the sailing, and has recovered the siege most wonderfully.'

25 January 1858

D.812/10/B/51

William S. Graham, Lahore, to his cousin, James Graham.

'I was not at all surprised when I heard of poor James's death and the sad way he ended his days. He often used to tell me he would do so, but when there were so many more nobler [sic] ways of dying at hand I must say my feelings were mixed with sorrow and disgust, especially as I know not why he committed this awful business, when as I said before so many finer and nobler ways of falling [were] at hand. He is gone now and his end will not enhance his memory. [? Mitties[13]] letter is most incoherent as well as one she wrote me. She told me of Manderson having sent a letter to James by his bearer after the servants were turned out of the entrenchments, to tell him to say good bye to me in case we never met, that they were all resigned, that Charlie Quin died of fever, that the same round shot that killed Dempster killed poor Nick Quin, and that she heard that Daniel was one of those gallant few who defended themselves in the temple, but although she dwells on this she never tells me anything of the end of my own poor brother. In fact so disgusted am I, that I have not answered her letter, which I don't intend doing until I know something more why he shot himself. I can't tell you my feelings, disgust is no name for them. I am on my way home and after this [I] am not sorry in getting out of the country. I want you to sign the accom[panyin]g like a good fellow, and send it to me to "Hope Hotel", Bombay by return of post please as I cannot leave the country without it. Good bye old fellow I will write you from Malta where my feelings will have improved a little.'

22 February 1858

D.812/10/B/52

Thomas C. Graham, Fort Allahabad, to his cousin, James Graham.

'Many thanks for your very kind letter which I received the other day, and ought to have answered indeed ere this. I herewith according to your directions return

13. *Wife of the late James Graham (brother of William), Mrs Sarah Ann Graham.*

H

the enclosed. I did not send it to you but I have not the least doubt
William was the gentleman, and as 35 [rupees ?] a month are not to be
despised, I shall be only too delighted, as you kindly say you will write
the requisite chits, to sign them, and the draft I am *ashamed to say* I must
permit of your getting just now for 54..12..4 [rupees, annas, pice ?] will it
not be? This of course I will square again the very first opportunity I may
have with you, and really you are a brick for offering this.

Let me hear from you again, and let me know what William's movements may be.
Has he gone to England? I have not heard from him since leaving Lahore, and
just before I got your letter had addressed a letter to Mussoorie for him,
so let me hear any news you may know about him. The Lahore l[igh]t horse
left this the day before yesterday to join Frank's brigade, and I am ashamed
to say I have been left behind here with another fellow "Prinsep", both with
the same complaint "babo's" sympathetic. I was unfortunate enough to get
like this just three marches from Futteyghur, but am nearly well now, and in
a week will be making my way most likely to join some other reg[imen]t back
in the Lucknow direction, as unless some reg[imen]t may be going out to
Frank's from here I cannot rejoin the l[igh]t horse. I have not received
any overland chit for a long time, but have no doubt they are running after
me somewhere or other. I never felt anything so much as when I heard of our
poor James's fate. To think if he had only spared himself he might now have
been alive [*sic*]. After I had seen his name down amongst the first list of
the garrison survivors, I looked forward when marching down country to think
I might meet him with some [? foudge] or other, but no, these have been hard
times for many.'

5 March 1858   Mrs Sarah Ann, Graham, Bishop's Palace,
                                Calcutta, to James Graham.
D.812/10/B/53

                                'I have been looking out for a letter from
                                you ever since I came to Calcutta, and as
you have not written I am afraid you did not get my last which I posted at
Dinapore. Write after you get this, and let me know where you are. We
arrived in Calcutta on the 5th of February after a very tedious voyage down
the river. We were met by Lady Jackson and Mrs Patton, who had prepared a
house for Mrs Gall and myself, and we lived there until the bishop and Mrs
Fealtry came to Calcutta. Mrs Gall lived in the same room with us in
Lucknow and I have been travelling with her ever since we left. My passage
is taken for the 17th of this month. I am going with the bishop to Madras,
and will remain there a week, [and] then proceed to England overland. I
shall be quite glad to see Sarah again. Poor James [? raved] about her, he
thought there was nobody like his little sister. He often wondered if she
was safe. All he brought with him from Secrora was a small prayer book she
gave him when at school, and a lock of his father's hair. Have you heard
anything more of William? I have looked in every paper for his name among
the list of passengers going home, but have not seen it. I wish Tom would
write to me. I would be so glad to have a letter from him. I hope you will
be at the taking of Lucknow. If you are go and see where James and my
darling children are lying and tell me what has been done to the graveyard.
They are all buried close to the church. I have a very good likeness of
James. It was taken by D[octo]r Dixon at Sealkote, and fortunately he had
one left which I got from his daughter the other day at Dum Dum. From the
relief fund I have got 2,000 r[upee]s and the wages and passage of a

servant to England. Why do you not try to go home now? You might get a
free passage or at least at the reduced rates overland which is 500
[rupees ?]. ...'

18 March 1858   William S. Graham, Club Bombay, to his
                                 cousin, James Graham.
D.812/10/B/54
                                 Graham informs his cousin that he is about to
                                 leave for his trip to England. He thanks
James for all his assistance in official affairs especially for sending him
the guarantee certificate, which however he requires in duplicate for
forwarding to various military and official bodies, so he asks James to send
another copy of the certificate.

Graham also thanks his cousin for his loans of money which he promises to pay
as soon as he can, although he has not as yet received the pay to which he is
entitled. Graham is worried that during his absence in England the Delhi
prize money will be paid out, and he asks James to 'look after my interests'
in that respect. William as one of the executors of his father's will has
received a letter from Daniel Cullimore, and he tells James that it is a
'devilish cold letter ... [which] ... contained not a word but business.'

4 May 1858   Thomas C. Graham, 'one march from
                                 Bareilly', to his cousin James Graham.
D.812/10/B/55
                                 '[I] have just come in from a douar so excuse
                                 this short chit. We found Shahjehanpore
evacuated by the enemy, left a small force in the jail there, and the
consequence is we hear they are now besieged by the enemy with eleven guns.
We go into Bareilly tomorrow where we fancy the enemy will make a good
stand. Penny was knocked over two days ago while his column was marching
thro' a village, he and his staff being at the head of all. Much to their
surprise they saw a fuse being rubbed on the ground ten yards in front of
them, and bang went a gun, and Penny whose horse evidently ran away was
found right on the other side of the village killed and hacked about. ...

[P.S.] Do you recollect when you wrote to me from the Kaiser Bagh dated
2nd of March? I got the letter at the Dilkoosha ten days after, and then
had in fact gone as far as the Iron Bridge on my way to see [you] but heard
you had gone.'

5 September 1858   Thomas C. Graham, Mountain's Hotel,
                                 to James Graham, Faizabad.
D.812/10/B/56
                                 'Many thanks for your kind chit which I
                                 received yesterday. Here I am still, but
have been very seedy of late and am now my wound tho' commencing at first to
heal fast has taken a wrong turn altogether, and is giving me a lot of dic
and bother. The res[iden]t surgeon here Macpherson who has been attending
me since my arrival sent me up to the board, and they have granted me
eighteen months to Europe, so that you will I am sure be no little
astonished when I tell you, I am all ready booked to revisit *once more that
sweet land* of my forefathers by the P & O steamer of the 8th instant; but

really holding the app[ointmen]t of adj[utan]t and q[uarte]r m[aste]r
besides my troop thereby bringing me in some 800 a month which I am at
present doing, you can fancy I am not over delighted at parting with this
in this way, but what other alternative is there when one's health is
really concerned.

I intend going to Grindley's tomorrow when I will desire them to send you a
draft for 55 [? rupees] which will square the amount you so kindly advanced,
with a slight int[eres]t James, but I make it here an even sum on acc[oun]t
of annas and pice not being generally granted in treasury drafts, do don't be
offended with the extra please. I like you indeed saying Sarah ought to be
much obliged to me for having executed all the needful regarding [the]
o[rpha]n's fund. I will take good care to let her know, who *was* indeed the
real executor. By the bye instead of drawing the acc[oun]t here myself,
finding, they would make it payable in England from the home agency, I
desired them to do this, so that Sarah will get the coin at once.

And James, regarding the *loss compensation* I sat down myself a few weeks ago
to endeavour to make out a sort of bill, but finding I was indeed unable to
enumerate any of the particular articles, knowing myself so little regarding
the contents of my poor governor's house I gave it up in despair. However
the paragraph you sent relating to it I will keep and will not fail on
arrival in England to set Sarah and William to work for I see six months
allowed for individuals in England to send in their claims. You asked me
how that noble regiment the l[igh]t horse behaved, admirably I assure you on
all occasions, but the great vices of the l[igh]t horsians are lying,
drinking, stealing, in a word everything bad you can imagine, they are
expert at, and Balmain and myself I assure you found enough to do in keeping
them in order, but I am very glad myself now that I have been serving with
them, for their being dealt with in every step similar to an English dragoon,
it has initiated me into the style in which I shall have to deal with the
five feet fours, hereafter, which is indeed a great thing. They have not
the least idea at all at home that I am about to join them, and will be
rather astonished when they see me I reckon.'

Graham ends discussing his future visit to Britain. He states that he
intends to visit the Lisburn Grahams, and he reflects on childhood experiences
during visits to his Co. Antrim kinfolk. Graham informs his cousin that he
is prepared to 'execute any commission' on his behalf whilst on his sick
leave at home.

14 December 1859   H. G[raham]-Smith, Fort William, to
                      his uncle, James Graham, Bareilly.
D.812/10/B/57

                      Smith informs his uncle that he has arrived
                      in India, and will be taking up his military
cadetship with the '42nd' [native infantry ?] at Bareilly. He describes his
'long passage' of four months and his shipboard instruction in Hindustani by
Lieutenant Birch who '... went through the siege of Lucknow ...'. Smith ends
discussing news from the family at home, and arrangements for his journey to
Bareilly.

HOMEWARD LETTERS

(30)   Sealkote 29th June 1857

My dear Anne

         I find this is the last to day
day for overland letters, now tho the
newspapers will tell you that we are
at War with our Native Army and
that the latter has been wreaking its
fury in brutal Massacres and oh
incendiarisms. yet they will not
give you and other friends the
great comfort of knowing that
all dear to you and them, are
safe and in the land of the
living. I will not attempt to say
any thing of the mutinous
spirit shewn by our Sepoys (and
which is wholly without provocation)
for the Press both of this country
and at home will give you all
                    your brother
ve details. I hear from James
every day and generally also
from William & Tom. They are
all well. I know your brother

16 May [sic] 1857

D.812/14/133

James Graham, Landour, to his sister Anne, Lisburn, Co. Antrim. Events mentioned in this letter indicate that Graham made an error in its dating, and that it should have been dated 16 June.

'For fear of letters via Bombay not going safely these disturbed times I send this via Calcutta, and shall send another via Bombay hereafter. By that time I hope to be able to tell you all about the fall of Delhi. Things are still in a very disturbed state, and we will require a good many more European troops to settle them again. A number of scoundrels who have been released from jail have been doing a great deal of harm in the different districts, but they will soon be caught again. The people to a man are quiet, and engaged in defending their property, and the disturbance confined to the army alone. We are fortunate up here in being released from the great imposure [sic] the troops are suffering from before Delhi, and us being in a place of such perfect safety.

The commander-in-chief reached Delhi on the 6th, and I have no doubt that operations were commenced the following day, but there being no direct post, we only hear news on the 4th day, and consequently know not what has occurred, though firing has been heard at Meerut, so the chief must doubtless be attacking the city. We may hear before I close this. 12 [o clock ?], the dawk just in from Delhi. The commander-in-chief advanced against it on the 8th. He found the mutineers had come out to meet him, with twenty heavy, and six light guns. They would not wait for him, left their guns, and bolted off. The whole affair lasted only five and twenty guns, they were in such a fright that they threw themselves off their horses and begged for mercy, very little of which they got. The remainder got into Delhi, and I suppose the city was attacked yesterday or the day before. There is only a wall round it with a ditch. The wall is not nearly so strong as that at Bomarsund[14], so you can fancy how long it will stand against about seventy guns, forty of which are of the very heaviest metal. All is quiet up here. Col Dickey still staying with me. Col Nuthall has two sons at a school here, very little boys. I have been down to see them, and they are to spend their holidays with me, the last Saturday and Sunday in every month. I have heard from their father two or three times lately, he was rather anxious about them, as the younger one has been unwell.

I heard from uncle about three days ago. All was then quiet at Sealkote. Sarah had not gone to Lahore as she first thought of doing. ...

I will try and send you a letter via Bombay, but remember, you must never be the least anxious at not getting my letters, as I never know when the posts are safe or not, and there are all sorts of delays. Now you must not be the least anxious if you do not hear from me for two or three mails. Where letters have to go such a distance on a bearer's shoulders, anyone can rob the dawk. To show how irregular dawks are, three days ago I received a letter from Col Nuthall dated the 28th May, and the following day one dated the 21st.

14. A Russian island fortress in the Baltic Sea, which was the scene of naval and military engagements during the Crimean War.

All is quiet in this neighbourhood and for a great distance in every direction.

I will write a long letter by Bombay mail in the hope of its reaching you, but don't expect it, as in addition to the post all the steamers here are employed in bringing troops.'

[17 May 1857]   James Graham, Landour, to his sister
                          Anne, Lisburn, Co. Antrim.
D.812/14/134

                          'I fired off a letter yesterday to you in
                          which I mentioned that a mutiny had broken
out among the sepoys between this and Bombay, so that I feared the dawks
might be cut off, and my letters not reach you, so I said I would despatch
one daily for the next four days in the hope of one reaching its
destination. The mutineers are at Delhi, and Meerut. They are only four
regiments, and as some of the regiments at Delhi fought well against them,
their numbers must be reduced.

The commander-in-chief is after them with four European regiments and a lot
of artillery. He will make short work of them. We are as jolly as crickets
up here, not the slightest danger, and only annoyed that we can hear so
little of what is going on below. Don't believe half of what you will see
in the newspapers. They always exaggerate, and don't let Mamma be the
least anxious.

I told you in my letter of yesterday that I had had long letters from
William, Sarah and my uncle. The whole three are gone on a pleasure
excursion for sixty days to a place in the hills close to Cashmere. Uncle
says it is a delightful spot, and they anticipate a couple of very pleasant
months. William has heard again from his lady love, and says (so Sarah
tells me) that *They may be happy yet*".

And so James Allen is really getting married. Well I believe, now that he
has got a sober married man, with something to employ his mind, that he will
be an altered being, and you all ought to countenance him as much as
possible. You never told me of the settlement of uncle's affairs, except
some very vague remarks. I am glad to hear that Lizzie was so much pleased
with her letter, and sad that it met with such an accident.

Col Dickey is staying with me at present, for change of air. He, as every
person who sees it, is quite delighted with the site of this house. Really
I cannot describe to you anything so beautiful as the weather is here at
present. It is something heavenly, mild summer without a breeze, and a
perfect calmness. Nothing can equal it, with these majestic mountains
[Himalayas] all round, and the snowy range in front.

I am highly amused with your parliamentary elections: you good people in
Lisburn, who used to be so thankful for the member that the Marquis of
Hertford sent you, to presume to have a choice of your own. I would not be
at all surprised to hear of the Lisburn ladies proposing to gentlemen, even
out of leap-years.

The mutineers at Delhi and Meerut, have murdered a good many Europeans, and a number of natives, and burned a great many houses, among others the Delhi Bank, and I fear uncle will lose a good deal. The manager and his wife lost their lives.

We are fortunate in being up here with a number of Europeans, where if there was any danger (of which there is not the slightest chance) we could defend ourselves against thousands, and tens of thousands.'

17 May 1857   James Graham, Landour to his sister
                               Anne, Lisburn, Co. Antrim.
D.812/14/135
                               'We have just heard the best tidings, about
                               the mutineers. The Meerut troops followed
them across to Delhi, and took possession of it before the commander-in-chief could get down from the hills. The native regiments at Umballah begged to be led against the mutineers, and the commander-in-chief took some of them with them [sic]. The Raja of [?Patiala] who lives in that neighbourhood sent 26,000 of his troops to assist the commander-in-chief if required, but the Meerut troops had settled the business. The reason for our not getting any posts, dawks, for some days was that the postmen (the men who carry the letters from station to station) were employed in carrying expresses from the different stations to the commander-in-chief. My other letters may have gone astray, and consequently I send you these few lines, to say that all is over, and everything and everybody in perfect safety, I mean at Meerut and Delhi (up here they never were in any). I fear you will see very sad reports in the papers, but you must remember there these things are always exaggerated, and do not believe half of them, nor be the least anxious. You will doubtless be surprized to hear me say that I think this mutiny most fortunate. The Queen's government would never allow the Company [East India Company] to have enough European troops. When they did not require them at home, they sent them out here to make the Company pay them, and when they wanted them they denuded India. Now however they will see the necessity, and the mutiny will teach them dearly bought experience.

I am afraid that my uncle will be a great loser by the burning of the papers of the Delhi Bank, and the murder of the manager of it. I myself will lose a small sum I had there, but it cannot be helped. We must all be thankful that it was no worse, and that we have no relations among the sufferers, I cannot say not friends. I fear I will have to mourn some.

I will write to you again the day after tomorrow, by which time we are likely to hear of the punishment of the mutineers, and I trust it will be a heavy one. The prisoners whom they let out of jail, and who have done the whole of the mischief are being caught in all directions, and will atone by a long confinement for their dearly bought (and short) liberty.

Now I must conclude again and must beg of you not to let Mamma or anyone at home have the slightest anxiety.'

19 May 1857   James Graham, Landour, to his sister
                               Anne, Lisburn, Co. Antrim.
D.812/14/135a
                               'Just a couple of lines to let you know that

all is quiet or nearly so. The news about Delhi being taken was a mistake,
but the commander-in-chief is marching against it, with a large force, and
the mutineers are so foolish as to think of making a stand there. The
c[ommander]-in-c[hief] is taking with him: 1st and 2nd Europeans reg[imen]ts,
H[er] M[ajesty]'s 75th and 9th lancers, and 1½ troops of horse artillery,
the 5th and 60th native infantry (who have begged to be led against the
mutineers) and the 4th light cavalry. He is to be joined 16 miles above
Delhi by the Meerut troops, consisting of: ½ a reg[imen]t of rifles, H.M.'s
60th, two squadrons 6th carabiners, the corps of sappers and miners, and the
[? Sirnoor] battalion (a corps of hillmen). With these he has a force
sufficient to march from one end of India to another, and to walk over anything that comes in their way. You will have very exaggerated accounts.
Don't believe half of them, and no matter what you hear or see, don't let
Mamma or yourself be the least anxious, for I can assure you there is not
the slightest necessity for it.

I trust some of these letters will reach you.

I only yesterday received yours of the 1st of April addressed to William's
care. I had a week previously rec[eive]d a later letter. Don't be anxious
about my health. I have not been so well for years. Indeed I only fear
(and I ought to say people tell me) I am getting frightfully stout. I can
walk up an ascent of 1000 feet without getting out of breath, and eat to an
extent that I am really ashamed of. I am thank God in perfect health and
strength, now I trust you will listen to nothing you hear about my health,
but from myself. When Col Nuthall saw me I had just passed my examination,
and had so much anxiety on this and other accounts, that I had quite
sufficient to make me ill.

It is more than probable that before this leaves Bombay, the telegraph will
have taken down the news of the retaking of Delhi, and the punishment of [the]
mutineers. ...'

1 June 1857   James Graham, Landour, to his sister
                               Anne, Lisburn, Co. Antrim.
D.812/14/136

                               'I can send off two or three letters by this
                               mail. Also, though to my great disgust, I
have just heard that no letters were sent from Agra by [the] last one, so
that I fear very much that you have been very anxious, as I know the first
outbreak was telegraphed home by the mail.

Since then there have been several outbreaks, but no European loss of life,
indeed the native corps have always shown an anxiety to protect their
officers, and the murders committed at Meerut and Delhi were by the scoundrels
that congregate at a large military cantonment. All the native chiefs sent
their contingents, and every man of respectability has assisted in keeping
the peace.

We have lost, if he can be called a loss, the commander-in-chief [General
Anson]. He died on the 27th [May] of cholera at Karnal, and as he was
dilatory and vaccilating it is looked upon as a gain. His delay has however
had one good effect. The mutineers at Delhi have had time to show how
little resistance the natives can set up against us. They have already
commenced fighting among themselves.

All this part of the country perfectly quiet. I have been ordered, and
have laid in a month's supply of food for the Europeans, though I don't see
the necessity for it myself. I hear from uncle daily, all quiet in that
direction. I had a note from Tom Graham a few days ago from Ferozpoor.
They had had a slight row there, but Tom's corps behaved first rate, and
has got great praise from the commander-in-chief. It is said that Sir
Patrick Grant is to be our new commander-in-chief. The necessities of the
time have shown that an Indian officer is required as commander-in-chief.
Sir Pat[rick] Grant belongs to the Bengal Army.

I think I mentioned to you long ago, that Smith of my corps was a great
drunkard. He was home, got married, and we thought had come out reformed.
However it is now proved that this was not the case. Drunkeness acted upon
madness, which was in his family, and he committed suicide on the 21st. It
is not to be wondered at, considering that his mother, sister and two
brothers did the same.

As I am going to write you, some two or three other letters by this mail you
must excuse the shortness of them, for though there is a good deal of Indian
news, there is very little that would interest you, except that you have not
the slightest cause for anxiety on my account. Here we are with some 200
Europeans, well provisioned in the midst of impregnable hills, where every
man is worth a hundred. The country all about quiet, and faithful troops
all round the foot of the hills, so I shall be very much annoyed if I hear
that you are yourself, or allow Mamma to be the least anxious.'

1 June 1857   James Graham, Landour, to his sister
                                 Anne, Lisburn, Co. Antrim.
D.812/14/137
                                 'I have just finished No. 1 for this mail,
                                 which I have sent to a friend at Seharnapoor
to be posted there, and I send this direct in the hope of its reaching you.

Everything is perfectly quiet up here, and likely to remain so. No cause
for any anxiety on my account. The mutineers are all assembled at Delhi,
where the troops will be on the 5th, I hope in time for the result to be
sent to you by telegraph by this mail. A number of scoundrels have taken
advantage of the row to plunder some villages, but they are being severely
punished, and their villages burned down as a punishment, but none of these
have approached within 70 to 100 miles of this place. The very name of
Gora (whiteman) makes them keep off. After the row at Meerut, the
Europeans turned out and according to the native's accounts killed the
scoundrels with their fists. Such a fright have they put the natives into,
that it is as good as if they had fought ten battles.

William Graham had got to Sealkote, and as the roads were not considered
safe for his return, he has been appointed to do duty with the 9th cavalry,
and is now marching to join the com[mander]-in-chief. As all the troops or
very nearly so have been withdrawn from Sealkote, Sir John Lawrence offered
Sarah the use of his house at Lahore, and his brother, Captain Lawrence,
asked her to go and stay with them, but she has not accepted their
invitation; she did not see any necessity for it.

I mentioned in my other letter that Smith of my corps had committed suicide from drink and other causes. His company volunteered to, and did carry him to the grave. As touching anything connected with a body is pollution to a native, their doing so at the present time is a good sign, and I hope they will behave themselves.

I will send you a newspaper by tomorrow's dawk, as I really will not know what to write about.

It is said that our letters by last mail were all stopped at Agra, which I trust was not the case, and that you were not anxious.

I hear from uncle almost every day. He is quite well, and all is quiet in that direction.

The c[ommander]-in-chief is dead, and we hear that Sir Pat[rick] Grant is to be the new chief. This is a great step for the Indian army.

When all this row is over, we must have a large increase of European troops, which I hope will do me good, both regimentally and departmentally.

Now remember you have not the slightest cause of anxiety on my account. Don't believe half what you will see in the papers. The greater number of the people the editors have killed have turned up.

I fear that uncle, and another, and much esteemed relative of yours will lose severely by the Delhi Bank. The manager and his wife were killed and I fear all the books burned. Though I had a small stake in it, you see my dear Anne, that it does not give me much anxiety, though I have lost every pice I have saved. However with health and a good appointment like mine, I hope still with God's blessing to have sufficient to take me to Europe in 1860.'

18 June 1857   James Graham, Landour, to his sister
                     Anne, Lisburn, Co. Antrim.
D.812/14/138

         'Though I think there is very little chance of this letter reaching you by this mail, as a number of the mutineers have assembled on the Bombay road, still I think it better to send a line on chance, as troops may be moving upwards and get the road cleared before this passes through Meerut. I wrote to you *via* Calcutta, and uncle I think wrote *via* Kurrachee. One of them may reach you, and I trust my former letters will prevent you from feeling anxious should letters not reach you for a mail or two.

Things will I hope soon settle, but even if they don't, we are perfectly safe here, in inaccessible mountains, with lots of provisions. We have not a thought for ourselves, but for those poor unfortunates fighting in such hot weather. The troops I am happy to say are enjoying the very best of health, and I have seen two or three letters which say that a blanket at night is most agreeable.

William Graham is by this time before Delhi. He is now doing duty with the 16th irreg[ular] cavalry, and will distinguish himself, I have no doubt, if opportunity offers.

Graham Papers

There are strange rumours about the com[mander]-in-chief's death, and some
say that he put an end to himself, which I am not surprised at. Prince
Albert's interest sent him out to this country, after having distinguished
himself by horse racing, and indeed in plain language he was a mere "broken-
down gambler", and quite unfit for his profession (the above between ourselves). The only sign of sense he showed was in making [a]way with himself,
when he knew he was perfectly unfit for his position. I hope he is the last
c-in-c sent out to this country from England, and that for the future they
will appoint men who have served, and know something of the country.

I have got a step in the comm[issaria]t by the death of Captain Howell. I
am gradually getting up the list. I expect to get two or three steps in the
regiment in the next year or so. Did I tell you that Major Richards has
sent me an offer to retire before the 1st of August 1858? My share of his
step money will be very small.

I hear from uncle almost daily, all is quiet in his neighbourhood.

You must still place no dependence to [*sic*] the exaggerated accounts you will
see in the papers day by day. The supposed lost and murdered are making
their appearance. One regiment at Delhi, of which the newspapers killed
every officer, has not lost a single officer, and several others in the same
way.

The governor general telegraphed up to the lieutenant governor of the North
Western Provinces that he will have 10,000 European troops in Calcutta before
the end of the month. It is said that the march on Delhi was to take place on
the 15th. The mutineers have made several sorties, but have been driven back
with great loss on every occasion. In the last they left at least 500 dead
on the field. The attack would have been made long ere this, but the
officiating commander-in-chief [General Barnard] does not wish to sacrifice
the life of a single soldier. The nat[ive] regiments, especially the ones
which went down from this area, of which we have a portion remaining, are
behaving nobly. The mutineers on making a sortie cried out to them "Come and
join us". They replied "We are coming", charged the mutineers, and poured
in such a volley that the greater part dropped where they stood. Such is the
corps of which we have some two hundred here to assist the Europeans. They
climb the hills like cats, and hate and despise the men of the country where
the mutineers come from. All the respectable natives are assisting government in every way. The disturbance is also in the regular army only. All
the irregular corps are behaving well, and some of the regulars also, *vide*
my own corps, of which I hear the best accounts. You of course have heard
the cause of all this row. Gov[ernmen]t were introducing the new Enfield rifle
into the army. The cartridges have to be greased. Well some scoundrels
disseminated a report that they were greased with cow's fat (to touch which
Hindoos lose their caste) and pig's fat (which pollutes a Mussulman's [? soul][15]).

Having a commander-in-chief who knew nothing of the country, and who was led
by his staff, young boys more ignorant than himself, no order or explanation
was ever given to the sepoys, and it always strikes me that he was quite as
guilty as they were ... . To show you how well disposed the people at Delhi
are, at the order of the commander-in-chief, 17,000 inhabitants have left
Delhi for [? Raotal] a place ten miles off.

15. Text defective.

The attack was to be about [the] 15th, and you may hear of it by this mail.'

25 June 1857   James Graham, Landour, to his sister
                                 Anne, Lisburn, Co. Antrim.
D.812/14/139

                    'I fear very much that you have not got my
                    letters by the last two or three mails, but
when my letters do reach you, you will find that I did my best, but the
mails have been so stolen, and stopped for safety in different directions
and places, that all my attempts *were* vain. This I am trying to send *via*
Lahore and Kurrachee. A number of scoundrels have taken advantage of the
mutiny to create little disturbances here and there, and as numbers of the
mails are carried on the shoulders of a single man, you can understand how
easy it is to cut them off.

At Delhi I don't know what our plan is. It is the great centre of attraction
for the mutineers, and consequently the greater the delay there, and the more
of the mutineers are allowed to collect, there will be less trouble in
arranging matters afterwards. Our troops have had already ten engagements
with them, in each of which they have been most successful, and have killed
at least 2,500, and as for every man killed at least four die of their wounds,
you can fancy how many of them have come to grief. The disaffection is still
altogether in the army, not one respectable native has joined them, and now
the Hindoos, of whom there are at least $\frac{3}{4}$ in every regiment, find that they
have been the tools of a few Mahommedans, and are mourning their folly in
sackcloth and ashes. Though it is such a season of the year, our men are
enjoying the very best of health (our loss has been trifling) and all
behaving nobly. In one of the sallies from the city the mutineers called to
the Ghorkas (little hillmen) to join them. They shouted "We are coming, we
are coming", and sent a volley of musketry at them. Then they threw down
their muskets, and flew at them with their bayonet knives (a most murderous
weapon), and it is said the havoc they committed on the mutineers was something frightful. The Sikhs of the Punjab are also doing their duty well.

For all this disturbance, we have no persons to thank but the Exeter Hall
people. In an army accustomed to despotism, the governor general and
commander-in-chief for fear of a lot of clergymen, and old women at home,
have attempted to rule orientals as they would Europeans, and the
consequence is that the natives think that Europeans are not what they were
one hundred years ago. Then your Exeter Hall people send out a lot of
missionaries who never attempt to convert by setting the people a good
example. They look merely after their own pockets, and trying to make as
many squabbles as they can amongst both Europeans and natives. Don't believe
one word you ever see in a missionary's report. It is all cooked up for the
English palate, a mass of lies. I know myself one missionary who is a pork
butcher, and instead of saving souls is employed saving bacon. I declare
most solemnly that every pice given for missionary purposes in this country
is a sin, much better to spend your money when you have it, or to give [it]
away in alleviating the distress, and converting the miserable outcasts from
humanity with which all our large cities at home are filled. The Exeter
Hall people have also been doing their best to force education upon a people
not ready to receive it, then the people's minds are bothered with everything
that can disturb their peace. As regards the army, a commander-in-chief is
sent out who knows nothing about the country nor the customs of the natives,

indeed who is only skilled in gambling and the turf, and perhaps a little
flunkeyism to Prince Albert. He attempts to command every regiment as well
as the army, leaves commanding officers no power, and the consequence is the
sepoys have nothing to look to from the commanding officer or officers of
their regiment; instead of, as in former days, a commanding officer knowing
everything that occurred in his regiment, the whole of this mutiny has been
concocted without their knowledge. It is said that Gen[era]l Anson put an
end to himself, and I do not doubt it, a man who knew nothing about his
profession, felt his own incapacity, and, poor man, it was not his fault but
those who sent him. He had lost every farthing he had on the turf and
wanted to save a little money. Thank God we are getting an officer to
command the army who knows something about it and his profession. I mean
General Sir Patrick Grant (Lord Gough's son-in-law), who has passed the whole
of his life in the ranks of the Bengal Army. No doubt the Horse Guards and
Prince Albert will not like such a piece of patronage passing out of their
hands, but they can scarcely turn him out now that he is once in. I dare say
they have a few more old women like Sir W[illia]m Gowan, to send out. He
spent his time in inditing sonnets to his wife's eyebrows, the day he first
met her, her birthday *etc*. Poor old man above seventy, he was in his second
childhood, but thought by the wise people in England a fit ruler for 300,000
men.

My corps is behaving very well, it has volunteered to go anywhere and everywhere, against Delhi, or the mutineers, and this is something in such times.

Since I wrote last I got a step in the commissariat, by the death of a Capt
Howell, you can rule him out of your army list.

I hear from uncle and write to him daily, all is perfectly quiet at
Sealkote.

I am afraid you have received very few of my letters, but I hope neither
Mamma or yourself were anxious, and I hope you will not be anxious if you do
not receive my letters for two or three mails together. Of one thing be
assured, that up here we are in perfect safety. We have nothing but
European troops, lots of them, arms and ammunition, and quantities of food,
and this is the very last place in the world to have any disturbance. You
can depend on my trying my best to send letters, but don't be surprised at
not hearing.'

29 June 1857

D.812/14/140

Dr James Graham, Sialkot, to his niece
Anne, Lisburn, Co. Antrim.

'I find this is the last safe day for overland
letters. Now though the newspapers will tell
you that we are at war with out native army, and that the latter has been
wreaking its fury in brutal massacres, much incendiarism, yet they will not
give you and other friends the great comfort of knowing that all dear to you
and them, are safe and in the land of the living. I will not attempt to say
anything of the mutinious spirit shown by our sepoys (and which is wholly
without provocation) for the press both of this country and at home will give
you all the details. I hear from your brother James every day, and generally
also from William and Tom. They are all well. I know your brother writes
to you by every mail. He has been out of this row, and in a fair hill

climate at Landour, so your Mamma need have no fears for his safety.
Stewart too has been equally fortunate in being absent from Meerut, and he
and his family are quite safe in the hills. Sarah has had a slight attack
of fever of late, her first indisposition since her arrival in the country.
She is now convalescent, and will in a few days regain her strength and
appetite again. This part of the country is quiet. The people have shown
no sympathy for the mutineers, and when we reoccupy Delhi the crisis will
have passed. No assault on this city however can take place before the 1st
or 2nd prox[im]o, as we have large reinforcements that cannot reach our head-
quarters before the end of the month.

The mutineers once driven out of Delhi will be to a great extent powerless,
for they cannot take with them for want of horses and bullocks any even of
our light field guns. A campaign we shall probably have next winter, but it
will be a mere walk over the country. We shall have no difficulty in
hunting them down, the people being with us. There is no want of firmness
and decision in our government, and what has occurred will lead to changes
and such an augmentation of European troops to our army in this country that
nothing of the kind will ever occur again.

I have no time to write more, but these few lines will tell you of the safety
of all dear to you, which is my only object in writing.'

29 June 1857

D.812/14/141

Dr James Graham Sialkot, to Daniel
Cullimore, [Ballyanne, New Ross,
Co. Wexford].

'... You will read all about our mutinies
and the brutal murders, that have been committed so I shall say nothing of
them.

Of the Delhi Bank nothing is yet known, but it is almost certain I fear that
poor Beresford, his wife and family are amongst the massacred. I fear too
we have lost our books, bonds and securities, and if this be the case the
result will be disastrous.

In our treasury we could not have had more than a lakh, this would not ruin
us, having a lakh and eighty thousand of a reserve fund, but it is the loss
of records and company paper I dread. We were prospering beyond expectation,
so much so that I had purchased seventy-two shares making the total two
hundred and fifty. The greatest number I believe held by any one proprietor.
I could have sold my shares in an hour (every one of them) for a lakh and
135,000. They were not to be had in the market. I have written to the other
trustees, and to the d[eput]y manager several times, but our dawks have been
cut off, and I have as yet had no reply. I have only discovered that this is
the last day for the mail, and as our dawk goes out at 9 am I have no time to
write more ...'.

9 July 1857

D.812/14/142

James Graham, Landour, to his sister
Anne, Lisburn, Co. Antrim.

'Another mail is going out, and I am not able
to tell you of the fall of Delhi. The

mutineers have been gradually getting into it, and our troops assembling [outside ?]. Its fall is however close at hand. The whole native army, or very near it, has gone, and the way they have been fighting shows what good soldiers they were. As each detach[men]t arrived at Delhi, the King, and the mutineers in the city, made them go out and fight before they would be allowed to enter, thus effectually making them participators in the mutiny. They all got a good licking, and each party was so disheartened that they never made their appearance a second time. The attack will now take place, and they will meet with most severe punishment. Here all goes on as usual, we are so completely shut out from the plains in these grand old mountains, that it is almost impossible to fancy sitting in such a natural fortress, and in such perfect quiet and safety, that there should be such pain, suffering and danger at Delhi. Great as their folly has been, one can scarcely help pitying the Hindoos, when we think how they have been led away, by a small party of bigotted Mohammedans, not one 1,000th part of their number. The present sepoys will rue in sackcloth and ashes. To them the only field of employment will be closed forever, and they will see stepping into their shoes, the, by them detested, Sikhs and Ghoorkas. They will from the easiest and best paid employment in India, lapse into mere tillers of the soil, and earn a mere existence with labour which after their life of comparitive ease will be worse than the treadmill.

The old men who looked forward to drawing their pensions, and passing their remaining years as small lords in their native villages, will now find that they also will have to work hard for their very bread, and most probably will be turned out to starve by their relatives, when otherwise if they had their pensions, their friends prize the latter too much, to let their lives be shortened by the slightest want of care and attention.

If it were not for the great loss and misery which has been entailed on so many, this whole mutiny has been a most fortunate thing for the British government, if it at last opens their eyes to the folly of denuding India of European troops. My dep[artmen]t must be doubled at least.

I hope you have not allowed mamma to be at all anxious about me. If you have you ought really to be ashamed of yourself, for here all is in perfect safety. I will not, and cannot be allowed to leave this [place ?] with so many Europeans to look after, and instead of being anxious you should feel pity for those who are sufferers. All will now soon be over. Troops are coming up-country in great numbers. Ten European regiments[16] have already arrived at Calcutta, and the native [army ?] has swollen them into forty. The King of Delhi, has it is said got into such a fright, hearing of them, that he has offered to give up Delhi, and the mutineers, if his pension was secured to him. If the old man escapes with his life, it will be all. His 100,000 [rupees ?] a year, the same which the Queen gets, will be reduced to a mere subsistence allowance, and his sons will all swing from the highest tower in Delhi.

William is still with the 16th irreg[ular] cavalry at a place called [? Trushinpoor] better that than being with his own corps which we hear has mutinied at Cawnpoor. Tom's corps is still behaving well, mine also is on its good behaviour. All quiet at Sealkote, from uncle I hear daily, and the

16. *At this point Graham adds a footnote 'To this:35, 53, 64, 78, 84, 1st Madras Fusiliers and others'.*

69

only relatives I am at all anxious about are James and his family. As our postal communications direct with the lower provinces are all cut off, our letters are very long in coming, but up to the last accounts we have received all was quiet in his neighbourhood and native reports are that they continue so.

I fear uncle will be a great loser by the Delhi Bank, I should say at least £20,000, as for my poor mite, it is scarcely to be taken into consideration, though it was every pice I had in the world. Still with good health, a good appointment, and perfect safety I am exceedingly thankful instead of feeling the loss at all. I am sorry to say that Sarah has been suffering from fever, but yesterday's letter from uncle said she was free from it, and getting stronger. I sent uncle the news from the neighbouring provinces and received the same from him, from W[illia]m also I hear frequently, and more seldom from Tom. Still I hear of both from his father, and Brigadier Jones, who now commands at Ferozpoor, and speaks of Tom in the highest terms, says he is in the best of health and spirits and a very fine young fellow. Col Dickey is still with me, he also hears frequently from Col Jones. ... P.S. Remember me kindly to the Garretts, and tell them that all is quiet at Peshawar, and indeed all through the Punjab, and that they need be in no anxiety about their brother, as they have four European regiments there, and are raising two more of civilians who are flocking in for service.'

Undated [probably July 1857]   James Graham, Landour, to his sister Anne, Lisburn, Co. Antrim.

D.312/14/143   The following letter is incomplete, with the first 4 pages missing.

'... the troops coming up-country under Gen[era]l Havelock met the Cawnpoor mutineers, completely defeated [them], took all their guns, and £110,000 sterling from them. The mutineers' leader was so completely defeated, that he rushed to his house, got his family to a boat, made a hole in the bottom, and all were drowned together. The news of this victory has confirmed in their loyalty all the native chiefs (some of whom were suspected, on no good grounds however). They have all come forward with their congratulations, and proffers of assistance. From the very beginning not one has joined the mutineers. The whole disturbance is confined to the army, and the camp followers, and for their being rebellious, we have to thank a British government, who sends out to command armies of hundreds of thousands: men like Gen[era]l Anson, who died some two or three days after he left the hills from old age; Sir John Gray, deaf and lame, who reviewed troops in an easy chair; a gen[era]l at Madras, who died from sheer old age in making a short trip to the hills; and as a writer last year described them, "Veterans swaddled, and slavering, crippled and broken down, worn out from the ravages of disease contracted on service, shattered by wounds received in action, tortured by the shivering from sciatica, handed over the side, trundled up to the hills, and soon peacefully expiring." Such are the men whom the British government send out to command the Indian army, and I wish you could get the newspapers in your part of the world to comment on them a little. Look at Gen[era]l Anson, a very good man no doubt on the turf, [who] knew little or nothing of India, and died before he became acquainted with it. He was succeeded by Gen[era]l Barnard about the oldest officer of the Crimean troops. Poor old gentleman, he subsided into a quiet grave.

Then came Gen[era]l Reed, poor old gentleman, a few days unfitted him for
active service. Gen[era]l Johnstone tried to accompany his troops to Delhi,
and how do you think this gallant officer proceeded? (These all belong to
H[er] M[ajesty]'s service remember.) Why in his carriage the upset of which
made him (if he could possibly be so) more unfit than he was before for
active service, and to look back to Gen[era]l Gowan, our last commander-in-
chief [sense ?]. He had long arrived at his second childhood, he spent his
time in writing sonnets to his wife, the day they first met, to her eyebrows,
etc. etc. These again I must repeat it, are the officers considered by the
British government, as fit to command an army in a conquered country. We
have at last got a man fit for the post, very little above fifty years of
age, if so much, one who has spent all his life in India: so strong and
healthy, with all his senses about him, [who] has seen numberless campaigns,
was adjutant gen[era]l of the Bengal army [and] is commander-in-chief at
Madras, I mean Gen[era]l Sir Pat[rick] Grant, but I suppose he will not be
confirmed in his appointment, as doubtless your "prince consorts" will have
another equerry to provide for.

If the road via Agra is open before the 14th or 15th I will write again,
that way this letter I send via Lahore to make [? sure] [sense ?]. Our
communication with down-country is completely closed, and has been for some
time.

I am happy to say that two companies of my corps which were not at head-
q[uarte]rs when they mutinied, have since been disbanded, and now I am
without a regiment. I trust my next will be an European one, but it does
not make much matter, as I am never likely to join any corps again, nor
serve anywhere except with European troops.'

13 July 1857

D.812/14/144

William S. Graham, Jullundur, to
Daniel Cullimore, [Ballyanne, New Ross,
Co. Wexford].

          'It is with the greatest sorrow I have to
announce to you my poor father's death. I just heard it this morning by
newspaper, but as for particulars God knows if such will ever come to light,
as he is amongst the murdered at Sealkote. I have heard nothing of my
sister, and have just this moment sent off a tel[egraphic] message about her
to Blackall who is some thirty miles off at [? Gogeranwallah] where he is now
stationed, to try and find out her fate. This is an awful calamity that has
befallen us, but God grant the latter is safe. I know not if there is much
hope, for you must have heard ere this what villains our soldiery have
proved themselves to be. To many of our country-women who have fallen into
their hands, death would have a thousand times been more preferable, for
their acts have been awful to these helpless creatures. I am in hopes she
is one of the few who got into the fort. I was doing duty with [the] 16th
irr[egular] cav[a]l[ry], but as this same has proved itself as treacherous
as other reg[imen]ts we were not allowed to go. Delhi was so hard applied
for to do duty with the [? guide] cav[a]l[ry], which had been granted, and
[I] was on my way down to Delhi, when I rec[eive]d the sad news here. I am
awaiting an answer, and if dear Sarah is still alive I will start upwards
there, and then by mail cart and see if I cannot release her. You of course
know the rup[ees] you have rec[eive]d by [the] Delhi Bank, this day not one
rup[ee] will be forthcoming. What my father ever had I know not, as they have

plundered his house, and papers are never to be found, I don't suppose much will be forthcoming. If you know anything of his affairs kindly let me know. No one can declare what the fate of this country will be, with so many enemies in our own camp. It is a hard fight that is being fought, but Britain's true stuff is being shown to the world here in every fight, and it will be a proud leaf in the history of British India. All our service here gone, but the 10th Tom's reg[imen]t, and after the news of today if John Company gave me treble pay to command blacks again I would not do it. Sooner than do so, I would take to cab-driving. My first act if Sarah survives, will be to assist her home at once, *via* Kurrachee and Mooltan.

I hope you will be able to aid me in the settlement of my poor father's affairs, as I know you are an executor to his will. Few parents have done for their family what he did for his, self he sacrificed for them in every way. Tell this to his many friends my good Uncle Tom amongst the number, and [I] know you will all commiserate with us in the loss we have met with. ... [P.S.] My reg[imen]t gone. The officers of Cawnpore brigade had to hold a barrack for some days fighting for their lives, until rel[ieve]d by Europeans that were *en route* from Calcutta. The 14th n[ative] i[nfantry] have been destroyed to a man, not one I hear left to tell the tale. Nicholson has started after the Sealkote brigade. I hope to be in time for the punishment of them if Sarah is alive.

James Graham and my two brothers [are] all right so far. Tom has been in one or two scrimmages and Jones the brig[adie]r has a good word of him in the soldier's line. James must have been in the thick of it too in Oudh. The news from down-country, we know nothing of, that is below Delhi. We are looking to the English newspapers for it. I don't know who is killed at 6 p.m. I trust my friend Tom is to the fore.

I send this under cover to Anne Graham, who will forward it to you as she will know your address.

I will erect something handsome to the memory of our good old father, but not in this country. The first thing the scoundrels did was to destroy such as: graveyards, churches, *etc*.

I would like your idea on this subject and where you think would be a suitable place.

Old Garrett all right - Nicholson also. In fact no Lisburn casualties, but our poor father.

I hope the next mail will tell you that the good old Saxon cheer will have once more rung within the walls of Delhi.'

27 July 1857   James Graham, Landour, to his sister
         Anne, Lisburn, Co. Antrim.

D.812/14/145

         'William wrote to you by last mail, and I am
         saved a duty to which I scarcely feel able.
Since his letter I have not heard from him, and I can give you no account of the sad occurrence at Sealkote. You at home my dear Anne know but little of my poor uncle, and I am afraid that I have never sufficiently informed you

of all his kindness and affection to me. He made no difference between me
and his own children, and not one of them feels the loss more than I do. In
every act and deed of mine, I worked for his approbation, and I cannot tell
you what a blank his loss leaves to me. We were in daily nay hourly
correspondence. There is now no one for me to look up to, no one to fly to
for advice, no guiding hand. It almost appears as if I was once more
separated from home.

William was then on his road to Delhi. Poor fellow, only the day before he
had written to me asking me if anything occurred at Delhi to him to beg of
his father as his last request to make peace with James, and some other
request. Poor fellow, how little he thought what a day would bring forth.
W[illia]m I hear joined the force under Col[onel] (now Brig[adier] Gen[era]l)
Nicholson, and took his revenge on the Sealkote mutineers. I do not know
where he is now, but if not with Sarah at Sealkote, he is escorting her
towards Bombay, on her road homewards. The poor girl her sufferings must
have been great, left totally amongst strangers at such a time. I trust she
will reach Europe in safety. I know nothing about where she is likely to
live, but my poor uncle always assured me that if anything happened [to] him
before her marriage, she would be well provided for. Though my poor uncle
died uncommonly well off, and some of his property will be easily realised,
his loss by the Delhi Bank will make a great change in the state of his
affairs. I should say that he had lost at least 20,000 pounds by its
failure. After Delhi is taken some portion of this will be doubtless
recovered, but I fear very little.

I am my dear Anne very sorry to say, that with the distressing news and so
much anxiety I think I quite forgot to write to you by last mail, but I
trust you were not anxious, and that you did not allow Mamma to be so either,
but rather prayed that all our poor fellow countrymen would soon be in such
safety, and like myself deeply grateful that my fate has been linked to
European troops, and must continue so.

I heard daily from Sealkote up to the day of the mutiny, which I believe
was the 9th instant. My poor uncle had written a letter on the previous
day, to be posted before the mail left that morning, and it reached me two
days ago, all torn and tattered, whether it had lain so long, in his own house
or the post office, I know not, but it is a precious relic. India will never
be the same to me again. Within another month all will be once more quiet,
the native army disbanded and things once more in their regular course, but
my loss is irreparable. Here or in Europe, he would have been a guiding star
to me, and I trusted to see him spending the remainder of his life in happy
ease and contentment: his feelings and motives appreciated, his children
reconciled, but God has been pleased to decide otherwise, and we must but bow
to his will. I must stop giving vent to my feelings, and not harass yours.

My corps has followed the bad examples, and mutined, but made no attempt, and
showed no wish to injure the officers, they are all safe, and the regiment
[has] been almost annihilated by the European and Sikh troops. I will never
serve with native troops again.

At Delhi the mutineers have made successive unsuccessful sorties, in all of
which our troops have punished them severely. On one occasion the 14th one
thousand mutineers were left dead on the field. Our reinforcements will I
trust be all assembled by the 15th proximo, and then the fate of Delhi will
be sealed. I would not be surprised if it were razed to its very foundations.

I have not heard from you since the 16th April, nearly four months. Your letters are all at Agra, and the postal communications between that and Meerut entirely closed, only private dawks are received.

I will most probable [sic] send you a few lines more, on the last safe day for this mail, but do not be disappointed at not hearing from me, as letters do not always travel safely.'

29 July 1857　　　　　　　James Graham, Landour, to his sister

D.812/14/146　　　　　　Sarah, Lisburn, Co. Antrim.

'I have just received your letter of the l[st] June, and am glad to hear that after all the suspense I have had that you are all well at home. The last letter I received was dated the 16th of April. I wrote to Anne a few days ago, and as I promised to write again on the last safe day for the mail, I take up my pen, though I have nothing or very little to write about. I heard from W[illia]m Graham yesterday. He is still at Sealkote at Sarah [sic] but I think he will shortly move to Lahore or Ferozpor to send Sarah down the river on her way home. Poor Sarah has had many trials. Poor girl she had been suffering from fever for some time before the outbreak at Sealkote. All is perfectly quiet there now. Here it has always been so. In our mountain eyrie we are far removed from all the troubles of the plains, and if it was not for our anxieties for our friends would have little to think about. In another month or two all will again be perfectly quiet, and our power in India be stronger than ever, but bought at such a price and wholly owing to the carelessness of governors general, and commanders-in-chief sent out from England who know nothing about the country. You may send as information to any of your editorial friends, that Lord Dalhousie received orders from home to raise eight light regiments of Europeans, and for economy's sake only raised three. Had those eight regiments been in the country, nothing of this would have occurred. It is also owing greatly to missionaries: poor illiterate country parsons who have never travelled twenty miles in their lifetimes, and whose minds are as narrow as their travels, come out here, and without the slightest respect for the religion of people who in their words and deeds are infinitely their superiors, commencing preaching Christianity, not by showing in their acts, not displaying that charity to others which is its vital principle, but with the wildest abuse of all other sects and denominations. They inflame the minds of the people against us. These narrow minded padres never think that they are inciting the minds of 150 millions of people. They think only of their own pockets, and of how they will be able to cook up their next home report, which is a mass of fiction. Yes, my dear Sarah, know yourself and let all your friends know that by your subscriptions to missionaries you are purchasing the murders of your friends and relations, and you are sending out a set of fellows who on their arrival try to make money by fair means and foul, who fight among themselves and with the people of the country, and who take to different trades and professions. I myself have purchased a swine, first rate pork, and hams from a German missionary who was far too busily employed in his own trade even to think of preaching.

Since I last wrote I have got another step in the commissariat by a Capt[ai]n Williamson's being turned out of it. He was a very quarrelsome person, and never did his duty, so he deserved his fate.

74

My next letter will tell you of the fall of Delhi. Troops (European) are [? swarming] up-country in great numbers. Delhi could have been taken at any time, but they wished to have sufficient troops to completely surround the mutineers, and not to let them escape.

I am very glad indeed to hear that you are going to have a visit from Eliza McKnight. You ought to make her stay until John would come over for her. I wish I was there to see her, you must get her to sit for a daguerrotype for me.'

11 August 1857

D.812/14/148

James Graham, Landour, to his sister Anne, Lisburn, Co. Antrim.

'Many thanks for your letter of the 16th of June. I suppose your happy party is broken up once more. I suppose the boys must have returned to school. I trust however you will soon have Eliza McKnight along with you, and I am most anxious to hear all about her. About the sale of Cottage Hill (except that you mention that it is sold) I know nothing, as the letters of three mails are I fear lost, so you must tell me all about it.

I have very little news to tell you, indeed you will see too much of it in the papers without my writing it. Our troops are assembling at Delhi as fast as possible, where now all the mutineers are collected. About the 22nd the troops from Calcutta the last to be there are to arrive. Your townsman Col[onel] Nicholson (now a brigadier-general with the Punjab moveable column) passed through Umballah on the 5th and is expected at Delhi on or about the 16th. We will I hope ere the end of the month have sufficient troops to completely surround the city, and prevent any escaping. We could take it at any time, but the difficulty is not to allow them to escape from a city so many miles in circumference, and with so many gates. However their doom is drawing nigh, and the longer delayed, will be only the more sure. We have the most distressing accounts from Cawnpoor, especially about William's regiment from which I fear not one has escaped, to tell the tale. William (I would not be surprised) is now third captain. Except three officers on staff employ and one in England, I do not think another remains. They were an exceedingly nice set of fellows, so kind and so hospitable, that I look on the two months passed at Cawnpoor this year as about the pleasantest I have passed in India. From William I heard some days ago before he started for Jullundur, where he was to join Maharajah Golab Sing's troops under Major Lawrence, Sir John Lawrence's brother. Sir John was a great friend of my poor uncle, and no doubt the offer was made him on that account. He is to have r[upee]s 600 a month. I don't think he will go to Delhi, but garrison some of the stations from which the troops have been withdrawn. I hope that appointment will lead to something, and it certainly would if William had passed. Tom and Sarah were still at Sealkote when I last heard. Of James, and his family I can hear nothing, but I trust they are safe in Lucknow. I wish you would write to Phoebe Fordyke and break her father's death to her, and tell her I would write but that I don't know her address. It is not impossible that I may stay up here during the whole of the cold weather, mind you it is cold weather indeed, sometimes eight or nine feet of snow. Would not that be jolly? The adjutant general has written to say that it is not intended to reduce the troops here, that if the recovered men are sent down, sick and wounded will take their place, so I shall most probably remain to take care of them.

Has Miss Walkington returned to Ballinderry, I hope so.

I am waiting patiently to hear when Sarah makes a start for this country. I fear Mamma may be frightened about these disturbances, but they are wholly confined to the Bengal and Bombay presidencies, and as for safety in India, India never was so safe before as it will be in the cold weather. The number of European troops will be trebled or quadrupled, and their number will never be so reduced again. Phoebe Fordyce[17] would I know gladly assist Sarah in every way, and though I fear there will be but little chance of my getting down to Calcutta to meet her, Joe would meet her at Madras, and you should also explain to Mamma, that ladies have no furlough regulations to be confined to the country by. I don't see why she should not make a trip now and again when I pay you a visit in 1860.'

25 August 1857

D.812/14/149

James Graham, Landour, to his sister Anne, Lisburn, Co. Antrim.

'The time has come for another mail to be dispatched, and as yet I am sorry to say things are not settled at Delhi. The gen[era]l there is determined to make things so sure that none can escape, and I only hope the mutineers will wait there until he is ready. The last reinforcement will reach him about the 29th inst. and if you do not hear of something decisive by this mail I will be very much astonished. Delhi once fallen, all will soon be once more quiet.

Down-country news we know little or nothing of, as the dawks are completely cut off. Troops have arrived and are arriving in great numbers, and the mutineers have been all well beaten at Cawnpoor. Gen[era]l Havelock has taken from them at least 100 guns, settled the country about Cawnpoor, and gone on to Lucknow. There were very sad doings at Cawnpoor before he arrived, and I greatly fear there is not one of William's regiment remaining. I would not be the least surprised that William was a captain, with one or two under him. From William I heard yesterday. He is now at Jullundur marching down with Golab Sing's troops. He expects to go towards Delhi, but Delhi will have fallen long ere he gets down so far.

Here all remains quiet as usual, and is likely to remain so. We appear in this mountain eyrie of our's to be quite removed from the troubled world below us, and one can scarcely believe how quiet we are with disturbances all over other parts of the country. I trust you have never felt anxious, nor allowed Mamma to do so, though I fear my poor uncle's [murder ?] must have been a great shock to you both.

There is really not a word of news up here, nothing but incessant rain and clouds. I don't think I will ever try to pass another season in the hills, it is really dreadful to see the way it comes down, and for the fog and clouds they are something frightful. We live in the midst of them, it scarcely repays one for the heavenly weather we had before, and I hear will have again after it has done.

Col[onel] Nicholson has arrived at Delhi and commands a brigade. His being

17. *Graham himself seems uncertain whether the lady was called Fordyke or Fordyce.*

Rather fanciful drawing of Indian mail carriers or dawk wallahs

put over the heads of so many of his seniors has I hear given great
annoyance, but in these days the right man is sought for the right place.

I have not heard from you since I wrote last, though the mail has been due
for a long time. We suspect that it has been delayed bringing more troops
out. You must excuse this for I really have nothing to write about. I
hope to send you a long letter by next mail, and if Delhi falls in time you
may hear from me again by this.'

27 August 1857   This letter is probably the enclosure
                                 mentioned by James Graham in his
D.812/14/150   letter of 14 September 1857. The
                                 signature and recipient's name have
                                 been scored out.

'I proclaimed through [? Roberts] yesterday the signal success gained at
[? Najafgarh] on the afternoon of the 25th. The victorious force returned
yesterday afternoon and thirteen guns were added to our park. Our fellows
were stuffed with plunder, and in great delight. The affair was excellently
managed by marching straight through. During the day Nicholson came up on
the enemy unprepared for resistance, and he yet allowed himself ample daylight, to obtain a complete success. They had only time to get their guns
r[oun]d to fire on the plain, and could not entrench themselves or occupy

strong positions. Having carried the guns their only line of retreat was
over a bridge, and our guns played upon them as they crossed. Our force
having out-stripped the baggage, remained without shelter, food or even
grog all night, and in fact had nothing but a [word illegible] from the
time they left camp until they came back on their baggage yesterday, but all
were content as the advantages of the rapid advance were obvious to all. The
division they attacked was the Neermuch force under Indhan Sing. The remnant
of the infantry escaped unarmed. The cavalry bolted as usual at an early hour.
The artillery are accounted for and everything they brought over with them
fell into our hands. Bakht Khan with the Bareilly division was at [? Pelun]
on the other side, the escape. He moved up leisurely to the assistance of
the Neermuchees, and fired some shot without effect at [word illegible], and
the other party occupied in blowing of the bridge. If Nicholson had been
less prompt, he would have had to fight both divisions strongly entrenched.
He had 1,600 men with him, and the strength of the two divisions was about
10,000. The fugitives on their return declared they had been fighting the
whole of our army, so an attack was at once made on our camp by the other
divisions, expecting to find it unguarded, but they fought off on seeing the
unwelcome faces of the rifles and Ghoorkas grinning over the breast-works.
Hodson had done gallant service against the Ranghurs at Rohtak.
He manoeuvred so as to draw a body of 1,500 insurgents into the Maidan.
They pursued with yells thinking he was bolting, but when they were
sufficiently in the trap he wheeled his 400 men round, and went down at his
pursuers like a shot and killed eighty-eight. For a cavalry affair this
was a good [word illegible]. The grandson of [? Shahenull] of [? Bujroul]
is trying to arrange an insurrection in [? Barrote]. It will be a local
affair. I hear of nothing above that the Pandees have detachments at
different places between Bagput and Delhi, but not at Bagput. They believe
they are stopping our supplies, or perhaps thought they could cut off our
escape across the river, when the other troops had driven us into it. I
got your note of the 22nd only yesterday, and will send this *via* Meerut.
It ought to travel faster. I am glad you have the reversion of the judge-
ship and that you can assist Keene so liberally.'

14 September 1857   James Graham, Landour, to his sister
                                  Anne, Lisburn, Co. Antrim.
D.812/14/151

                      'I do not intend to close this until
                      tomorrow, when I hope to hear of the fall of
Delhi. We may not have the news in time for the mail, as we only expect
that the assault took place this morning, but it will reach you by this
mail, as the telegraph will take it to Lahore some three days later than we
can write. I sent you a few days ago a *Punjabee* which gives a fair account
of the commencement of the mutiny. In this I enclose a copy of a letter
from the l[ieutenan]t governor's agent in camp at Delhi, giving an account
of a fight in which our troops were commanded by your townsman, now
Brig[adier] Gen[era]l Nicholson[18]. You can send it to his mother, and
afterwards to the provincial papers. I will ere closing this also add the
last news we have from Delhi. I have just posted a *Lahore Chronicle*, which
will give you an extract of the orders issued by the general commanding at
Delhi on the return of Col[onel] Nicholson [sic]. It will show that the
fight was excellently managed, and that it has won great honour.

18.   *27 August 1857, D.812/14/150.*

78

Send it to Mrs Nicholson, and then to both your newspapers, and newsroom.
I hope it will have a better fate than the last paper I sent about him.

William has reached Delhi, but I have not heard from him for some days.
The troops which he accompanies will most probably guard camp during the
assault, as they are likely to remain in this neighbourhood. I hope to see
him when I get down in the cold weather. I would like to get Bareilly as a
station. It is a very quiet part of the country, and close to the hills.
Sarah has got as far as Mooltan on her road home. Taylor of my corps is the
only fellow passenger of hers down the river, and will I am sure pay her
every attention.

There is again great talk of a staff corps, and I hope this will at last
turn out a fact. It will enable me to take a much longer furlough, and
remove me completely from any military duties. I am not anxious ever to
rejoin a regiment, and to tell the truth, years on staff employ does not fit
one to return to it. I think I have got two more steps in the commissariat,
since I wrote last, one by the death of the man immediately above me, James,
2nd grenadiers, and the other by Malleson getting another staff appointment.
I am very glad indeed to hear that Sarah is coming out. All Madras is
perfectly quiet, and likely to remain so. Indeed to tell the truth neither
sepoys nor people, are likely to fight as they are not fit to do so. One
regiment of our sepoys would eat up a dozen Madras regiments. Though our
regiments are mutinous, they were very fine men, and good soldiers. The
Madrassees are most wretched beings. I fear there is very little chance of
my being able to get to Calcutta to meet Sarah, but I trust to see her
either by going down on a couple of months leave, or when I go home.

I am glad to hear such good accounts of Eliza McKnight. We must pay America
a visit when I go to Ireland. If the staff corps is formed I dare say I
will be able to get two or three years furlough, and it would make a very
nice trip for us.

I have now got all your letters but one, and I dare say it will soon turn up.
I was glad indeed to hear that Miss Walkington was back again in
Ballinderry. Give her my best and kindest regards, and the same to her
uncle and brother if they are there.

Extract from a letter dated 9 Sept[ember] 1857 from, and to, the same person
as the enclosed letter.

"The siege operations are progressing very favourably. The secret was so
well kept that the enemy had no idea of our designs, and were thoroughly off
their guard, and they were not a little astonished yesterday morning to find
our troops, in firm possession of the Koolseagh Bagh within 250 yards
of the wall on the left, and of Ludlow castle on the left centre, and
two batteries armed with ten heavy guns thrown up within 650 yards of the
wall bearing on the Moree and Cashmeeree bastions. All this was actually
done during the night of the 7th without their knowing anything of it. Their
attention was diverted by a heavy fire from the ridge batteries, on the right,
to which all their bastions replied firing clear over the heads of our
working parties. 800 camels were employed in taking down the fascines, and
300 in carrying ammunition. When day broke four of our guns were on their
platforms, and ready for action. The platform of the other six had to be
laid during the day. This battery had at first to sustain a very
formidable fire, and was well supported by the ridge batteries, and by

79

midday we had established a superiority of fire. This is but the beginning
of all things. There are now twenty-two mortars in position, and a
considerable number of heavy guns for which batteries are being prepared in
advanced positions. These will remain silent until all [is] ready, as the
working parties are thereby allowed to work unmolested, the enemy being in
happy ignorance of these preparations. In the meantime the ten guns under
Major Baird are doing excellent service. They have made a great example of
the Moree, and have knocked the Cashmeeree well about. Their return fire
is not what it was. They have had to run their guns there back, and fire
at random."

The friend whose death you will see mentioned is that of poor Trotter, a
nephew of Col[onel] Dickey's. He died in my house.

15 Sept[ember]. I am afraid the post will not be in time to let you know of
the fall of Delhi, but I will write tomorrow in the chance of its reaching
you. I will not delay this, as I know how anxious you must be, though you
have really no cause for anxiety, about me at least.

I had a letter yesterday evening from William written in very good spirits
from Delhi. The troops he is with (the Cashmeeree ones) are behaving well,
and everything going on satisfactorily. We had on the 12th forty-six heavy
guns, and mortars playing on the walls. So you can fancy it must be very
disagreeable inside. Once Delhi has fallen, all the country will soon be
quiet again. The mutineers confess to have lost 11,000 men, since our troops
arrived to look after them. I do not say the siege commenced, for that only
occurred a week ago, and the first night we were within six hundred yards.
The second or third, at some places we had established ourselves within two
hundred and fifty. It is said that we have got letters implicating the
Kings of Delhi, and Oude, and the Nawab of Moorshedabad. If this is the
case pensions to the tune of £410,000 sterling will lapse to government.
A letter has also been intercepted between the Queen of Oude and her son,
which explains Her Majesty's visit to England. She is there as a spy, and
writes that no troops are coming out, and there are but few to send, so they
may commence the mutiny at once. I wish they may get her at Barclay and
Perkin's brewery, and treat her as they did Marshal Haynau.'

27 September 1857   W[illiam] S. Graham, Delhi, to Daniel
                           Cullimore.
D.812/14/152

                           'Delhi gone fhut at last, and I was there and
                           had a little to-do in the business. I had
the command of one hundred of Punjaub mounted police, and though we in one
attack with some of the Cashmere inf[antr]y were obliged to retreat, there
being only five hundred of us in all, and [we] were surrounded by some 3,000
of the enemy, I did not get off before I lost twenty-two men, and twenty-
nine horses, which was a good lot out of one hundred. We went to take the
East [word illegible], and I was sent with cavalry through the [? Subzie]
Mundie, which is nothing but walls, and gardens and brushwood, quite unadapted
for cav[alr]y, there was not one hundred square y[ar]ds where we possibly
could [? act on]. But thank God I got all serene out of it, not without one
or two nasty patches. One ball through my pugry, and the other a spent ball
hit me on the heel. I was riding a 1,400 rupee horse which I was in such a
state about, I had not time to think of myself.

The British attack at Delhi

Lisburn has to mourn over the loss of the finest soldier John Company could boast of; this is Nicholson. He commanded a brigade in the attack, and he never stopped until they reached the Jumma Masjid, but one of our other columns of attack having failed, they were obliged to recross the Chandni Chouk again, when poor Nicholson got wounded through the lungs, which proved fatal. India has met with an awful loss in him, for such men as he was, and [? Mackeson], and Sir Henry Lawrence are not to be found. It is useless my holding forth on him. His loss is greater than 2,000 Europeans at the present moment and these are of no small value, at the present crisis. You ought to see the conglomeration of fellows we have fighting our battles for us now: Affreedes, Affkhans and all the different race[s] of border tribes, who have for so many years p a s t been giving us so much trouble. All our horses were taken away from disarmed reg[imen]ts, and these fellows put on them with arms *etc.* complete, and sent down under their own chiefs, and the latter looked upon poor Nicholson as their head. He was the only one that had the slightest control over them; his name and they quaked. The Delhi Bank think they will make a better wind up than I first expected, but I doubt it much, and you know my dear Cullimore what the army are to trust to us a body - rogues who will be only too glad to take advantage of the bank's misfortunes. In fact I know it so well that I have heard lots give it out that they felt the bank had no further call on them, and it was not their intention to pay now that their bonds were destroyed. Others who were in the same box backed them up, and said they were going to do likewise. I

fear the bank [? must agree]. Mr Hobson is too hopeful, and you know as
well as I do, what the world and the bank debtors in this country generally
speaking are; men with their better feelings blunted, and if they have the
opportunity won't stick at trifles. My poor governor had something about a
lac and a half in it, and I w[oul]d (if it were in my power to act) take
half that for it tomorrow. Of course you have seen the copy of his will,
which is at Coutts's, as he has made you one of the executors, and I trust
you act as such. James[19] and I are also [executors] having arrived at
twenty-five years of age. Fordyce is another. Nothing can be done here
until the roads open, but if you are near Fordyce I would like you to talk
over matters with him. Everything is to be sold, and put in Bengal and
Bombay banks, but I say don't sell out of Delhi yet a while, and see if
matters improve. The manager expects only the loss of a six months'
dividend, but I fear he is [*at this point at the bottom of a page part of
the letter has been cut away, and some of the text lost. The text resumes.*]
[? vent] to such opinions from him to be little fit for bank manager. The
bank is open at Meerut. My poor father's house and property also I propose
letting stand, as there is no one at Sealkote now. It ought to sell well at
any rate. I would wait a little. Sealkote is sure always to be a large
station, on acc[oun]t of it salubrity, but troops may not go there next year,
and as its a house all pukka, and will require no repair, I would let it
stand over also. Old Parson has got an idea that now James and I are twenty-
five he is no longer an executor to the will. At Lahore I cannot find this
out, but I don't think so. Misfortunes they say never come singly, and not
only have I lost the best of fathers, but everyone of my own reg[imen]t gone.
Is not this awful, to have swept away at one swoop those you have been with
so long? Poor Charlie Quinn amongst the number. I assure you I can't
realize it, but thank God we have got the scroundrels out of Delhi, which
they were in [in] overpowering numbers with ground and everything just
suited for their sneaking cowardly fighting, and the next news you will hear
I hope will be that we have met them on open ground, when I [? pities] them.
I saw the King of Delhi, and abused him like a pick-pocket, and treated him
anything but as the Great Mogul. I saw his three sons also after they were
killed, lying at the Kotwali, where the Europeans were treating their
remains with every indignity.

Delhi is completely looted, but I hope they will re-sell it, which will give
us a good dollop of prize money.'

1 October 1857   James Graham, Landour, to his sister
                          Anne, Co. Antrim.
D.812/14/153

                          'Here is another mail going out, and I have
                          not heard from you since I wrote last.
However I suspect this will be the last time that I will have to complain of
any delay in the arrival of English letters. Last mail took you the news of
the assault on Delhi on the 14th ult[imo]. The whole city, citadel, palace
and magazine were in our possession a few days after. The effect on the
country was great, all around this neighbourhood became at once as quiet as
before the outbreak. The King surrendered himself into our hands, and as he
is about ninety years of age his life will I think be spared, [? two of] his

19. *His brother.*

82

Above: the capture of the *King of Delhi* by *Lieutenant Hodson*

Below: Sikh troops dividing loot

sons, and a grandson, one of the former the commander of the mutineers, were taken prisoners and shot without a trial. All was successful. All the guns in the magazine, nearly two hundred, fell into our possession. The mutineers were dispersed in every direction, and are being pursued. A column followed hard at their heels, and if it overtakes them will knock them to pieces. For such a success we of course expected great loss, but it was not so much as we had anticipated, but I regret to say Brig[adier] Gen[era]l Nicholson was badly wounded, and died a few days after. He was first in at the breach, and his name for cool courage, and gallant conduct will keep his fame in the annals of the Bengal army a lasting one. I send you a *Punjabee* which gives Sir John Lawrence's order concerning him. The governor general's has not as yet reached us. He is a great loss in every way. No officer in this army showed more signs of a noble future. For the victory he won at [? Najafgarh] he would have been made a [? companion of the bath]. I sincerely pity his poor mother, tho' she has much to be proud of, for no soldier lived who was more honoured, nor died who was more lamented.

William was in the very thick of the assault. He was commander [of] one hundred men of a mounted Punjaub police corps. He describes the fight as very severe. Out of his one hundred men, twenty men and twenty-six horses were killed, and wounded. William was not very well, and after the city was completely in our possession, the doctors recommended that he should take a few days leave for change of air, and I am glad to say that he is now at Umballah. From the number of dead bodies, there was great sickness in the city, and he will return before active operations again commence, and with the weather much cooler.

I cannot describe the beautiful weather we have now here. The mornings have a cool refreshing breeze, and the mountains look so like, or at least makes one think so much of, the Mourne Mountains, that I can almost fancy myself at Newcastle.

You will be glad to hear that there is every hope of recovering a great part of the Delhi Bank property. If successful it will make all the Grahams very wealthy, by the time they come into their property. The cold weather is now commencing, and I expect shortly to go down, but where I don't know. Col[onel] Nuthall will give me a good station, I have no doubt. Did I mention that two of his sons were at a school here. They come up to spend their holidays here, and I regret much to say when they are here I always feel I am getting an old bachelor. Though very fond of children, the old bachelor, does not like to be put out of his ways, and his [? traps] to be turned topsy-turvy.

The last *Home News* brought the intelligence of a commissariat staff corps, but how it is to be formed, and what it is to consist of we know nothing about, but we expect the details in the next *Home News* which should be in here about the 2nd or 3rd. I am of course very anxious to see it, and as the commissary general Col[onel] Ramsay is now in England, I expect it will be very favourable to present commissariat officers. A few days now will settle it, and I hope to be able to tell you all about it in my next.

We have heard nothing yet of James and his family, but as the troops were to leave Cawnpoor for Lucknow on the 16th ult[imo] every day ought to bring us intelligence.'

17 October 1857   James Graham, Landour, to his sister
Anne, Lisburn, Co. Antrim.

D.812/14/154

'Since my last, everything in every quarter
of India has been brightening. Delhi I think
I mentioned has been taken. Shortly after, the King, two of his sons, and a
grandson were made prisoners. The three latter were shot at once without a
trial, or certainly only a drumhead one, as they were caught in arms against
the state. The King has been tried, and is waiting his sentence. Two more
of his sons have been taken, and shot immediately after the taking of Delhi.
Our troops separated in all directions. One force went to a place called
Kewarree; took a fort of that name, a large number of guns, a gun foundry,
and large munitions of war. A second pursued the mutineers at Bolundshupur,
took five guns, and had a complete victory, followed them to Allyghur, and
took a like number of guns, again to a place called Akrabad, took as many
more, when the mutineers dispersed and made for Oude in small parties. The
columns again returned, left a small detachment at Allyghur, and made a
forced march to Agra, arriving the very day that a third body of the
mutineers not knowing of their movements attacked that place. We had another
complete victory, took thirteen guns, treasure and lots of baggage, and I now
believe that there is not a body of disciplined mutineers in our own
territory. Of Gwalior we have no certain intelligence, but the rumours are
of the very best kind. It is said that the Maharajah has with his private
troops quite overawed the mutineers, and holds possession of the fort, so
that there will be no trouble there. To all these, I have to add the good
news of the relief of Lucknow, which took place in the end of last month.
We have not as yet heard from James but I believe he is all right. The ladies
and children who were there are being sent off to Calcutta, and that part of
the country will soon be settled. Up here and in the neighbouring districts
everything is as quiet as if the mutiny had never occurred.

You will be glad to hear that William reached this [place] a fortnight ago
to pay me a visit. He was seedy at Delhi, and as there was a good deal of
sickness, his doctor advised him to come away. As he got no better at
Umballah I asked him to come up here, and he is nearly well again. However,
he now intends to apply for leave, and remain up here for six months if
possible. As yet I hear nothing of my own movements, and as the weather is
beautiful I am not anxious to leave this [place]. I cannot describe to you
anything like the beauty of the scenery, and the delightful weather we have
at present. I was out about thirteen miles into the hills yesterday, and
enjoyed the trip excessively. Where we had our tents was just over the spot
where the river Jumno bursts from the hills, and we saw five rivers falling
into it at different places. Our tents were on the site of an old Nepalese
fort, on the last ridge of hills nearest the plains, and 7,000 feet high.
So you can imagine the view we had. On the one side the plains, on the other
the finest view of the snowy range I have seen here.

William has written his last proposal to Miss Roberts, and I think if they
come to [? terms] he will go home to be married, and leave the service.
With what she was to have he would be very well off until he is of age (34).

By the bye the houses my grandfather left (in Lisburn) to my poor uncle are
by his will to be sold. For a stranger to have them might cause considerable
inconvenience. Would William be able to buy them? If not, I will make an
offer for them, and will make William Graham who is one of the executors
give William or myself the first refusal of them. If the purchase money was

J

allowed to be paid by instalments, at a moderate interest, I could do it with ease. My uncle valued them at about £800, and placed the rental about £40 per annum. You will however know better what they are worth, and kindly let me know all about them.[20] [* They are] so [? mixed] up with William's property [* that if] they got into a stranger's hands, [* there] might be some disturbance about them. Let me know all you would advise and recommend.

Delhi Bank affairs, are looking up, and I trust to be able to get out of it with but little loss, so that the above purchase would not put me to [? much] inconvenience.'

15 November 1857

D.812/14/14/156

James Graham, Landour, to his sister Anne, Lisburn, Co. Antrim.

'Though tomorrow is the last day for the mail, still for fear of any mistakes, this time I sent off a newspaper to William several days ago, and I will continue to do so every mail if possible.

Everything is now very quiet up in these provinces, but down below, that is, in Bengal and near Calcutta there is still a good deal of disturbance, but now that the reinforcements are beginning to arrive all will soon be over. Delhi, and the King were names to get hold of, but now they can only look upon themselves as "without a head". This part of the country is so quiet that we have already sent one force down country from Delhi, and another starts about the end of the month. I would like very much to accompany it, as this place is now getting bitterly cold, too much so to be agreeable, and the place is quite deserted. Even ladies and children are going off in different directions, where a few months ago all was riot and confusion. I would have tried to get away ere this, but I am afraid that Mamma and all at home would be anxious, notwithstanding all I have explained to you about commissariat duties, and I will again tell you that we are non-combatants, and except a military uniform, we are mere civilians. Everything is now so quiet as far as Cawnpoor, that I am seriously thinking of asking Col[onel] Nuthall to let me go down into the plains, and I think if I do I will most probably take with me as far as Cawnpoor, his two boys who are here at school. Below Cawnpoor I will not go, but will easily send them to Allahabad, and from thence down the river [Ganges] by steamer. If I do go you must remember that I go only with European soldiers, and it is a considerable body of them, with whom a commissariat officer is sent, and my taking two helpless little boys about eight and ten years of age will show you even more than anything else, how little danger there is. However it is very likely I may not move at all, for I don't know whether Col[onel] Nuthall will let me. I have heard from him several times lately, and he has not mentioned anything about removing me from this [place].

William is still here, and now looking very well. I don't know what his future movements will be after April next, when his leave expires. I think it very probable that he may then go home, if all things go straight. He has written finally to Miss Roberts, and of course everything will depend upon her father.

20. *At this point part of the letter has been torn, and parts of the text are missing. An attempt has been made to reconstruct this missing text. Reconstructed text has been placed in parenthesis and indicated by the use of an asterisk.*

I am sorry to hear that Mr Garrett was at Cawnpoor, but I did not see his name in any list, and he may have been at Lucknow, which I think is more likely, for I think you mentioned it was a railway in Oude on which he was to be employed. I will [? sharp] at every list, and let you know at once if I see his name mentioned.

I am glad to hear of the pleasant trip you had to France. What travellers Sarah and you are become, first to Manchester, and then to the continent, not to mention your previous visits to London and Dublin. Well you will be the better able to show me the world when I visit Europe.

You do not mention the rows in Belfast, where they appear to have gone mad. I am quite surprised to hear of quiet sensible Northerners going mad in this way. What can have come across them? I don't much admire Dr Hanna for persevering when he found it was creating so much ill-feeling, it was very unbecoming in a clergyman. William had a letter from your very affectionate brother-in-law at Ballyanne, by land mail, but it only referred to my poor uncle, and his affairs, and you were not mentioned at all.

William hears frequently from Tom, who is now in the Lahore light horse, but from James neither of us have had a line. He is one of the worst correspondents I ever came across ...'.

17 November 1857

D.812/14/157

William S. Graham, 'Club Mussoorie', Mussooree, to Daniel Cullimore, Ballyanne, New Ross, Co. Wexford.

          'Very many thanks for your kind letter, as well as for yours and Eliza's condolence with us in the sad loss we have met with. There were few parents like my poor father. His everything was the welfare of his children, and not one selfish thought was in him. Everything was sacrificed for our future happiness, and had he, as most parents in his circumstances been in England, he would have been spared us now. As you say, now when gone we see more clearly the motives of what in life, we looked upon as his eccentricities, all was [for] our welfare. When I reached Sealkote it was my wish to have him moved from where he was buried, to have his body placed in consecrated ground, but he with Brind and eight others were the inhabitants of one grave, close to the fort, and my poor father's body before burial I heard was much decomposed. I proposed having it moved [*word illegible*], and had ordered a large coffin for the purpose, but was advised against it, as they all lay together. If it were possible I would do as you propose, and would myself like my mother and he to be buried together, but such was impossible, and so now I have had a wall built round the spot, and I intend to erect either in the Sealkote church or at home something handsome to his memory. This has been a sad year out here, and no one can have met with more serious losses in the shape of friends than myself. The good old second all gone, and with it my warmest friends!!! Friends of years, proof and trial [*sic*], providence protected me most wonderfully; escaping Cawnpoor massacre, getting through Delhi three days before [the] outbreak there, and escaping at Delhi during the assault. On the day of the assault I had command of one hundred Seikh Police, and lost twenty-two men of these, but I had a charmed life. I had my pugry ripped open, a spent ball hit me on the temple, and one on the heel, and I and a 1,400 rupee horse I was riding, [? Jalaff], all serene. If anyone ought to think and reflect on God's mercies I ought. I cannot realize the past, there is a vacuum left which nothing but time can fill up. Poor Charlie Quinn, what a [? state] his father and mother will be in, but England must be in [? mourning], but she has reason to rejoice, and be proud of many of her children, and the noble way they met death.

Now my dear Cullimore I know my poor father used to think well of your powers of reasoning. [At this point part of the letter has been cut away, and there is a consequent short gap in the text] ... either and the question I have to put to you, is what ought I to do? Put everything into the scale, and remember at [the] same time what my feelings must be towards niggers. These it would be difficult for you to realize either. I can never have revenge sufficient to satiate my thirst, and its a thing I can't and won't do again, command black men of any sort. By the time I am thirty-four I will have the money I have been left as it is to be laid out, some £1,200 a year. That will calculating on [? 8%] hereafter ... . I hope after everything is sold and the Delhi Bank gets on a little, there will be about 4½ lacs to be divided amongst us, which is to be divided into 30 shares, and I believe my share is to be 6½ shares, which will make my share about a lac, and this with six years growth will I hope give me about £1,200 a year then. Is there anything I can do till then? I wrote by [the] same mail as this to my only love Miss R[oberts]. My prospects can never improve. I have explained this, and put the old question to her, to be my wife. I tell her that if an answer in the negative comes that it is all up with me in that quarter, and *entre nous* after all that has taken place I think it time I should give up old ways, and lead a respectable life. I must have a little money, and Mr Roberts if he likes, can do the needful. At any rate I will have a few thousand rupees in hand, and will come home for a year when furloughs are open, whatever comes or goes. The next thing is, such appointments as adjutants of yeomanry reg[imen]ts, Irish mounted police, and other gentlemanly appointments, are [they ?] open to purchase; and as I think I will be able to sell after I am appointed to some reg[imen]t when a remodelling of the service takes place, and ought to get 20,000 [? rupees] step [money ?], as I am sure of my capt[ain]cy, I would be able to give £400 or £500 for the like. Do you think is such comeatable? Tell me what you think of this, and if I would have any chance of getting it.

I want you and Fordyce to send me a power of attorney to enable me to act out here. I see no mention of James's two butchered at Lucknow, so suppose poor little things they have not been able to stand the hardships they had to endure.

Here rumours from Lucknow; one all the ladies murdered, another Lucknow all ours, but with a loss of 1,000 killed and wounded, and all their guns taken except eight.'

23 November 1857   James Graham, Landour, to his sister
                                    Anne, Lisburn, Co. Antrim.
D.812/14/158

                                    Graham concentrates in this letter upon a
                                    discussion of family affairs, and a trip he
has made to the government tea factories at Deyrah. He gives his sister
details about the cultivation of the tea plant, and its preparation into
the finished product, and the variations of tea that can be produced.
Mutiny references begin in the latter half of the letter.

'... you will see by the *Times of India* I send you that James and his wife are all right at Lucknow, but I fear that they have lost their children: who are not mentioned, not by the water being cut off, my dear Anne, but by living on parched grain, which these poor little children, I fear, could not digest. These stories which get into the English papers about water being cut off are sheer nonsense. If I were shut up in my own house in any part of India, except the deserts, I would dig a well before twenty-four hours, if I had as many people to assist as were at Lucknow. However now, thank God, they are all right. We have just heard that Lucknow is completely in our possession, and the sepoys have at last met with the punishment they deserve. In the one spot 1,500 bodies were counted, so their loss must have been great.

I still want to get down to the plains, so [don't] be surprised if you next hear from me from some place on the march, and keep in mind, and in Mamma's too that the commissariat officers are non-combatants, and only accompany European troops, which I think are two guarantees for my safety. I am also glad to see that the interruption in the dawks did not cause you so much anxiety. Remember there are 10,000 causes for a bag of letters getting astray or late, so if mine don't reach you just think that a thief has seized it, a bridge of boats has not been repaired in time to allow it to come by the right mail, but that another will bring my next very valuable epistle. I have now I am happy to say got all your letters but one, and as it contained the news of the sale of Ballinderry, the name of the purchaser, and the amount he gave, I must beg of you to send me this information.

I have got two or three tea seeds, to send you packed up in a pill box, but I am not sure whether I can send them by post. If they reach you put them at once into damp hot ground, and if you keep them [in] the latter, you can hardly give them too much of the former. William is here, all jolly. He desires me to thank you for y[ou]r kind letter rec[eive]d one or two mails ago, which he will shortly answer ...'.

14 December 1857

D.812/14/162

James Graham, 'Fort Allygurh', Aligarh, to his sister, Anne, Lisburn, Co. Antrim.

'As you will be expecting a letter from me by this mail, I take up my pen though I have very little time to do so. Shortly after writing my last letter I was ordered down to take charge of a convoy of stores proceeding to Cawnpoor. My services were asked for as a favour by Major Scott a[cting ?] c[ommissary ?] gen[era]l at Cawnpoor under whom I acted at Wuzeerabad, and I had the high compliment paid me by Col[onel] Thompson dep[ut]y com[missar]y gen[era]l of the upper [? circle], "that a better man could not have been selected". The work is hard, and I have a good deal of responsibility. You will think this when you know my charge: above 2,000 carts laden with 25,000 mannds grain, 70 mannds salt, 2,500 gall[on]s rum, 1,500 m[ann]ds soojee (flour), 106 of ghee *i.e.* clarified butter, each m[ann]d is 50 lbs. Then I have: 11,500 camels laden with 166 tents, each for 16 Europeans, 35 pair camel trunks, 32 mujawas (panniers); and 2,000 doolie bearers ([a] doolie is a bed for carrying the sick) with doolies then I have 1,400 men being the establishments of servants required for the six European regiments. The carts cover twenty miles of ground when in one row, and ten when we are able to get them into two. We were escorted here: by the first European regiment, one Sikh regiment, one squadron of the 6th dragoon guards carabineers, several detachments of cavalry going to join their regiments down-country, one regiment of native cavalry the name of which you may have seen mentioned, Hodson's Horse, six [? nine pound] guns (one troop [of] horse artillery), and two eighteen pounders. So we are very strong, but notwithstanding, we are ordered to remain here until the troops from below clear the road up, and come here to escort us down, which we expect will be very soon.

The payment of my charge amounts to 10,000 pounds sterling *per mensem* all of which passes through my treasury chest in hard cash, so you may imagine what sort of a business it is.

We expect to move downwards very soon, for we daily receive native reports of a great victory won at Cawnpoor over the Gwalior contingent, in which one of their regiments was completely annihilated. The whole suffered severely, and we took one of their guns.

You must make Mamma fully understand that there is even here not the slightest reason to be anxious about me. We are now a pursuing force. If this victory is a true one, and you will have a full account by this mail, we will have nothing to do but to clear our old provinces of a few stragglers.

I have charge of about 15,000 camp-followers, and I can assure you my tent which is pitched inside the fort is like a small pandemonium, from the number of people, and the work going on; so you really must not expect me to write, but I will send you as many papers as I can, and write on them the dates and places.

The weather is delightful. I have an office tent, which is intended for sixteen European soldiers. It is double poled about sixty feet long by thirty feet broad, and this beside my own private tent of about fourteen feet square. I have with me about 1,000 spare camels, and 500 carts, all of which I am allowed to use if necessary. So I travel like an alderman.'

25 December 1857   James Graham, 'Fort Allygurh',
                             Aligarh, to his sister, Anne, Lisburn,
D.812/14/164   Co. Antrim.

                  'May you all be spending as happy a Christmas as I am doing, but with less to do. I have fortunately been able to shut up office for the day, but it will entail I fear double work tomorrow. My charge now amounts to above 4,000 carts, most of them with four, five and six bullocks, so you may safely say I have 16,000 of those animals to keep provided with food, beside about as many camp-followers. We have been here for about ten days, but hope to be off shortly now. Since I wrote last, victory and success has [*sic*] been following our foot-steps. At Cawnpoor which the Gwalior mutineers attacked, we took the whole of their guns, carriage *etc.*, and killed thousands of them. Another column came across a few scoundrels who had crossed from Rohilkand, and took all their guns, sixteen in number. Before the cold weather has passed India will be as quiet as ever it was, and will have got a lesson it will never forget. Now there is not one body of insurgents assembled in any place. Dispersed bodies, and those in not large numbers, will have of course to be broken up and punished. These are but a matter of time. Once the troops reach them all will be over. There is now but one place occupied in our old territories, "Fattehgurh", but from it, since the discomfiture of the Gwalior troops at Cawnpoor, they are bolting sharp.

I have had another letter from you since I wrote last, and I am glad to hear for his poor wife's sake that James Allen has once more given up drinking, for ever so short a time.

The ladies and children from Lucknow have reached Allahabad in safety. They passed through Cawnpoor when the Gwalior troops were attacking that place, and Sir Colin Campbell allowed the latter to have their own way until the ladies and children were safely on their way, if not arrived; then he went at them, and drove them out with a loss of only twenty men.

At Delhi they have hanged an independent Rajah [? of Hanjjur] who was implicated in the mutiny, and another will follow in his footsteps. The King's life has been guaranteed, and he will be allowed to spend the brief remainder of his life in prison, without attendants or any consideration. Five of his sons have already met their deserved reward, and more are continually being brought in, so that the root and branch of the wretched breed will soon be cleared off.

William is still at Landour. I had a note from him a few days ago.

When at Meerut (between ourselves) I saw Colonel [? Stannes] and his children. The former was speaking to the friend I was driving with, but I neither made myself known to him, nor wish to do so. He is far too disagreeable a person for anything of that sort. His children are three very nice looking little girls.

I did not tell you in my last that I had run over to look at Delhi. In the deserted city I stayed four days. In one of the streets, a few shops are allowed to be open for our own convenience, but for the rest every house is empty. You can roam through street after street without meeting a single soul. I went into several houses, but they were perfectly cleaned out, and the only thing I found was a dead mutineer.

Now my dear Anne, with my best love to Mamma, yourself and all at home, and ... [*text defective*] you a happy Christmas and new year ... P.S. Address your letters to Cawnpoor *via* Calcutta for the present.'

December 1857   James Graham, to his sister, Anne,
                       Lisburn, Co. Antrim.

D.812/14/166

                       This letter is undated, but has been endorsed
                       'probably December 1857'. The endorsement
was most likely added when the papers were being arranged and bound. Graham has also omitted to address the letter with the name of his military encampment. The letter is headed 'Private and Confidential', as Graham wished certain of its contents to be secret from his mother. His reason is clarified in the transcript.

'I have just heard from W[illia]m about his father's will. You must not repeat what I tell you. My poor uncle left (without the Delhi Bank in which he had 20,000 pounds, and government paper and E[ast] India stock *etc*. of

which the papers have been lost) some 30,000 pounds to be divided, to which
I hope some of the Delhi Bank money will be recovered and added. He has
divided it into thirty shares of which Phoebe gets three, Sarah seven until
her marriage, when four go to W[illia]m and James, who each get seven and a
half, and Tom four and a half, which will be about the same for the boys as
they can neither draw interest nor capital until they are thirty-four years of
age. My poor uncle explained this to me a long time ago. The will is a very
long one, sheets and sheets of paper, Fordyce, Parsons and your affectionate
brother-in-law (Daniel [Cullimore]) the executors. By the bye the latter
individual must have lost the greater part of his money in the Delhi Bank.
I myself lost 600 pounds, my little all, of which I fear none or very little
will be recovered.

When this mutiny broke out, fearing that I might be sent down, for your sakes
I sent my will to my poor uncle for safety. It may have been lost among his
papers, but should it reach home (it is addressed to you) take care not to
let Mamma see it or it might frighten her to know I had written such a
thing ...'.

The letter ends with Graham discussing the sale of some family property at
Ballinderry, and hoping that a family quarrel has been ended.

15 January 1858   James Graham, Kanpur, to his sister
                               Anne, Lisburn, Co. Antrim.
D.812/14/167

                       'You will be surprised I suppose to see
                       Cawnpoor at the head of this letter, but I
have been here for the last three days, and as I am off again tomorrow
morning, and as I may not have another opportunity to write soon I take up
my pen. I arrived here three days ago, and have been lost in astonishment
ever since to think what could have made the general think of taking up such
a position as the entrenchments were, in which our poor fellows suffered so
much; exposed on three sides to buildings from which a murderous fire of
musquetry poured upon them. They had only a trench you could step over by
way of shelter. The buildings they were in are so pierced by musquet balls
that there is not one square yard without holes.

I fear you must have ere this seen how we have lost poor James Graham also.
He during one of the engagements at Lucknow, got a stroke of the sun which
brought on a touch of apoplexy which affected his mind, and he, I am sorry
to say put an end to himself, but between you and me my dear Anne, William
and I had been expecting this for some time. James had of late years taken
to eating enormously. It produced violent dyspepsia and his temper was
really dreadful. He could not bear society. He did nothing but shut
himself up in his own house, and we both felt convinced that something of
this sort would happen. We did all in our power to show him the folly of
his ways, and I know William spoke to his wife often, but it was all to no
purpose. He would not listen to anyone. When he got his stroke of the sun
(Mittee writes to me), he told her he could not take care of himself. Poor
girl she lost one of her children, and was just confined of another when this
dreadful affair took place. She is in a dreadful state poor girl, and is
much to be pitied. I have just written to her offering her every assistance
in my power, but I trust she by this time is on her way to England. I did
not hear of James's death until about a week ago when her letter reached

me[21] * from this.

William is I hear going. * I have not heard from him for a long time
though I have written often. When I last heard from him he was in the hills.
I believe he is still thinking of matrimony, but I do not know if Miss
Roberts is still in the same mind. By poor James's death he will become a
man of independent fortune. I think uncle's was a curious will, but I think
after making an ample provision for the widow and daughters the rest went to
his sons.

I have got rid of my convoy at last, and now start for an easier time of it.
I think it not unlikely I may be posted to Fattehgurh where troops are to
remain, and I would like it very well.

I have not now heard of you for three mails, my letters being like myself,
wandering over the face of the country. I daresay they will reach me in time,
but I do not practice well what I preach to you about having patience.'

21 January 1858   James Graham, Fategarh, to his sister
                                    Anne, Lisburn, Co. Antrim.
D.812/14/168

                                    'It appears to me I am to see the whole of
                                    the places where mutiny has been worst after
they have got safe and quiet. I was only five or six days at Cawnpoor when
I was told to proceed here by the first opportunity. So, being all ready to
start off I came the following morning with a detachment of troops coming
here: such fun (to me!!!) for I had nothing to do, and to see what griffs
my companions were was most amusing; all Queen's officers they could not
speak one word of Hindostani, and poor devils they did suffer in consequence.
I did my best for them, explaining how they would get on with greater
comfort, but they were so full of English notions, and "the way this was done
in the Crimea", that where[as] I had my tent pitched, and [had] comfortably
bathed and breakfasted before 9 o'clock, they generally had their breakfast
and dinner in one at 5 p.m. I used always to share my little breakfast with
one or two of them, but of course I could not attempt to feed the whole party,
for I had only my own cantonment establishment of servants, and poor
creatures after they have marched twenty-four or twenty-five miles (we made
double marches) [and] have pitched my tent, prepared breakfast and I have
dressed, they have in my opinion done a good days work.

I travel with great comfort. I have got two tents: one for my office a
large soldiers' tent which is allowed for sixteen Europeans. I send it ahead
one day after office is over; and my own small one. The [office ?] tent is
always on the ground ready when I arrive. I send a couple of office
[? chuprassies] ([? dugliee] messengers) and one tent pitcher. I am allowed
two to my office. I have altogether six camels. Four of these are employed
in the office, are paid by government [sic] and carry the office tent, a pair
of camel trunks filled with office books and papers, and the office tables
and chairs. The other two carry my private property, my tent and traps, but
besides these, I have: a mule which carries a pair of Peshawar mule trunks
(which William made me a present of), with all my clothes; and a bangley
burdar (a man) who carries two light tin boxes, which bring up sufficient

21.   *The letter has been torn and parts of the text are missing. The
resultant gaps in the transcription are indicated by asterisks.*

traps to make and give me my breakfast, at once, on arrival at the
encamping ground.

Well the rest of my establishment consists of: my bearer (or valet) who
dresses me and takes care of my clothes (don't think me luxurious, we have
not comfortable basins and jugs to wash in and things of this sort, you must
have someone to pour the water over your hands as it falls into a great
brass basin); then my khudmutgar (or butler), my dhobie (or washerman), my
mehta (or sweeper), and my bheestie (or water carrier) complete my household.
My only other servants are my sais (or groom), and my two grasscutters, one
of whom leads the mule on the march. The other brings the grass for the
horses and mules. You will think me very extravagant, and perhaps
luxurious, but I could not do without one of the above, and if I could get
an assistant butler I would be very glad to take him.

The above is a complete establishment which every officer has to keep, and
not one in excess, and the whole of their pay does not amount to 40/- a
month. We Bengalees are supposed to be luxurious and extravagant on account
of having so many, but I prefer them to the Madras method of having only two
at perhaps 20/- each, which comes to the same thing, and is not so comfortable,
for the more servants you have your tent is the sooner pitched. Well I told
you above how one of my tents always goes ahead. The rest of my servants
bring up the other. I am allowed two men mounted on camels for my office.
When I get up in the mornings I mount my butler off behind one of them, and

British troops breakfasting on the road between Allahbad and Kanpur

94

off he goes to the next ground to prepare breakfast giving me always a cup
of tea before he starts. Behind the other camelman I mount my groom. As
soon as I have walked sufficiently and the camel keeps up with my borse as
he canters along, so as I get off him the groom is ready to take care of him.
Such is my march everyday, and as you may suppose I travel very comfortably.
I sold my horses when I went up to the hills, and was very fortunate in
getting another on my arrival at Meerut. He is a very handsome, strong,
powerful arab, and even at the end of a double march is full of fun, and at
the same time so gentle, that it is quite a pleasure to ride him. At
Cawnpoor the other day the noonday gun was fired in his face within twenty
yards. He merely looked up in astonishment at its impudence, but start him
into a gallop, and it is all I can do to hold him.

You had better continue to address your letters to Cawnpoor, for I don't
know as yet what will be my final destination. For another month or two I
will be marching about with the troops, and will enjoy it much. You must
not think yourself or allow Mamma to think that I am likely to do any
fighting. I am a mere civilian if you strip off my uniform and military
rank. So little have we to do with fighting that an officer in the
commissariat department though of a colonel's rank, if all the officers were
killed but an ensign, could not assume command of an army ...'.

The letter ends with Graham giving his sister news of two friends serving in
India; Graham Huddlestone and Tom Graham. The latter he notes is serving
with the Punjab light horse.

23 January 1858   Sarah C. Graham, 26 Dorchester Terrace,
                           [London ?], to Daniel Cullimore.
D.812/14/169

                           In this letter Sarah discusses her brother
                           William's broken romance with Miss Roberts,
and the latter's character. Sarah mentions that William has '... not been
long in finding another very nice good girl ... at Mussoorie ...'. William
has told her not to be surprised if he gets married and leaves the army.

Sarah then discusses the impossibility of having her father's body removed
to Kanpur and buried in her mother's grave. This she blames on the padre at
Sialkot during the rising there, whom she claims was lax in getting her
father buried, and eventually had him interred in a mass grave without a
coffin. She also thinks the Kanpur cemetary has been destroyed, and mentions
that communications with the city are also still closed. She regrets
William or Tom had not been at Sialkot to arrange her father's funeral.

2 February 1858   Sarah C. Graham, 26 Dorchester Terrace
                           [London ?], to her cousin, Anne,
D.812/14/170   Lisburn, Co. Antrim.

                           The letter opens with Sarah Graham regretting
she cannot accept Anne Graham's invitation, probably to visit Lisburn. She
then discusses the suicide of her brother James at Lucknow.

'... You will I am sure be sorry to hear that I received by this last mail
the very melancholy tidings of the sad end of poor dear James. Poor fellow,
his death so unexpected, is indeed another heavy blow, and I feel it more

than I can express for he was my favourite brother. My sister-in-law's
letter is dated from Cawnpore, but she has I see by the *Times* reached
Allahabad, with her child. Poor thing she has lost her two other
children also. Their only food for three months of the siege she says was
horse flesh, and a few ounces of wheat, so we can imagine what they must
all have suffered poor creatures.

I trust you have had good accounts from James, these are sad anxious times,
and I am now waiting anxiously for the arrival of the Southampton letters
to hear from William, and Tom, and I sincerely hope I shall have good news
of them both. The latter I trust is still safe at Lahore, but they were
expecting the order to march down country, cavalry being required
there ...'.

The letter ends with further apologies for not accepting Anne's invitation.

9 February 1858   James Graham, Kanpur, to his sister
                                Anne, Lisburn, Co. Antrim.
D.812/14/171

                                'I have now not the slightest idea of when
                                the mails arrive and depart, so I send
papers as often as I get an opportunity, and letters whenever I have a
moment to write. I last wrote to you I think from this place. Since then
I have marched to Fattehgurh, seen that station, and come back again. I
went up by double marches, but with no commissariat duty, so I enjoyed it
much. I came down with some troops returning to Cawnpoor, and have very
little to do.

William has started for England. I had a note from him the other day, and
he asked for my reply to be addressed to Bombay to await [his] arrival.
Tom may be here but as I have just arrived I have not been able to find
out, but perhaps may ere I close this.

I see Col[onel] Garrett is made a b[reve]t col[onel] in the army, and I dare
say will now retire. He will get the rank of major general when he does so,
and he must be entitled to his full colonel's pension long ago. Col[onel]
Nuthall also has sent in his papers to retire. I would not be surprised if
he left for England by the steamer of the 20th inst, or at latest the 8th
proximo.

I have had another note from James's widow. She is now I trust on board ship
for England. Poor James, his end was a melancholy one, but between ourselves
it was one I had long expected "*De mortuis nil nisi bonum*", but I tell you
what I would not repeat to others. His temper for some years was quite
unbearable. He fancied all sorts of slights and insults, never went into
society, nor would he let his wife do so, and the consequence was that both
William and I anticipated something like this for a long time. William told
him, told his wife, and did everything he could to no purpose. James stuck
in his house, gorged himself with food, and had a chronic attack of dyspepsia
(he had a sunstroke at last) which affected his brain, and made matters worse.

About Sarah I am really rather glad than otherwise that she is not coming out to this country. For years no part of[22] ... .

William goes home a captain, and I suspect will not return to this country. It will depend however a good deal on Miss Roberts. You are I suppose aware that government are raising four European cavalry regiments. Once raised William will get a sum for his step which will give him a sufficient maintainance until he comes into his property, which will give him all that he ought to want.

12 m[idday ?] Tom has gone towards Lucknow, so I am not to see him for the present.

I have been trying to find out in all directions whether there was a Mr Garrett here or at Cawnpoor during the outbreak, but I have never heard nor seen his name mentioned, so I hope he will soon turn up. I am very busy so you must excuse a few hasty lines. I am working at my desk from the moment I rise in the morning until I go to bed at night.'

20 February 1858

D.812/14/173

James Graham, Camp Poorale, four marches from Kanpur, to his sister Anne, Lisburn, Co. Antrim.

'Where I wrote to you last from I really do not now remember, but I should suppose from Cawnpoor, which I reached about the 10th inst, and left again on the 13th. We came out here to look after that scoundrel the Nana Saheb[23], who after all his atrocities is now almost without a follower, and as the rebels in Oude will not let him join them in trying to escape into central India he has run away from this part of the country, and I fear he will never be caught unless by the treachery of his own people. It is so difficult to catch a single native so easy is it for them to disguise themselves, but caught he will be at last some way or other, and meet the just reward of his crimes.

I always feel it quite unnecessary now to tell you anything of what is going on in this country, as the *Times* correspondent has arrived, and you will have everything so much better told than I could do it. I daresay you will soon have Mr Russell abusing us all out here. I am told that he has a very good opinion of the commissariat, and I am anxiously looking forward to see his opinions of it published. All the Queen's officers who have come out speak of the commissariat in the highest terms, and I think they deserve it [*sic*]. Do you know how many commissariat officers are with the whole of Sir Colin Campbell's army? Only four permanently in the department, the rest picked up as best they could from mutinied regiments, and knowing nothing about their work.

Tom Graham is at Allahabad on escort duty with the governor general. We hear Lord Canning is so much pleased with even Allahabad, the very first station

22. *The letter has been torn at this point, and much of the text lost. Graham seems to be saying that women and children are safer and more comfortable at home at present, and can come out to India again once things are quiet when the mutiny has been completely crushed.*

23. *Graham's note: 'not Nena.'*

in the upper provinces, that he never intends to return to Bengal as long as he can help it.

Ladies from the upper provinces are now flocking down on their homeward journey. Lady Wilson passed by today. I suppose you remember my telling you that she (then Mrs Wilson) stayed at my house for some weeks in May last. We hear that there are fifty ladies one march behind us. They will overtake us tomorrow. They are taking advantage of a large number of government tents going down for the troops and are travelling in them [sic].

William is I suppose *en route* to England ere now. I expected to have heard from him from Bombay, but I suppose he has not had time to write. Do you know I have not heard from you for three or four mails. Your letters must be wandering over the country. The last one received was of the 1st Nov[ember], and though I have got a *Whig*[24] of the 15th Dec[ember] I have had no letters. I hope mine reach you more regularly, for although I now never attempt to write by any particular mail I believe I write more frequently than I used to do, and send papers also.

I saw in the Lahore newspaper a few days ago the departure of a Colonel Garrett for Kurrachee. I dare say it is our Colonel Garrett on his way home. Now that he is a b[reve]t colonel and has served for his full pension, he had little else to wait for, and I should think will take his pension at once, and become a major general.

[25]I have just got your letter of the 31 Dec[ember] for which many thanks. I thought I was never to get your letters. Just fancy I got on the 14th inst a letter from Calcutta dated 8 June. However the dawks are all open, and this goes direct to Bom[bay].

Col Nuthall's two sons are going down with the ladies to accompany their father home. He is leaving the service.'

19 March 1858	William Graham, Bombay, to Daniel Cullimore (/174). William Graham, I.N.S. Club, to Daniel Cullimore
D.812/14/174 D.812/14/175	(/175).

        An undated letter (/175) explains that Graham intended to post the letter (/174) dated 19 March 1858 in Bombay, but he 'was late in posting'. Graham also discusses his father's will and Cullimore's position as executor. He states that another executor Fordyce has decided to leave all questions regarding the will to Cullimore for execution.

In the letter of 19 March William Graham discusses the arrangements he has made for executing his father's will regarding his Indian property. He then discusses his own financial position in the light of the will, and his future plans.

24. *Probably the Belfast newspaper* The Northern Whig.

25. *Graham has dated the last two paragraphs of this letter 22 [February 1858] in the margin.*

'... I am well aware we do not come into the interest on our respective shares for some time - the age of thirty-four by the codicil in lieu of thirty-six - and a more sensible thing my poor father could not have possibly done, which assures us all at a mature age a handsome income, and it is now when he is no more that his sense and all his acts towards us generally shows how he sacrificed himself in many ways for the benefit of his children. I can assure you Sarah, Tom and myself who on talking over the past fully saw and appreciated his goodness [*sic*].

I am sorry to say that constant exposure to rain and heat, having been all last hot weather under canvass, has shattered my constitution, and I am now on my way home, where I hope to reach in May [*sic*]. I start a week from this date, and intend wending my way slowly home through the continent. I have my [? compensation] six months [? batta], Delhi prize money, and having been gazetted as a captain and the value of my step some 20,000 [rupees ?] (should I retire) have ample to keep me until I am thirty-four, and I doubt much if I [will] return to this country where I have lost my every friend. My engagement with Miss R[oberts] I am glad to say broken off, and if I can but get a good and purely religious girl in the shape of a wife I think I will be a better and happier man. The last quality she must have for without it I am afraid there is little happiness. I have had some frightful warnings within the last year, and God grant that I may benefit from these, and that God's wonderful mercy shown to me in not being at Cawnpore will not be turned to bad account.'

11 March 1858

D.812/14/176

James Graham, [Lucknow ?], to his sister, Anne, Lisburn, Co. Antrim.

'If I was not afraid of Mamma and your being frightened at such times as these I would not take up my pen for I have so much to do, and so little to write about.

I only received your letter of the 16th December a few days ago. I think William was right in making an offer for the houses, for it would be a nuisance to have a stranger for the owner of them considering how they are mixed up with his ones. Believe me, I have no wish to be a house proprietor.

Our troops are getting on famously at Lucknow. All the troops have arrived and surrounded the greater part of the city. It will be a very short affair, after Delhi. There are so many troops. The Nepalese have arrived, and everything is going on well. The troops have already a great part of the city in their possession. I have not time to write more, but you may expect a very long letter by next mail ... P.S. I cannot let this go without a copy of a circular order of Col[onel] Ramsay's which I hope will quiet your uneasiness about me hereafter.

No. 1030
From the com[missar]y gen[era]l,
to the dep[uty] com[missary] gen[era]l,
Fort William, 19th Feb[ruary] 1858.

I have the honour to request you will remind commissariat officers, who are now or may hereafter be employed with troops in the field, of the great importance of the duties entrusted to them, which should not be neglected for strictly military duties. The proper place for a commissariat officer in the field is with the stores in his charge, on the safety of which the efficiency of an army so much depends, and that place must not be deserted unless under the positive orders of the commander of the force.

Any infringement of this order will be seriously noticed.'

15 March 1858   James Graham, Lucknow, to his sister
                         Anne, Lisburn, Co. Antrim.
D.812/14/177

                         'As you may have suspicions of my whereabouts
                         I think it as well to send you a line though
I have little or no time to write. I have been through the siege of
Lucknow, which was completely evacuated yesterday, and [? am] to say though
I had a stray ball passing disagreeably close to me now and then, and was
several times under fire, I have never had a scratch of any sort. I am at
present equipping columns in pursuit of the fugitives from the city so [I
can ?] give you but a short account of our last eventful week. About ten
days ago we arrived before Lucknow and I crossed the river Goomtee
yesterday week as principal commissariat officer under Sir James Outram G.C.B.
We had a slight skirmish the day we crossed. They attacked our camp the
following day, and then we attacked them completely clearing them out of this
side of the river, and taking them in the reverse, which had the most powerful
effect in our getting the city.

The first day we had the balls flying not only over the heads of the soldiers,
but right over all our camp followers. The second day, when our camp was
attacked, in the very centre of it in my go-down (where my supplies where
kept), a camel was killed, and the balls going through the camp in all
directions, but by God's good providence we have had very little loss.

Until last night we have had the music of shells, and cannon balls without
intermission since Sunday last, and in so short a time do we become
accustomed to these things that I am now perfectly ready to sleep under a
gun.

We have taken forty-five of the king's wives, sixty heavy guns and
munitions of war without number.'

31 March 1858   James Graham, 'Camp Lucknow cantonments',
                         to his sister, Anne, Lisburn, Co.
D.812/14/178   Antrim.

                         'You will have long ere this received some
of my former letters, and the papers themselves will have told you of the
fall of Lucknow. We are now off to other fields, not to fight, but quietly
to occupy them. All fighting is I think over. Our destination will be I
think Bareilly, and I will rejoice if it is, for Bareilly is the favourite
station of the Bengal army.

Lucknow is fallen indeed: the handsomest city in India, famed for its
beauty, swarming with gilded domes and pinnacles, towers, minarets, stately
trees and everything which could add beauty to such a heap of buildings, has
its towers falling and fallen from our destructive missiles. Its gilded

The Lucknow Residency after the siege

domes have only left vestiges to tell where they were, its trees are
stripped of foliage, in some places by our shot and in some by the more
destructive fire. For the last ten days exactly I have been wandering
through the palaces of kings, prime ministers and princes strewn with the
refuse of what once has been Indian grandeur: marble couches and thrones,
magnificent pier glasses, chandeliers of every kind, all in ruins, first by
the mutineers afterwards by our soldiers looking for plunder. I have got a
few articles as memorials of Lucknow, a china cup of the late King's with
his name inscribed on it, several papers and books from his library, and
other things of this sort not very valuable in themselves, but valuable as
memorials. Plunder valuable in the eyes of natives was to be had in
abundance , but nothing that I thought worth encumbering myself with. I
brought away among other things a carriage, for the prize agents were not
very active in their performance, and everyone was allowed to bring away
what he chose. Yet notwithstanding this it is said we are to have prize
money and that mine will be two or three hundred pounds, very acceptable if
it comes, but I do not expect [it ?]. We will be sure I think to get six
months batta of which my share is about seventy pounds.

I received two days ago your kind letters of the 15th and 30th of January
both together. I am sorry that you were frightened on my account, I will not
say are, for I cannot conceive you being so now, after all I have told you of
my being a non-combatant ...'.

The letter ends with Graham discussing the personal affairs of friends and relations in India and England. This discussion includes the affairs of William and Sarah Graham, and William's romance with Miss Roberts.

5 April 1858

D.812/14/181

J. C. Chadwick, 26 Dorchester Terrace [London ?], to Daniel Cullimore.

The letter opens discussing William Graham's romance with Miss Roberts. Chadwick expresses the view that he is 'delighted' the engagement has been broken. He mentions that he has informed William of 'all her tricks', and generally deprecates her character. This has had the desired effect as '... his engagement with Miss R is all over, he had received our letters giving him information of all her goings on, and which he gives us every credit for, and says he will never see her more . ...'

Reference is then made to the settlement of Dr James Graham's affairs: the sale of his house in Sialkot for 14,000 rupees, and other matters relating to the execution of his will. The letter concludes noting the 'sad end' of James Graham, the Lucknow suicide, and the return of his widow to Britain.

10 April 1858

D.812/14/182

James Graham, 'Camp Murriaon, Old Cantonment of Lucknow', to his sister Anne, Lisburn, Co. Antrim.

'Nothing of any importance has occurred since I last wrote. The army has broken up to a great extent, and is off in different directions. I for the present am settled down in the old cantonment of Lucknow, and have got very comfortable quarters in what was once a merchant's shop. It is very cool, and very agreeable. Can you fancy Tom Graham is arrived at the other side of the river, about four miles off. I was quite too lazy to attempt the trip, and he has not come out. Perhaps I should not say lazy, but too much afraid of the heat. I can never afford to spend a whole day out of camp, and to go and return in one morning without great exposure is impossible.

My present charge consists of; the 1st Bengal fusiliers, 2nd batt[alion] rifle brigade, Her Majesty's 38th reg[iment], one Sikh infantry and cavalry regiment, Her Majesty's hussars, one troop Bengal horse artillery, one royal battery, one company of royal artillery with the siege train, and an unlimited supply of engineers, sappers and miners. You can fancy what trouble all these give when you consider that the greater part are new-comers to this country. They have got at least 1,500 camels, and about two hundred elephants, with bullocks and horses innumerable.

William has by this time arrived. Tell him I hear that the Delhi prize money will be something considerable. I am afraid we will not get much at Lucknow, and even if we do it does take such a time to collect, and distribute it. I dare say we will get six months batta, which will be something near ... [text torn] pounds, seven hundred for a lieutenant.

We are all very anxiously looking forward for the new Indian Bill. It may seriously injure our future prospects. The commissariat is to be at once remodelled, but the main part of the change is a large increase ...'.

25 April 1858

D.812/14/183

James Graham, 'Camp Nawabgunge', [Nawabganj ?], to his sister, Anne, Lisburn, Co. Antrim.

'They tell me it is time to send off letters by another mail, so I take up pen though I have so little to write about.

This country is being gradually settled. The last stronghold of the mutineers will be attacked in a few days, as two strong columns have entered Rohilkand and are making for Bareilly. The year will not have elapsed since the commencement of the outbreak before they will not [sic] have lost every single place of note. Then will come the hunting out, and punishment of the chief marauders, and such are the rewards offered by government that I doubt very much if even their own followers could resist them.

Since I last wrote I have been out with some troops receiving the guns of repentant landholders, and blowing up [the forts ?] of others who had fled26 ... a good many are being blown up now, and the cold weather will see the whole country disarmed. Their passion for keeping some cannon is really extraordinary. The other day one landholder came into our camp just as we march[ed], and told us that his guns were waiting to be made over at the next encamping ground. Can you fancy that although the fellow knew it would cost him his estates, he had not sent them at all. Fortunately the general thought of going himself to see the fort, and just as we were leaving it we discovered in a retired courtyard the three guns. ...

It is now getting precious hot in tents, [the] thermometer something above 115°, but as I have two good tents, a punkah, tatty and thermantidote, I fare uncommonly well. I daresay you do not know what they are. The first is a large fan that hangs from the roof, and which being pulled forward and backward keeps the air in motion. The second is a curtain of a particular kind of grass which being kept constantly wet cools the air coming through it, and the last and best is a wooden machine very like fans for cleaning corn and quite as large (mine is carried on an elephant). The air is drawn into it through a wetted mat of the same grass as the tatty, and the fans drive it out. There are thousands of poor fellows here without any of these comforts, nay necessaries of life ...'.

5 May 1858

D.812/14/184

James Graham, 'Camp Murriaon', Lucknow, to his sister, Anne, Lisburn, Co Antrim.

'The time I believe has come for writing again, and though it appears as if I had just laid down my pen from my last letter, I take it up again though I have

26. At this point the letter has been torn, and part of the text lost. Graham in this section would appear to have been discussing the problem of disarming landholders, as he continues on this subject.

103

really nothing to write about. I am now in com[missaria]t charge of a
force under the command of Sir Hope Grant, and we are marching about the
country receiving the arms and destroying the forts of the rebels. They
are never occupied. As we advance they fly. They say they would have
stood, but that we took a base advantage of them in bringing mortars to
shell them out. We are to continue marching about thus until the beginning
of the rains, and strange to say we do not find it disagreeably hot. We
never make a march above six miles, and get into our tents shortly after
the sun is up.

Did I tell you in my last that we are to get a medal for Lucknow, such is
the report. We have got already six months batta, which in my case, a
subaltern's, amounts to £73 odd shillings. The prize money collected is
immense. They say that £605,000 pounds is already collected, and that a
subaltern's share will be about £250, something for our trouble. We are now
marching to a place called Dalanow on the Ganges. It is nearly opposite to
Futtepoor about halfway between Cawnpoor and Allahabad, and you will most
probably find it marked on your map. From thence on we go to Roy
Bareilly, and there remain until the rains are over.

Our troops are now closing up on Bareilly, and in a few days you will hear
of its recapture. It is the last stronghold of the rebels, and one year has
not yet elapsed since an army of 150,000 well trained men, train[ed] both to
use muskets and artillery stood in arms against us. We always feared that if
they would ever fight in unity our reign would be ended. They have done so
and proved themselves wanting, so our fears are at an end for the future.
They may rise and have some temporary successes, which will soon be
followed by certain defeat.

I wish you would now address your letters to Lucknow. I think I am very
likely to remain in Oude until next cold weather at least, and your
addressing it there instead of Cawnpoor will save a day or two's delay.

I have not heard of you since I wrote last. Your letters are wandering some
place or another over the country trying to [find ?] me. Well may they,
when I tell you that country newspapers do not reach me until they are a
month old, and frequently not at all.

This is really a beautiful country, covered with trees. There is not a
quarter of a mile without a mango tope, and such topes, in which a whole
regiment can get shelter, and covered with fruit. They are not yet ripe
enought to eat, but we have mango fool which is quite as good as its
gooseberry namesake, stewed mangoes, and [we] are eating the ripe ones in
anticipation, so they are useful in many ways.

This marching about does not put a commissariat officer to many expenses.
All my carriage is paid for me, and I have no expenses except mere food and
servants. I use two elephants for my own, and my office tents, six camels
for my own traps and office records, and I allow my English writer, native
ditto and treasurer to ride on another. I have altogether twenty-three
spare elephants.'

18 May 1858

D.812/14/185

James Graham, Lucknow, to his sister
Anne, Lisburn, Co. Antrim.

'Though I have dated this Lucknow, I write
it from two marches distant from it, but as
we are ordered in there, and will reach it in two days it does not make
much matter. I have been wandering about the country in charge of a large
force under Gen[era]l Sir Hope Grant K.C.B. taking guns and destroying
forts. We have taken about thirty guns since I joined him. I daresay you
will see my name in some of his despatches, although there is a report
abroad that the officers of the civil (military) branches of the army are
not to be mentioned for the future. However we will see when they appear.
In the meantime a supplementary list of the officers who were recommended
for conduct before Lucknow has been sent in and mine is among the number.
It has not yet been published. In the first little affair I accompanied this
force to, Gen[era] Grant thinking that the senior officer must be senior
departmentally, mentioned one of my subordinates because he was a captain.
The matter was so trivial and getting it corrected would have given so much
trouble that I did not trouble myself about it.

In the meantime I have got seventy pounds donation batta for Lucknow, and
the commissariat has shone so well here that the government has called on
the commissary general for a plan to remodel it as a staff corps, and have
sent the plan submitted to them home strongly recommended. I hope it will
pass the India House before their sway is over. It must benefit me for I am
so unfortunate in promotion, and I think the pay instead of being now
military and staff, will be a consolidated sum suited to the rank in the
department, which my military rank will I fear never equal. I believe we
are close to another line step which will raise me one more in the list of
lieutenants, but I really never think of military promotion now-a-days, I
believe in the staff corps we will have a sort of official rank of which
captain will be the lowest grade.

Tell William that government has allowed a second six months donation batta
for Delhi, which he ought to draw. Nothing has as yet been declared about
the Delhi prize money, nor likely to be for a considerable time. As for the
Lucknow I really know nothing whatsoever.

I had a note from Tom a few days ago. He was then within a march of
Bareilly. He has been appointed adjutant of the 2nd Punjab cavalry, a very
fine corps. He has got some steps I believe by officers being removed from
his corps to fill up vacancies in others which suffered during the mutiny.
I have only heard of it, so do not know how much he has benefitted. I
believe I am likely to gain some steps in the same way.

We are to have a medal for the campaign with clasps for Delhi, Lucknow, *etc*.

As you may imagine it is very hot in tents. Generally the thermometer is
between 100° and 115°, but I have never enjoyed better health, and as a body
we are much healthier than the troops quartered at Lucknow. We had a great
laugh the other day at an Irishman, a Col[onel] Kelly, who declared, that a
rifle in the hands of one of the soldiers of his regiment had a sunstroke,
and went off of its own accord, though uncapped, and the hammer remaining
at half-cock. As powder explodes at 600° fahrenheit you may believe as much
of this as you like.

I do not know when I heard from you. It certainly cannot be within the last two months. I do not know where your letters are wandering. Kindly direct to Lucknow for the future, and perhaps they may reach me.

Part of Col[onel] Ramsey's new plan is I believe a very large increase to our numbers and to our pension, so that if it passes I will benefit immediately in promotion, and hereafter when retiring.'

5 June 1858   James Graham, 'Camp [? Poowrah]', to
                               his sister, Anne, Lisburn, Co. Antrim.
D.812/14/186

                               'Since I wrote last I have been so
                               fortunate as to receive three of your
letters (dated respectively the 17th and 31st March and 17th April), the last came direct without stop or stay, and I am now in hopes of hearing from you regularly every mail *via* Bombay. I trust my letters reach you all right now. They should for the road is perfectly open.

I am still marching about, and notwithstanding the heat and exposure I have never enjoyed such health since I came to India. You can fancy what the heat is when I tell you that we consider ourselves fortunate when the thermometer in our tents is under 100°, and it is only reduced to that degree by artifical means. Where they are not used the thermometer varies from 105° to 115°.

I send you a copy of a letter which the General Sir Hope Grant sent me the other day. I daresay it will be published in general orders, but I am not sure.

I am quite astonished about William Graham's proceedings with regard to Miss Roberts. Between you and me Phoebe disliked the connection from the very first. She thought that Miss R was making a convenience of William and (as [? Ben Gaultin] says) "kept him off and on in hopes of higher game", as for Lord Castleross that matter is finally settled, for by the last home news I see he is married to the sister of a poor fellow I knew very well, and who was killed the other day at Lucknow, Thynne of the rifle brigade, a son of Lord Charles Thynne the Dean of Westminister. Well if Miss R has gone to Paris to meet William I think they are very likely to be married, but of one thing I am certain, that William will not marry if she has not something for them to live on for the next nine years, as until then he will have to live on his pay, and William has no anxiety whatever to return to this country. He will I have no doubts in another year get a good round sum for retiring from his regiment, the now 2nd European light cavalry, but until then what is he to do?

Tom has resigned the appointment he got, the other day. He is determined never to serve with natives again, especially now as his has become one of the European regiments. He now belongs to the 4th European light cavalry, and only fancy within the last month he has got no less than five steps. Four officers of his reg[iment] have been removed to other cavalry regiments, and one has been killed. In the same way I expect to get some steps, as soon as the new European regiments for Bengal are officered. The orders have came out for three, but I believe as many as seventeen are to be raised at the same time. However I do not know whether military promotion will be of any use to me. That will altogether depend upon the

new commissariat rules, a plan of which highly recommended by the Indian
government has been sent home for sanction. One part of it is a large
increase which must benefit in some way your honourable servant ... .

This is a most magnificent country, I have now been marching about for
the last three months, and it is literally covered with groves of mango
trees covered with fruit, and only to think that with all its beauty, for
the last one hundred years there is not on the face of the world another
country in which so much blood has been shed, and so much oppression
carried on. When it is to end now God only knows. Everything looks like
as if a guerilla war was to be carried on for ages. However one never knows
how soon it may end, and a piece of news we have just heard may be the cause
of its becoming immediately quiet. It is that the Queen is anxious to come
in with the boy prince she put on the throne, if we will only guarantee her
an existence allowance. She is the mother of the prince now in Europe, and
the second Queen, so it is really wonderful that she should have tried to
set upon the throne a son of the king by another wife. I have in my book
of odds and ends a photographic likeness of the King and three of his wives,
which I found in one of the royal palaces, and you can have no idea of what
a nasty, low, dissipated brute he looks, and how by no means handsome they
do.

Still continue to write to Lucknow. My next letter will I suspect be from
Lucknow cantonments, or somewhere in its neighbourhood. We are making
Lucknow very strong, and are building a great fortified city at Allahabad.'

[*Enclosures to the above letter.*]

31 May 1858   [*Enclosure 1*] Copy, 'From major general
                               Sir Hope Grant commanding Lucknow
D.*812/14/187*   field force to the dep[ut]y adj[utan]t
                               gen[era]l of the army, Camp [? Barree]'.

I regret through inadvertence I neglected to mention the names of Capt[ain]
Vaughan commanding the 5th Punjab rifles, and Lieutenant Graham of the
commissariat in my despatch at Barree of the 24th ult[imo], and I have the
honour to request I may be allowed to correct the omission. Capt[ain]
Vaughan on this as on all occasions since he has been under my command has
displayed great energy, and coolness, and I consider him well worthy of the
fine command he now holds. L[ieutenan]t Graham has been most perservering
in his efforts to obtain supplies throughout the country, and has given me
the greatest satisfaction in every way.

I have the honour to request you will do me the favour to lay this before
his excellency the commander-in-chief.'

30 June 1858   [*Enclosure 2*] Copy, 'Extract'.

                   'General orders of the gov[ernmen]t of India,
No. 242 of 30th June 1858, publishing Sir Hope Grant's despatch No. 104.58 of
17th June 1858.

"I beg to bring to his excellency's notice my personal and divisional staff

...*27* and Lieut[enant] Graham dep[ut]y ass[istan]t com[missar]y gen[era]l, a most active intelligent officer whose name I inadvertantly omitted to mention in my despatch from Barree on the 24th April last."'

[This last enclosure was added later when the papers were being arranged. Thus the confusion of dates as it is dated 30 June 1858 in a letter of 5 June 1858.]

25 June 1858   James Graham, 'Camp Nawabgunge',
                                    [Nawabganj ?], to his sister, Anne,
D.812/14/188   Lisburn, Co. Antrim.

                        'I do not think that since the outbreak, I have once taken up my pen to write with a heart as light as I do today. I really and sincerely believe that the Indian insurrection will soon be at an end. The last week has been so great with results. [The] last mail will no doubt have given you the news of the fall of Gwalior into the hands of the Calpee fugitives. Sir Hugh Rose (*our only general*) though sick and worn out, could not let his own victorious troops go against them without him, and I enclose you his message [*not present*] from the palace of Gwalior, dated the 19th instant. A general action of five and a half hours duration cannot have passed without the enemy's receiving a great blow, and you will be happy to hear it was not a solitary one, for on the 12th this force under Sir Hope Grant (of which I have the commissariat charge) left Lucknow and commenced a second march at 11 o'clock that night.

Just as day broke on the 13th we reached this place where a force of 16,000 men with fifteen guns had come down to threaten Lucknow. Our force did not amount to 4,000, but before 8 o'clock the enemy were scattered and strewn, and flying far, leaving five hundred dead bodies and eight of their guns to mark where they had been. If it had been at any other season of the year they would not have got off so easily, but our fellows were dropping in every direction from sunstrokes, and we lost ten times as many men from the heat as we did from wounds. This battle has had a great effect over all Oude, and now that it has been followed so quickly by the blow at Gwalior I hope to see great results follow, for between ourselves blows to the enemy have been very scarce since Sir Colin Campbell reached this country. He is very careful, and very skilful in manoeuvring, but he always leaves a hole for the enemy to escape. Sir Hugh Rose has earned a peerage, much better than the Baron of Lucknow [*sic*].

Nor have we alone to count on the results of these two successful engagements. We have to add to them the death of that fiend the Ranee of Jhansee, who has been killed at Gwalior, and of the famous Lucknow Moulvi, a priest who has been our most bitter enemy, whose head now graces a pole at Shahjehanpoor. To these are also to be added the surrender of the Rajah of Mynpooree, and several petty chiefs, who feeling that their day was run came in to try by a late submission to save their lives. I confess I think them foolish. To me at least, a death on the field would be infinitely pleasanter than a life in the Andaman Islands, where you would have perpetually before your eyes the pleasant expection of filling some day the paunch of one of the savages.

27. Graham has in this extract from government orders deleted the names of the other members of Sir Hope Grant's staff mentioned in the despatch.

I believe you will see my name in the despatches regarding this engagement here. As long as I am a lieutenant my name being mentioned can do me but little good, but if it takes place frequently it gives a good claim for a brevet majority on becoming a captain.

We are to remain here until after the rains (so please continue to address my letters to Lucknow) and are raising huts. I am building no end of a palace; raised two feet above the mound I selected for its site, and am at pleasant [sic] living in an European soldiers' tent (intended for sixteen privates, 24 feet x 18) in which I have got a punkah, a tatty and a thermantidote. It is perched on high ground in the shade of a mangoe grove, with outriggers on all sides protecting it from the sun's rays, and I can assure you I have really good reason to be thankful for my luck, as I believe it is the largest, coolest and most comfortable tent in camp. I always run on so much about myself that I am perfectly sure any stranger would think me very egotistical, but you I trust set it down to your oft repeated wish to know everything about me.'

8 July 1858   James Graham, 'Camp Nawabgunge',
                                [Nawabganj ?],'Faizabad Road', to his
D.812/14/189   sister, Anne, Lisburn, Co. Antrim.

                                'The time has come for another mail, and I
have so little to write about as usual. Things are getting quieter, and I
have at last got into a house in which I am uncommonly comfortable, and
fortunate in getting into, considering we have had a commencement of the
rains, and there is lots more coming.

The despatch regarding the battle at this place has been published in the
Gazette, but not as yet in the newspapers so I can only send you the
following extract[28]. ...

... You see he promotes me to a deputy a[djutant] c[ommissary] g[eneral].
Unfortunately he is only prophetical, not historical, but there is a good
time coming, and my promotion to at least an officiating d[eputy] a[djutant]
c[ommissary] gen[era]lship cannot be far off.

Did I tell you of my house. It is very like a long barn!!!, and consists of
two pretty lofty rooms, each eighteen feet by twenty-one, with a four feet
broad verandah in front and rear. It is well situated on high ground with a
little hillock in front on which to sit in the cool of the evening, and I
can tell you that your humble servant's habitation is an object of no little
envy, especially as it does not leak, and considering that he has the command
of ninety-five elephants, 1,550 camels, seventy-two ponies and unlimited carts
and workmen did not cost him much.

I was sorry to hear of Henrietta and Graham's disappointment, but trust
he may be successful still. I see the competition examinations for the
royal artillery and engineers are still to continue. Perhaps he may be
successful if he tries for one of them. You certainly astonished me by
telling me Graham's age, for notwithstanding my grey hairs (!!!), nearly

28. *This extract has been quoted previously, see James Graham's letter of
5 June 1858 enclosure 2.*

bald head (!!!), and no teeth (!!!), I had no idea I had a nephew so old [19].

I have not had a line from William Graham since he left Bombay, but from all I hear Miss Roberts is no loss. Phoebe Fordyce did not like what she saw or heard of her at all, and I believe she has been making a convenience of William and would have thrown him off any day if she could make a better match.

I hear nothing of Tom, indeed to tell the truth I am getting a most wretched correspondent. I have so much writing, nearly always five or six hours daily, which I must do, so you can imagine how gladly what is not absolutely necessary is put off day after day, until it is put off altogether.

Things are settling down so rapidly that I would not be the least astonished to see all quiet before the cold weather sets in, but whether [*sic*] or not, I expect to have some most agreeable marching over Oude when the civil officers are settling the police arrangements, and collecting the revenue. Fyzabad will I think be our headquarters and they would be most agreeable ones. It is a large old native city, with lots of houses, and on a river which steamers can come up easily, and only six marches from where we are now ...

... P.S. I had almost forgot to tell you that my corps has got the line step. I believe it makes me 8th lieutenant.'

3 August 1858   David Beatty, Lisburn, Co. Antrim, to
                       Eliza Graham.
D.812/14/190

                       Beatty discusses various personal and family
                       matters, including 'Willy's' attempts to gain
an East India Company post.

'... As to the hopes I have to obtain an appointment for Willy they are now "fading away", but if there should be (as I expect) competitive examinations for commissions in the East India Company's Service, I will be quite reconciled to adopt that course, and so will Willy, as we both feel that it would be more honourable, and more reputable to obtain it by his own exertions. ...'

[On the last side of this letter there is an extract from an undated letter, discussing Graham Smith's career. The writer and recipient are unidentified.]

'extract from Mr S[mith]'s letter.

I heartily wish that Mr and Mrs Cullimore had not agitated Graham's mind about India without having the power of realizing their professions. If they had let him alone he might have done very well in Ireland, and it is not fair when they have blown out his brains, to put the bad fellow upon me.'

3 August 1858   James Graham, Faizabad, to his sister,
                       Anne, Lisburn, Co. Antrim.
D.812/14/191

          Graham begins discussing the India Bill of
          1858 which removed all power from the East
India Company, and placed the government of India under the direct control
of the British government and crown.

'Yes I am no longer a servant of the hon[orable] Company, and I can assure
you I regret the change much. From all I have seen of Her Majesty's service
I do not much admire it. It was a fortunate thing that the clause was added
to the Indian Bill securing to us all our rights. New-commers will have many
a change for the worse. ...'

Graham then goes on to discuss the affairs of his nephew Graham Smith and
states that he feels Smith could make a reasonable career in India. He then
informs his sister that he should like to invest his savings in Britain,
'... things are now so unsettled in this country, and are likely to be so for
years that I should like to invest my little savings at home, not in any
company, railway or others, but in the government funds. ... Mind you it is
no great sum, only a few hundred pounds I have at my disposal. ...'

The affairs of William Graham and other members of the Graham family are then
discussed. James gives the opinion that William will soon squander his money
and have to return to India '... very hard up, with nothing but his pay to
fall back upon ...'. He regrets the murder of his uncle James as he kept the
Indian members of the family in line, preventing the excesses of William etc.
'... His approbation was what we had all to look for, and always got when
doing right, and his reprehension kept us from doing wrong. ...' James also
thinks that his cousin Sarah is unlikely to return to India, and that her
income from her share of her father's will may be less than expected, as
his investment in 'dividends' is yielding decreasing returns, and his Delhi
Bank shares have been devalued by the loss and destruction of the bank's
property during the mutiny. James then refers to the affairs of 'Mittee'
the widow of his cousin James. As in former letters he puts James's
suicide down to his violent temper, enormous appetite and consequent
dyspepsia. He notes that Mittee's 'frettish' nature clashed with the bad
temper of James. He also puts part of the blame upon Mittee's family whom he
implies did not approve of James. The eternal saga of William and Miss
Roberts is also discussed, and the character of her whole family denigrated.
Her brothers are described as '... drunken and gamblers ...', and her
relationship with William is related as follows '... but the worst of her I
know is that she did not care one straw about him, and only kept him
dangling on, until better would turn up. ...'

Graham then assesses the prospects of Graham Smith again. He does not hold
out much hope for him if he has to sit '... direct appointment ...'
examinations for the Indian service (whether civil or military is unclear).
The reasons he gives are the shortcomings of the Irish educational system,
which specializes in the teaching of '... dead languages with an eye to
Trinity College ...'. As the examinations will include German, French,
'Hindostani', history, English and geography he reckons Smith's classical
education is singularly inappropriate. Graham then describes how he
overcame this deficiency in his own education, which was produced by the
classical education he received at Dungannon (the Royal School Dungannon).
He acquired knowledge in subjects relevant for the Indian examinations

through '... my own fondness for reading ...'. He notes that his historical knowledge especially was superior to that of his 'compeers' and that '... I was always referred to when any historical point was disputed ...'. Irish schools he views as superior to English ones in the teaching of English, but inferior in the modern languages, and the '... top-dressing which bring him [the scholar] up to the examination mark ...'.

Graham then begins to discuss affairs relevant to the continued disturbances of the mutiny.

'... I heard from Tom the other day. He has been down in Calcutta. His wound was behind the shoulder, where a Ghazee fired his musket into him after Tom had tried to cut him down. In doing which [his] sword was broken in his hand. By the bye I find I am reversing the thing. Tom got shot first. Then finding himself not disabled he rode at the fellow, and his sword broke in trying to cut him down, but one of his men polished him off. Tom (at the doctor's advice, recommending a change of air) and at Gen[era]l Parson's request went down to Calcutta to take out probate on his father's will. He also at my urgent request (I wrote the letters for him), applied to the orphan's fund for Sarah's pension, which William thought she was not entitled to on account of being so well off, but I knew the change of the rules and made them apply for it, and the application has been successful. She will get £35 a year until she marries, and £150 then. Tom is also trying to get her passage money home, but I don't think she is entitled to it.

Things are getting daily quieter and quieter, and I really believe all will be over before the cold weather. I trust so as I may in that case have a chance of remaining at this delightful station where I am ready and willing to stay until I can pay you a visit. ...

... There is not a word of news. The papers have doubtless told you about Gen[era]l Roberts having attacked and beaten the Calpee refugees. That will quiet central India. If we had a governor general like Lord Dalhousie we would soon have India quiet, but Lord Canning is a sleeping old creature who has done those things which he ought not to have done *etc. etc.*'

3 August 1858   James Graham, Faizabad, to his sister,
                       Anne, Lisburn, Co. Antrim.
D.812/14/192

                       Graham begins by discussing life at the
                       Faizabad station.

'I fear I have lost a mail, but you must excuse my silence, as I have been marching again, and really too busy to write. I am now I think finally settled, and [have] got such a beautiful station, that it atones for all the discomfort I have had in coming to it in the middle of the rains. I have also got a palace, of one of the Queens' of Oude to live in. It is situated on the banks of the river Gogra, and I anticipate a very pleasant time of it, though lots of work. I have been however provided with an assistant in the shape of a Capt[ain] Graeme who will do all the drudgery, which is something.

Steamers are to commence running at once, so that we will only be four days from Dinapoor, and at this season about six more from Calcutta.

I am greatly afraid Tom has been wounded in an engagement near Allahabad, I have not seen any despatch about it, and the newspapers merely gave the rumour, so I know nothing about the extent of the wound. ...'

Graham then discusses the frequency of the Indian mails. He mentions that two days previously he received a letter from Anne dated 30 November 1857. A few days prior to this he had received one dated 16 May 1858. The discrepancy he ascribes to the confusion of the mutiny period, especially his frequent change of address, whilst on campaign. He advises his sister to address his mail to Faizabad in future, '... where I am likely to remain for some time. ...'

Graham mentions that he only managed to see their mutal friend Graham Huddlestone on one occasion at Futtehgurh, as '... I left the following morning and before I returned his corps had gone off to Agra ...', and that he had as yet failed to meet his cousin Tom since his arrival in India. He mentions that when stationed at Nawabganj he had built an extra large house to accomodate himself and Tom, as Tom's regiment the 4th European light cavalry were to be stationed there. However Tom was ordered away and did not arrive with the rest of the regiment. The house only cost 50 rupees to build, and Graham when moved to Faizabad received compensation from the Indian government.

Graham hopes William has managed to purchase the houses in Lisburn, formerly owned by William's father, and he offers to lend William £100 towards their purchase, as he does not want William to get into debt. He again expresses pleasure at the end of William's romance with Miss Roberts, as she was a '... most disagreeable person, and one that would never make a good wife, and I believe she has been keeping him "off and on in hopes of higher game" ...'.

The letter ends with Graham mentioning the formation of three new European regiments in the Bengal army. He also notes that '... the unlucky officers of all corps are to be removed to fill up vacancies in those which have been cut up, and that it may run me up the list a little ...'.

24 September 1858   James Graham, [Faizabad], to his
                           sister, Anne, Lisburn, Co. Antrim.
D.812/14/195

                           Graham opens the letter telling his sister
                           that Tom Graham has left for England, as
when he reached Calcutta '... for change of air and to take out probate to
his poor father's will ... his wound continued so unhealthy that the
doctors ordered him off home ...'.

William Graham's wife-hunting exploits are then discussed, '... I suppose
he is still wife-hunting, and I fully expect to hear that instead of
marrying a young lady with money, he will get one without a rag to her
back ...'.

At this point Graham begins to refer to the reorganization of the Indian
army created by the mutiny, and other issues related to the mutiny.

'... Since I wrote last the army has been to some extent reorganized (I mean the officers) and I have benefited. Two of my seniors Armstrong and Beggs have been removed to fill up vacancies in other corps, so that I now stand 6th lieutenant, and as soon as the royal commission now sitting at home complete their work and decide what is to be the new formation of the army I expect to get two more.

Perkins has written to me that he wishes to go to the invalid establishment, and Richards now a major wishes to retire. Even then I will only be 4th, very unlucky. Tom will be third within another month, and if I am not mistaken Joe Beatty under the reorganization of the artillery and engineers is a 2nd captain. Well I must not grumble. I dare say there is a good time coming. We will see what the new formation of the commissariat will do ...'.

Graham Smith's career prospects in the army are then discussed, and Graham feels that he should try for an appointment in the artillery or engineer sections of the 'royal army', as these have been thrown open to competition. In regards to the Indian army Graham notes, '... there is to be a very large number of appointments (direct) given away this cold weather ...' Graham states that Smith should not '... let the time slip away ... [as] ... if he has any interest at all, now is the time to use it ...'.

Preparations for the coming winter campaign against the remaining mutineer forces are also mentioned, '... things are now being got ready for the winter campaign in Oude. There will be such a collection of cavalry and light guns that, fast as the enemy were able to fly away from us before, they will now find a difficulty in doing so. Long before the end of this cold weather their game will be played out, but at what a cost of blood and treasure to us and themselves. I have seen here some men of my corps who were on leave when the outbreak took place. They declare that of the whole regiment not a man has got to his home. Those that have not lost their lives are wanderers on the face of the earth, their homes empty, and a much greater blow, they have dragged down with them into poverty those relatives of theirs who having served their time, were spending the remainder of their lives in what was to them luxury on the handsome pensions given them by government, for whose protection not one of the latter raised their hands.

We are greatly pleased to hear of the successful laying down of the Atlantic telegraph. It makes us the more sure of one to India. We are daily and daily getting nearer to you. The railways in this country are being pushed on rapidly, and successfully. The governor general has just opened a line one hundred and twenty miles long between Allahabad and Cawnpoor. It is pushing its way upwards towards Meerut and the north, and the Calcutta branch is making rapid strides to get hold of its fugitive child at Allahabad. ...'

Graham ends discussing his commissariat duties at Faizabad. He has collected a large amount of stores, and more are constantly coming by steamer, and he notes '... this is to be a great station apparently ...'. He reports that he has received a copy of a letter from the commissary general to the deputy commissary general in Oude stating that his report has been very good, and that he has shown 'zeal and energy' in his duties.

26 August 1858

D.812/14/196

James Graham, Faizabad, to his sister,
Anne, Lisburn, Co. Antrim.

Graham begins lamenting the fact that his
sister's last letter was sent *via* Calcutta
and not Bombay and had 'lost a week' in consequence. He then makes some
general comments regarding the state of Indian affairs. '... I am sorry
the English papers' are still in low spirits about India. We are
brightening up. I believe the country is settling down quietly and that
before the cold weather there will be no one to go against ...'. Reference
is then made to a dinner held in Lisburn in honour of Walter Trevor Stannus
J.P., Lord Hertford's agent. '... I have also received your two papers, one
with the dinner to Walter Stannus, which I read with great interest. It is
very amusing to see how people can humbug each other after dinner, and their
fulsome praise of Lord Hertford, especially as regards his generosity during
the famine when they used to abuse him like a pickpocket. Has he yet given
back the lower part of the assembly rooms for the newsroom ...'.

Graham's thoughts then return to India, and he describes the beauty of the
country around Faizabad '... situated on the banks of the Gogra with a
country most beautifully wooded ... [with] tamarinds ...'. It is also a
very convenient station '... only four days from Dinapoor, and from it about
a weeks sail from Calcutta ...'. Graham regrets that he may have to leave
such a 'comfortable' station, but '... I am getting so high up in the
world (*i.e.* so many of my seniors have gone home on furlough) that without
promotion I may expect to be removed almost immediately to some of the
large stations ...'.

For the present however he has to remain at Faizabad although his force
has gone to Sultanpur, halfway between Faizabad and Allahabad. '... I
proposed to go with them but my chief Fitzgerald wrote back that he thought
my proper position was here. So here I am for the present, and I have to
thank the river mostly for it, as I have steamers coming with stores, and
the General (Sir Hope Grant) for the remainder, as he has made this his
headquarters, and must have a commissariat officer of some experience with
him ...'.

Graham mentions that he has as yet not heard from his cousin Tom as
writing '... is not one of the whims to which the Graham's devote themselves
...'. He also mentions two members of his regiment who are leaving for home,
Perkins and Armstrong. He referred to their leaving in a previous letter.
He notes that as far as promotion goes '... it will not make much difference
to me ...'.

Graham then finishes making some comments relevant to the mutiny. '... I am
glad to hear that my letters are beginning to reach you with some regularity.
We have a mail robbed occasionally in this country now-a-days, but otherwise
all goes right. I hope you have commenced writing to Faizabad.

And so, Joe Beatty is going to be married to a Miss Young. Well I am glad
it is so. India though in outward appearance getting round to its old
appearance is much changed, and I think ladies are well out of it. The link
is broken which bound the natives to us. Now we may always expect little
disturbances, which will not annoy bachelors, but will give many an anxious
moment to those encumbered with wives and families. Mind you I do not mean

to say that there will be any more mutinies or disturbances, but I mean that
formerly we used to settle down into a quiet home (as much as India can be a
home) life, now we will be always soldiers in camp.'

17 October 1858   James Graham, Faizabad, to his sister,
                                Anne, Lisburn, Co. Antrim.
D.812/14/199
                                Graham begins informing his sister of the
                                interruption of the Bombay mail by continued
rebel activity. 'I had almost given up hope of hearing from you by last
mail, as the papers had announced that the telegraph wire had been cut, and
the postbags carried off by some scoundrels crossing the Bombay road.
However your letter came in all right two days ago ...'.

Graham then refers to the purchase of the cottages in Lisburn by William,
and thinks it a good thing as it will consolidate the family's property.
He also discusses Graham Smith's future, and notes that if he is going to
enter any of the open examinations for a post in either the Indian or the
British armies he will have to look 'sharp about it' or he will soon
be over age. He deplores the attempts of Smith's mother to force him into
the church for which it is obvious Smith has no call, and Graham
comments, '... I really do not know a heavier punishment she could inflict
upon him ...'. He also wishes she would send her younger children to an
English public school as '... you have no idea what a gain it is in after
life. They there make friends who have the power, and do assist them in
their future career. Besides brought up at a public school [they] are far
more manly, and much better able to fight the battle of daily life ...'.

Graham then discusses tongue in cheek the insidious effects of old age which
he sees creeping over himself, friends and relations. Regarding himself he
notes '... in another few years, when sunk into inevitable bachelorhood, I
will have to mount a wig, a new set of teeth, and with the addition of a
little paint (the wig will cover the few grey hairs which remain) I dare say
I will be able to get myself recognized again ...'.

A recurrent theme, the retirement of Colonel Garrett is then referred to.
'... Col[onel] Garrett will doubtless retire in the cold weather, once the
winter campaign is over. Retirements now prohibited will again be allowed,
and furloughs opened. You must not be making love to the major general as
he will then be ...'.

Graham then discusses a family squabble over his uncle's will. It appears
that his cousin Phoebe felt her sister Sarah had come out of the affair
better than herself. He enquires after his cousin Tom and hopes his wound
has healed. The remainder of the letter is devoted to the continued
disturbances of the mutiny, and the imminent defeat of those rebel forces
still holding out against British authority.

'... I do not expect to move from this until I am transferred into one of
the large offices in the upper provinces. The commander-in-chief has now
commenced the cold weather campaign in a style that will bring all
disturbances to an end at once if he carries it out as he has commenced. He
has an enormous force round the very hotbed of the insurrection, instead of
as last year, one enormous army. He has now encircled it with fourteen
strong columns, all sweeping all before them to a common centre, where it is

expected there will be no stepping away this year. Nothing but surrender or death. To them [the rebels], the former, I should think, they have shown as little liking for the latter as they do for fighting with the white faces [*sic*].

We have now the railway open from Cawnpoor to Allahabad, and besides the telegraph from Calcutta, *via* Agra, and from Calcutta *via* Madras to Bombay, we have now another line *via* Lahore and Kurrachee, and the superintendent of the electric telegraph has just announced that he has completed a line to Ceylon, and last but [not] least the papers announce that he is at once to lay down a line from Lucknow here, which will be a very great convenience.

I ought not to have commenced at the end of my letter to ask you have you seen the comet? Here it has been a world's wonder, and the talk of everybody. I first saw it about the 14th of September, and it is still visible, though it is rapidly getting invisible. The natives say it brings misfortune to them. It will scarcely be invisible when grief will be in many a house especially in Oude. Upon a moderate calculation there is not a day passes now in which a hundred of them do not go to their long account, many from the sword, but numbers from the exposure and starvation in the jungles to which they have had to fly for protection. No person however pities them. Government has offered pardons free and unlimited to all who have not the blood of Europeans "*murderously shed*". This you will remark does not except those who have even fought against us, only those who committed murders. The children and children's children of those who are still in the field will tell with a shudder for many and many a day of the sufferings, and well deserved punishment which fell upon them in the year in which appeared the [*? jhara ke tara oz*], star of the [? broom].

We feringhees who know better tell them that it is a sign that Her Majesty's assumption of the rule of this country (to be pronounced this month) will remain in the hands of her descendants for ever, or as Lord Dalhousie would have said, "so long as the sun shines in the heavens, so long will the province of Oude remain one of the British possessions in the east".

We have now beautiful weather: the sun of course strong as it ever is in India during the heat of the day, but in the mornings and in the house delightfully cool.

I must now conclude wishing Mamma, yourself and all at home many a happy Christmas and New Year, and with best love.'

24 October 1858   James Graham, Faizabad, to his sister,
                     Anne, Lisburn, Co. Antrim.
D.812/14/200

'I had quite made up my mind not to write to
you until I would be able to tell you a
piece of good news, but have been forced to give up my determination.

I have been told on the very best authority that the commissary general's scheme for the reorganization of the commissariat had come out sanctioned,

L

and that it entailed a large increase. So I was in hopes of it appearing in
orders, and of my being able to tell you that I had got a step, but [I] have
been disappointed. There is no doubt that it has come out sanctioned and
all right, but the government have delayed publishing the order for some
reason or other. Most probably it has to go to the governor general at
Allahabad, and as the c[ommissary] g[eneral] never lets out any information,
we don't know how much we are to get.

Many thanks for yours of the 31st August received two days ago. There
appears no doubt that William is going to get spliced. The lady is a Miss
Mew, a niece of a great friend of his L[ieutenan]t Mew of the 74th n[ative]
i[nfantry], whom I found stopping with him when I passed through Cawnpoor in
1857. I don't think he is likely to get much of a fortune. If William
married it may turn out the best thing that could happen to him. That is to
say if she is a sensible girl, for William is very extravagant, and unless
kept in order he will very soon dissipate all that his poor father left him.

We are I think to get another step in the commissariat by the retirement of
Col[onel] Ramsay, whose health will not allow him to remain longer in the
country. This is most probably the reason of the delay in publishing the
increase. The report I heard was that Colonel Ramsay's resignation had gone
in so the governor general would have to be consulted about the selection of
an officer to fill so r[espons]ible an appointment.

We are still in the same state here, little fights, and always successful,
frequently occurring. Indeed I ought scarcely to call them fights, as the
enemy run away as soon as we appear. This week we took from one party alone,
all their guns (two), seven ammunition carts, three elephants, sixteen
horses, and forty-five gov[ernmen]t bullocks without the loss of a man.
All will be settled before the cold weather is over.

We have had an event here: the arrival of the first steamer which ever
came up the Gogra. The natives streamed to the banks in thousands. The
laying down of a telegraph wire has also been ordered, so you see Fyzabad
is rising in importance, and likely to remain so, while the river Ganges is
so dry this year that steamers cannot get up to Benares, the steamers can
go above one hundred miles above this on the Gogra ...'.

The letter ends with Graham discussing the proposed retirement of Colonel
Garrett, whom he feels '... has been long enough in this country ...'. In
a postscript he makes an interesting comment on the standard of English
newspaper coverage of Indian affairs '... P.S. We have been as much amused
with your story of Jung Bahador and the rings, as with your former one of
Jessie Brown, and the Highlanders. You have no idea what lies they publish
about India in the English papers ...'.

7 November 1858   James Graham, Faizabad, to his sister,
                             Anne, Lisburn, Co. Antrim.
D.812/14/201

             Graham starts informing his sister that the
             proposed plan for the reorganization of the
commissariat has not yet been published. He also mentions that Colonel
Garrett sails for home in two days time, and refers to a visit made by his
sister to Killarney. He wishes longingly that he had been able to accompany
her but comforts himself by looking '... forward to the good days which are
coming ...', when he returns home on leave.

Graham then describes the manner in which India has reacted to the assumption of Indian government by the British crown and parliament. '... On Monday last Her Majesty's assumption of the government of India was proclaimed with all the honours. A royal salute fired at every place where there was a gun to do the needful, and the day closed with fireworks, and an illumination. Her Majesty on assuming the throne of Hind, gave a pardon full and free to every rebel with the exception of leaders, murderers, and harbourers of the latter. Report says that, though by some mistake the vernacular copies of it have not been distributed, it has already had a good effect, and that the less guilty of those still opposed to us are rapidly coming in. The day after the proclamation was read the commander-in-chief left Allahabad to join the forces in Oude, and now some six or eight moveable columns traverse the land, and we have strong chains of posts in all directions. Every fort in Oude is to be levelled, and every man disarmed, every jungle cleared so that willing as they may be in future years to disturb the country again, they will have no place to retire into if they do so. The commander-in-chief moves in this direction, and I expect lots of work. Already two officers, both captains, and one of them my senior departmentally have been ordered here as my assistants. I do not move from this myself. You will not understand my saying that I am to have a departmental senior under my care, unless I tell you that he is a bad officer, and comes here to learn his work under the hands of that distinguished officer L[ieutenan]t Graham. If report says true he is not likely to benefit much by the increase, as all his juniors are to pass over his head.

There is not a word of news. We hear of little fights daily, but they are always the same. The rebels bolt, and we take their guns, and so it will be for another month or two, until they are completely dispersed. Unless shut up in a fort they now do not wait for the sight of an European, but walk off at once. ...

I must bring this to a close for sheer want of anything to write about which would interest you. Nothing is talked about but marchings and countermarchings, and how well General This does so and so, which General That does not do at all. So excuse this and with best love ... .

P.S. The weather here is delightful, much cooler than expected down here. Altogether the climate here is very fine. Fitzgerald our chief and Oude [sic] says he will keep me here as long as it is in his power, so I do not expect to move, and am thinking of writing for all my traps now lying at Meerut.'

11 November 1858   James Graham, Faizabad, to his sister,
                            Anne, Lisburn, Co. Antrim.
D.812/14/202

                            'The promotions in the com[missary]
                            dep[artmen]t are just out. I am d[eputy]
c[ommissary] gen[era]l, of the 2nd class, and officiating in the first
class. I will either draw 450 or 500 [rupees] staff allowance a month now
for some time, and will get 400/- permanently.'

27 November 1858

D.812/14/203

James Graham, Faizabad, to his sister, Anne, Lisburn, Co. Antrim.

'I have no time to write a long letter, merely to send this that you may not be disappointed. I got my promotion as I told you. I am now deputy a[ssistant] c[ommissary] gen[era]l of the 2nd class, and officiating 1st class. I draw permanently 400/- staff pay per mensem, and at present 50/- additional officiating pay from the 5th of next month. I get 100/- a month officiating allowances probably for the next [few ?] months, and with every chance of continuing to draw it from a long time to come. Col[onel] Ramsay has retired and Col[onel] Thomson [has] been appointed commissary general. This has given me another step. Col[onel] Ramsay in a reply to an address presented to him at Calcutta let out that a royal commission had been examining into the English commissariat department, and had recommended that it should be reorganized on our system. Is not that very complimentary to us?

I have just finished equipping General Grant's column prior to it going over the Gogra. I have had very hard work, but it was repayed by the sight of the column crossing the bridge, and my knowledge that I pulled the string to set the mighty mass in motion. For four and twenty hours the bridge of boats more than half a mile long was a mighty living stream. First the troops, three infantry regiments, three cavalry regiments, two troops sappers and miners *etc. etc.*, and then camels, elephants, bullocks, tattoos and carts, all laden with tents and food. Fancy what a stream. It was one of the most magnificent panoramas I ever saw or expect to see ...'.

Graham ends hoping William Graham will register the Lisburn houses with the [Irish Land Judges Court ?] so that the family will have no future problems over the title to the property.

16 December 1858

D.812/14/208

James Parsons, [? Aleuroh], to Daniel Cullimore, Bally Ann Park, New Ross, Co. Wexford.

Parsons begins discussing his position as one of the trustees of Dr James Graham's will, and developments over the Indian property, especially the Delhi Bank shares and the Sialkot property. Parsons asks Cullimore to consult with Fordyce and William Graham, and to send him detailed instructions regarding the Indian property so that he will know, '... what is to be done respecting all the property, and let me know clearly all that should be done, and I will have it done at once, for I wish to act up strictly to what is said in the will, and so incur no risk or responsibility. ...' He then states that he hopes that William Graham is clear that they must adhere strictly to the terms of the will regarding the Delhi Bank shares. Parsons advises that the best way to dispose of the Sialkot property would probably be by auction, '... after having given notice in [the] *Delhi Gazette* and *Englishman* newspapers. ...'

Parsons is determined that there should be no ambiguity over his instructions as he reiterates, '... if you will then just take the trouble to write to me explicitly what I ought to do to carry out the instruction of the will *to the letter* I will do it ...'. He fears that it will '... prove hopeless to get so many (as the four trustees or executors) to agree in all points ...'. He

then states that he will agree to anything Cullimore decides, and like
Cullimore is concerned that whatever happens the settlement must be legal,
'... as you say "the law must be obeyed" ...'. (Parsons seems here to be
alluding to his fear that William Graham cannot be trusted to keep to the
terms of the will.) He then makes a telling comment on his view of William
Graham, and his scheming nature. '... What brings William Graham out to
India again? He is so well off I wonder he did not stay at home. I daresay
he gets [? some] money with his wife, for he knows well what he is about. ...'

Parsons next describes the continued disturbed state of India. '... Matters
are far from being settled yet, and only a few days ago the Nana - Feroze
Shah - Bahadur Khan and several thousand men gave our *very slow* com[mande]r-
in-chief and others the slip, crossed the Ganges between Cawnpore and
Futteyghur, and we shall probably have another hot weather campaign ...'.

Parsons concludes asking Cullimore, '... now like a good fellow write
explicitly what I should do respecting all the property, and I will do it,
and you may tell this to William Graham, for I am resolved to incur no
responsibility, but to act up strictly to the restrictions of the will as
far as I am concerned ...'.

19 December 1858   James Graham, Faizabad, to his sister,
                          Anne, Lisburn, Co. Antrim.
D.812/14/209

                          Graham commences informing his sister of
                          military operations in the Faizabad region.
'... I am afraid I have been very remiss in writing of late, but you will
not be surprized at all when I tell you that the whole of the commander-in-
chief's army passed through here within the last ten days, and all had to get
something from me. I really did not know whether I was standing on my head
or my heels for some days. We never knew he was coming until one morning, as
I was getting up I had an express in to say that he would be here that day.
Such a row! He crossed the bridge the following day, and the day after with
one brigade. It was one perpetual stream from sunrise to sunset. Some police
at the bridge made a calculation of their number, and found that the first day
sixty seven thousand men crossed. You can judge from this what an Indian army
consists of. This was only one of the five brigades which accompanied him.
...'

After referring to a vist by Tom and William to Lisburn, Graham thanks his
sister for her advice regarding investment of his savings. He mentions
that he has put his 'small savings' into government stock which he hopes
will supplement his captain's pension. Reference is then made to Graham
Smith whom Graham fears is too old to enter the [artillery ?] at Woolwich.
He suggests however that some of Smith's younger brothers could make a career
here. Graham also mentions another acquaintance, 'young Birney', who has been
posted to the 'Northwest'. Graham however notes that the post-mutiny
confusion has produced a situation in which, '... one can never be sure of
the whereabouts of the officers in India at present. Why, I was nearly moved
from this place. Capt[ain] Fitzgerald the principal commissariat officer in
the field left it to my option to go with Sir Hope Grant trans-Gogra or not.
Fortunately I had at my disposal two captains (commissariat officers), one
of whom I thought sufficiently up to his work to place in charge of the column,
so I remained here.

Infantry travelling by cart during the mutiny

Everything is settling down even faster than I expected. I think that all
will be [? done] before the 1st proximo, so that the remainder of the cold
weather will be at our disposal for throwing down forts, and disarming the
population ...'.

Graham ends discussing personal matters, affairs of friends *etc*. In a
footnote he describes the military development of Faizabad. '... Orders
have come to form a large station here; two Eur[opean] inf[antry] reg[iments],
two squadrons [European ?] cavalry, two companies Eur[opean] artillery, one
reg[iment] of na[tive] inf[antry], and one of [native ?] cavalry. These with
a magazine will give lots of work, and if I remain here I will have an
assistant. I am totally indifferent about my movements. To counterbalance
anything disagreeable in the change, I would have less work at any other
station.'

7 January 1859   James Parsons, [? Aleuroh], to Daniel
                          Cullimore, Bally Ann Park, New Ross,
D.812/14/212   Co. Wexford.

                          Parsons opens wishing Cullimore and his wife
a happy new year, and then discusses Dr Graham's will. He informs
Cullimore he has written to Mr Parry telling him to sell the Delhi Bank
shares, and to Judge [? Watkins] asking him to submit the will to council

respecting the Sialkot property. He continues, '... If it should be that W[illia]m Graham cannot have it [the Sialkot property ?] as his at law I have told [? them] to take immediate measures for selling it, and I have written all this to [William ?] Graham *etc. etc.*, and I hope all will now be right, and as you may well say - [Dr ?] Graham with all his knowingness has been completely outwitted, and what was the good or happiness either of all his wealth to him? ...'

The meaning of this passage is unclear, especially when compared with the letter between Parsons and Cullimore of the 16 November 1858, when Parsons was concerned to adhere strictly to the letter of the law. From the above however it would appear that Parsons and Cullimore managed to circumvent, perhaps by a legal loophole, the spirit of Dr Graham's will, and at the same time defeat William Graham's schemes.

Parsons proceeds discussing his purchase of a wig, and his efforts to obtain *via* his wife and friends in Delhi various silk shawls and scarves for Mrs Cullimore. He also outlines his plans for their package, insurance and despatch to Ireland. He then states he would like to visit Cullimore and his wife at Bally Ann, but due to the post-mutiny military situation he feels he cannot leave his post. The letter concludes with Parsons discussing friends who are joining various regiments, taking Hindustani examinations, going hog-hunting *etc.*

9 January 1859   James Graham, Faizabad, to his sister,
                        Anne, Lisburn, Co. Antrim.
D.812/14/213
                        Graham starts referring to the visit of Tom
                        and William Graham to Lisburn. He hopes,
Anne, '... will have found Tom in the best of health, as for William if his ailments only are to kill him he has a long spell of it before him. I suppose he will soon return to India. He is fortunate in having his corps at such a good station as Meerut, though it is in no way superior to this, to which I hear I am immediately to be permanently posted, and made independent. At present all the offices in Oude are under the Lucknow one (branches of it at least); now we are to get our own charges, and mine is to be the largest. [I] am fortunate in getting such a climate. I have found none which agree with me so well in India. I am fortunate in having a palace to live in, when all the troops are in tents. However fine barracks are now going to be built for them.

My traps arrived from Meerut yesterday, and on getting out my thermometer this morning [I found ?] that it was far from anything like the cold ones we have had. I found that it stood at 47° F., fine weather is it not for troops? The whole business in this part of the country is nearly at an end. Today the naval brigade under Capt[ain] Sotherby passes through on its way to Allahabad, from that to Calcutta *en route* to England. The siege park has returned to Allahabad also. The engineers' park has been taken into stores here. All the remaining leaders have hidden themselves in the jungles on the borders of Nepaul; their troops have dispersed, their guns taken. The commander-in-chief has taken eighteen guns within the last fortnight, [and] Gen[era]l Sir Hope Grant fourteen or fifteen. The forts are being levelled, the people disarmed, the jungles cut down, and the people of Oude who have lived in a state of constant warfare for one hundred years if not longer must war no more. Their swords must be turned into ploughshares, their spears into pruning hooks. ...'

Graham then discusses the affairs of friends at home, including William Graham's coming marriage. He comments that he is '... glad to hear such good accounts of William Graham's wife to be. I wish for his sake she were a little older. My poor uncle when he first came out made a bet with me that I would be married before W[illiam] and James. Even William is going to set me an example. So now that my ten years service is drawing to a close it is almost time for me to take a trip home and follow it. I hope when they reorganize the army they may do something for us, for my present furlough including the passage there [home] and back would now only be six months, scarcely giving me three to be with you, but if they will give nothing more I will avail myself even of that the first opportunity. We have a great number of commissariat officers at home now, but their leave will soon be beginning to expire, and then it will be [my] turn I hope. The short time is a terrible blow considering the expense. I could not do it under six hundred pounds, whilst if I got a medical certificate I would have my passage paid, and have when at home about [£ ?] 500 a year. However I must not be ungrateful for the good health God has given me.'

13 January 1859 *D.812/14/214*	Delhi Bank order of £50 from the account of Captain James Graham, Faizabad, made out to his sister Anne.

21 January 1859 *D.812/14/215*	James Parsons, [? Aleuroh], to Daniel Cullimore, Bally Ann Park, New Ross, Co. Wexford.

This letter begins with an extract from a letter to Parsons from his wife in Delhi. It describes her efforts to buy silk scarves and shawls for Mrs Cullimore. Parsons uses this to introduce the topic of the silks which dominates the letter. A list of the silks is drawn up in an enclosure, their total price being £564.

In the latter half of the letter Parsons discusses more developments over the will and property of the late Dr Graham. '... I have *blank* endorsed the Delhi Bank shares, and Mr Parry will dispose of them as advantageously as he can, and when we get the opinion of council respecting the Sealkote property I will act according to it and sell or not as may be. ...'

The letter continues with Parsons describing the doings of various friends in India including [? Quinlin] who had '... just returned from a hog-hunting party where they had capital sport: twenty-nine real good *fighting* hogs in five days, and lots of horses *cut* and [? Quinlin's] little mare very badly. ...' Parsons closes mentioning that he is moving to Mysore, and he asks Cullimore to address his letters there in future.

23 January 1859 *D.812/14/216*	James Graham, Faizabad, to his sister, Anne, Lisburn, Co. Antrim.

Graham informs his sister that he has sent by

the last mail a bank draft for £50 (D.812/14/214), and that he encloses a
second for the same sum. He then thanks her for her last letter, and its
description of the Lisburn visit of the Graham brothers, and proceeds
to discuss the marriage of William Graham. '... I suppose the next mail
will bring me news of the latter's [William's] marriage. W[illia]m will
make a most affectionate husband I have no doubt, but I do hope his wife
will have some hold on the purse for he is really too extravagant for his
present means. I don't suppose she will bring him anything ...'.

Graham continues discussing the career of a friend in the engineers, and
then moves on to his own prospects. '... Since I wrote last there has also
been published a warrant reorganizing the commissariat dep[artmen]t of the
royal army, has been published [sic]. It is now formed completely on our
system. I do not think it will make any change in ours, except that we will
get an official rank if it is followed up by our gov[ernmen]t. I ought to
be by it an official capt[ain], and when promoted to be an ass[istan]t
comm[issar]y gen[era]l, [and] in the good time coming, an official major.
These official ranks do not give pay, but persons holding them get batta -
prize money *etc.* at the rate given for those ranks in the army.

I have now been here within a few days of ten years out of England. My long
voyage round the Cape now begins to tell. Had I come out overland I would
have been entitled to my furlough in six weeks, but I now will not be until
the 26th of June, [when the] weather [is] hot enough to drive out of one's
head all ideas of travelling. I doubt also if I would get it now if I asked
for it considering the great number of commissariat officers we have now
sick at home. They will however be coming out again in the beginning of the
next cold weather, and then I will make play for even a six month's furlough
if I can get no more. When the time taken up in going and coming is
deducted from it, it does not leave much time at home, three months would
be the very most, but what else is to be done? These wretched doctors are
troubled with a disease called conscience, and will not give me a sick
certificate.

I sent you the other day a *Delhi Gazette* showing the chief commissioner in
Oude's opinion about the war being over. The commander-in-chief has gone
back to Lucknow. Ladies have got permission to come to all the stations in
Oude, so that matters look bright. ...'

Graham goes on asking his sister to get Tom and William Graham to sign his
security bond as a deputy adjutant general, and to make sure it is returned
to him, as he feels they may lose it if the responsibility for its return is
left in their hands. Without it he can still draw his pay, but the '...
auditor of commissary accounts has the power of cutting it until the bond is
sent into government ...'. He then makes a brief reference to the
continuing freedom of rebels in the hills. '... We have had a few days hot
weather, which have changed again to some so very cold that I have lost the
use of my fingers. Not very pleasant for the enemy who have fled into the
hills, they will suffer dreadfully. ...'

Graham concludes referring to various friends in India, Britain and the
United States of America. He mentions that he has not written yet to Mrs
[? Clemence] who was offended he did not call to see her when stationed in
Meerut in 1857. He tells his sister that he was working so hard during the
day organizing a convoy at this time that he could only call on her late at

night, and he did not like 'calling at such irregular hours', especially
as she was sharing a house with another lady.

12 February 1859   James Graham, Faizabad, to his sister,
                          Anne, Lisburn, Co. Antrim.
D.812/14/217

Graham begins stating surprize that he has
not received an invitation from William Graham
to the latter's marriage. He goes on to mention that he believes William
has as yet done nothing to obtain compensation for the damage done to his
father's property during the Sialkot mutiny. Graham fears it is now too late
to lodge such a claim with government. He comments '... I have written to
both Tom and him [William] repeatedly about it, but I believe they have
both allowed the time for sending in the claim to pass by ...'.

Graham then tells his sister that he has sent her another bank draft
similar to the one he despatched by the same mail last month. He then moves
on to the topic of the career prospects of Graham Smith, who is trying to get
an Indian army appointment. '... Henrietta [Smith's mother] has every
reason to hope for the best. My only fear is that Graham be above the age
before Lord Stanley can do all he wishes. There will I think be a great
number of appointments to be given away on the reorganization of the army,
and you ought to hear something about that before this letter reaches you.
We have numerous rumours here, but nothing I can believe as fixed about it.
All the appointments to our artillery and engineers are now thrown open to
competition. Don't you think Graham might have some chance? Mr Sherret
ought to be a judge; and to get one of [them ?], even artillery, would be a
prize indeed. They do not require as much reading as the civil appointments,
and as for the first year no preparation will have been made for them, the
contest for them may not be so hard fought as it will be hereafter ...'.

Graham continues describing the post-mutiny prestige of the commissariat,
and then he refers to the continuing campaign against the rebels who took
refuge in Nepal. '... I sent you a *Friend of India* this mail, which I wish
you would send to Col[onel] Nuthall if you know his address. It will show
him what the Indian papers say of the commissariat now-a-days. You of
course have seen what the *Times* correspondent says, that it is No. 1. A son
of Col[onel] Nuthall's stayed with me for a couple of days on his way to
join Her Majesty's 56th at Belgaum in Bombay. He is an uncommonly fine
young fellow, and a great favourite. He was here some time as a field
engineer assisting in building a bridge of boats for the army to cross and
got great praise. ...

All is very quiet here now. When the enemy were driven over the Nepaul
frontier, government would not cross over after them, as native states
consider it such an indignity. They have since however asked Jung Bahadoor,
if he had any objection to our doing so. He says not, and that he will not
only be glad to see them do so, but that he will co-operate in every way. I
suspect he finds the scoundrels no end of a nuisance, as they must be eating
up his country. The only thing he wishes is for us to avoid killing cows if
possible in his country. So we have been sending no end of sheep. Sheep as
I suppose you know Hindoos eat, but cows they worship.

The year is once more on the turn, and the hot weather approaching. A very
different state of affairs however since we came down country last year.

126

Then Rohilkand and Oude were (with the exception of as much ground at the
Allambagh near Lucknow, as Sir James's Outram's army could stand upon),
completely in hands of the enemy. They had guns by hundreds, forts
innumerable and arms and ammunition in abundance. Now not a fort in Oude
is in their hands, and 350,000 arms of all descriptions have been given up.
They are supposed to have taken a few light guns with them to Nepaul, but
they are few indeed. I send you by this mail the commander-in-chief's order
summing up the campaign during the last few months, by which you will see how
much has been done. The forts are being rapidly dismantled, the jungles cut
down, and they must either give up their arms and become peaceful citizens,
or die. They have no alternative here. We have a report that the old King
of Delhi is fast going to his grave, and it would have been fortunate for
him both in this world, and in the next, if he had gone there years ago.

By the bye I am told that a Mr Cullimore, a nephew of your dear brother-in-
law passed through here last month with the 6th Madras cavalry. I don't
know but that I would have tried to have seen him if I had known at the
time [*sic*].

I think I told you in my last that I am permanently posted here. There is
now no chance of my being moved until I ask for it myself, and I trust that
my first move will be towards old England. I have now finished my ten years
in the army, but my ten years counts from the date of [my] arrival, the 26th
of June. There would be no chance of my getting leave this year when there
is so much to do, and so many of our officers sick at home, besides it would
be impossible to move at that season. I trust that the beginning of next
year will see me at home.'

27 February 1859   James Graham, Faizabad, to his sister,
                                Anne, Lisburn, Co. Antrim.
D.812/14/218

                        Graham commences mentioning William Graham's
                        marriage, and then he mentions that he has
enclosed a second bank exchange note. He then thanks his sister for
congratulations on his promotion, '... You are right in thinking I am
appointed a 1st class d[eputy] a[ssistant] c[ommissary] g[eneral], but it is
only officiating. However I am so well up, that I expect to continue
officiating till I get the promotion permanent. We await the report of the
commission on the reorganization of the commissariat which I expect will
make us a staff corps and bring us some advantages. ...'

The temperate nature of the Faizabad climate is Graham's next topic, and he
hopes it will continue during the ensuing hot weather. Faizabad he notes
has, '... a beautiful view of the hills and snowy range, and one envies the
Nepaulese enjoying such a climate. In a few years I dare say we will have
a sanitorium in them, but now they are unapproachable, as the last remnant
of the sepoys are wandering about the lower range. Jung Bahadoor whom you
have heard of in England is behaving very well, and is driving them into our
clutches. They are completely disorganized, without guns, and nearly
starving. They are all in the Nepaul territory. We have completely driven
them out of ours. ...'

Graham then begins to refer to his possible furlough in the summer. '...
Retirements and furloughs are at last open. The latter however on a very

small scale. ...' He then describes the post-mutiny military reorganization, '... nothing is being done but building barracks and housing troops. There is not a station from one end of India to another, but that some additional buildings are required for them, and the quantity of money being expended is enormous. It will far exceed the bill for the war (the commissariat one), and will be a continual drain on the finances of the country for years to come. Some of the oldest regiments have been sent home. You are all so warlike looking there, that we consider you will require all you can get[29]. I trust that [England ?][30] will not be drawn into any of the quarrels that are abroad. War I think there must be if only to help the Emperor of France, but England has had enough of war lately I think. I cannot make out what your Belfast Phoenix Club people want; a landing of the Americans in Ireland to assist them in getting what ! They ought to be put down with a strong arm. Give them [the authorities] a special commission as they did formerly, and hang not only all concerned but everyone that harbours them. They will then have met the just reward of their ingratitude.

This is I feel an awfully stupid letter, but write I must of course, and having nothing to write about, as the natives say "Kya Kareya", *what can be done*? ...'

10 March 1859   James Graham, Faizabad, to his sister, Anne, Lisburn, Co. Antrim.

D.812/14/220

         Graham thanks his sister for her congratulations on his further promotion, and he discusses how his position has been affected by the retirement of a number of commissariat officers. He states that he hopes his position as a temporary 1st class deputy assistant commissary general will be made permanent, and describes his recent promotion as trivial, then comments, '... but every little makes a muckle, and I am glad to get even one step. ...'

Graham then refers to the improvement of the mail service, which means that there are now four regular mails each month. This he reckons will cause confusion as '... it will be quite impossible then (as indeed it is now) for anyone to be certain of the arrival and departure of the mails ...'. Graham promises however to write to his sister as soon as he receives her letters under the new postal arrangements. He sends her a newspaper praising the work of the commissariat during the mutiny and comments that he feels '... proud to think that I have been even in a small degree, instrumental in getting it such a good name. ...' He states that despite the general reorganization of the Indian army the commissariat is likely to be left basically untouched. He also reports a rumour that '... all pay is to be cut by one fifth ...', and he thinks this will prove true in the case of all staff and civil appointments, but military pay he thinks will be exempt from any economies. Reference is then made to the parliamentary commission on Indian affairs, and Graham hopes it will establish the commissariat as a staff corps. This development he is awaiting with every mail to India.

29. *Graham is referring here to the Franco-Piedmontese war against Austria which created general European unrest, and which was part of the movement for Italian unity.*

30. *Text torn.*

Graham closes describing how he is decorating his Faizabad house, and referring to the mildness of the Faizabad climate.

27 March 1859   James Graham, Faizabad, to his sister, Anne, Lisburn, Co. Antrim.

D.812/14/221

Graham opens lamenting the death of a friend mentioned by his sister in her last letter, and then he goes on to joke about his stoutness. He mentions a rumour that he is to be posted '... to bring up arrears of account in the Cawnpoor office ...'. He finds the idea of moving troublesome but such an appointment he takes as a compliment to his ability and he thinks it would '... be a nice appointment as I will have no executive duties, be quite independent, [and] have nothing whatever to do with the station duties ...'. The Kanpur post he believes will last until 1860 when he can apply for home leave. This would be beneficial as he would be able to leave for home directly on the conclusion of his work there, due to it being a specific posting of limited duration. If he remained at Faizabad he would have to await the arrival of a replacement commissariat officer before he could begin his journey to Britain.

Graham then refers to the new postal system which has speeded up mails, and he mentions that he has sent some tobacco seeds home to Lisburn. He continues discussing Col[onel] Garrett's leave and states that Garrett must be awaiting the commissariat reorganization before retiring, so that he might reap any benefits under the restructured commissariat. Graham proceeds on the same topic when he airs the view that the commissariat reorganization proposals being prepared by the British government have been extremely slow making their appearance. He also reiterates his view that the commissariat should be made a staff corps, on the the new British army model.

Graham complains about the lack of interesting issues on which to write, and then declares that the only event of significance he has yet to refer in his letter is, '... a bill which has just been passed for taxing everything imported for the use of Europeans in this country. It is generaly abused of course, and the Europeans think they are very badly treated, and the natives favoured, but I myself am of a different opinion. The finances of the country must be put on a firm footing, and I would infinitely prefer Europeans having to pay part of them by a tax on luxuries, than that the government should carry out a scheme which it was rumoured the other day they intended carrying into execution; to reduce all civil and staff pay [by] one fifth. ...'

Graham concludes noting '... the commander-in-chief and big-wigs are moving towards Simlah. Lord Clyde is not I suspect in such vigorous health as his friends wish him. ...'

8 April 1859   James Graham, Faizabad, to his sister, Anne, Lisburn, Co. Antrim.

D.812/14/222

Graham starts by saying that he may be posted to Bareilly instead of Kanpur. He has mixed feelings about this prospect as although Bareilly is '... one of the best stations ...', close to the hills, being posted there might affect his chances of leave as, '... I would have charge of the Rohilkand division and would find difficulty in slacking it off ...'. This disadvantage he feels is balanced by the proximity of the hills which he can reach in two days[31].

Graham continues referring to his Delhi Bank shares which have fallen in value due to the bank's mutiny losses, and the fact that Dr Graham's shares were sold and flooded the market. He states that his six shares were previously worth £50 each, but had now dropped to £42. He hopes they will recover their former value once compensation is paid for the destruction suffered by the bank during the mutiny.

Graham then writes of the coming of the hot weather, and how he regrets the proposed move to Rohilkand under such conditions.

A paragraph is then headed with the date 10 April, and Graham informs his sister that he has received an order posting him to Rohilkand and he suspects '... from the way it is worded that I am to open an office of account there under a new system that has lately been introduced. By it I will have no outdoor work, and no anxiety ...'. Graham then tells his sister that he will be the central accounting officer for the whole Rohilkand division, responsible for collating all the accounts of the local offices where, '... there will be officers at each of the stations to do the executive work under me, who will have all the hard work. ...'

The letter proceeds with Graham describing a Hindu festival at Faizabad. '... Today there is a great festival here, it being the anniversary of the birth and disappearance of a god. There cannot be less than 50,000 people assembled here; young and old, men and women, halt and lame, blind and deaf, all come in the hope of getting some good from bathing in the sacred stream at the place where the birth took place, and besides these I spoke to one poor old creature carried in, one out of many, who told me he had come to die, to give up his last breath at the sacred spot. Among the mass are to be seen specimens of every class of devotee. I saw this morning creatures who have held their arms above their heads until they became fixed and withered in that position, some with uncut nails, all with uncut hair. Part of the ceremony today is caused by a belief that for every hair cut off on the sacred spot they will have a million of years in paradise, so every village has brought with it the village hereditary barber, and I saw actually little hills of hair on the banks of the river. There were hundreds and hundreds among them who had never seen a European's face before, and gazed at me with wonder. You have no idea of the utter helplessness of natives, especially of the women. I have no doubt that today or tomorrow at least a hundred women or children will be lost, from getting separated from their families, and not knowing the names of even their own villages. Some told me that they had come a month's journey, some three hundred or four hundred miles. Such is the strength of superstition. ...'

Graham ends referring to his departure for Bareilly. '... My servants start tomorrow and all my household goods are packed up. I have got two carts made out of captured gun carriages, and these take all my worldly goods.

31. *This was important during the hot season when the hills offered a cooler more congenial climate to Europeans serving in India.*

Twelve gov[ernmen]t bullocks take them and they are to go twenty miles a day, my servants trudging along with them, and thinking it nothing.   I myself will stay eight or ten days here, and three or four at Lucknow, and then [go] straight on to Bareilly from which place you will next hear from me, your most affectionate brother.'

COMMISSARIAT LETTERS

M

Simpson's first letter after the outbreak at Meerut — May 1857

My dear Graham —

We have had a dreadful time of it here for the last week. On Sunday the 10th at ½ past four a six o'clock the 3 [...] broke out into open mutiny shot down such officers as they could lay hold of, fired all the bungalows assisted by the Suddur Bazar rascals & the [...] population from the surrounding villages. I had just time to [...] the carriage which was ready to go to Church when the rascals about 200 came into the Compound fired our bungalow, fired at us as we were driving off, burnt my house, the office with every thing in them to the ground & plundered my treasure chest of some [...]. There is not a single house with hardly a [...] that has escaped. [...] Macdonald & his wife of the 20, Taylor, Patten & Henderson [...] of the 11th & Mrs Chambers, Phillips, Macnab Dawson & his wife of the [...] cavalry. The poor pensioners have been butchered fearfully. Some 50 persons murd[ered]

Letter from Col C. W. Simpson to James Graham,
c.May 1857, Mic 305 Vol. 2 (see p.135 opposite).

[May 1857]   Colonel C. W. Simpson, [Meerut ?], to
                              James Graham, Landour.
Mic. 305 Vol. 2

                              This letter is prefaced by the following
                              endorsement in Graham's hand, '... Simpson's
first letter after the outbreak at Meerut ...', and it is clear from the
contents of the letter that Simpson is describing his experiences during
the initial outbreak of the mutiny at Meerut.

'We have had a dreadful time of it here for the last week. On Sunday the 10th
at half past five or six o'clock the three reg[imen]ts broke out into open
mutiny shot [? down] such officers as they could lay hold of - fired all the
bungalows assisted by the [? suddubazar] rascals and the goojur population
from the surrounding villages. I had just time to get out the carriage
which was ready to go to church when the rascals, about two hundred came
into the compound, fired my bungalow - fired at us as we were driving off,
burnt my house, [and] the offices with everything in them to the ground and
plundered my treasure chest of some 60,000 r[upee]s. There is not a single
house in the native lines that has escaped. The butchery has been great,
Macdonald and his wife of the 20[th], Taylor, Patch and Henderson junior of
the 11th and Mrs Chambers, Phillips, Macnab, Dawson and his wife of the
cavalry. The [? poor pensioners] have been butchered fearfully. Some fifty
persons must have been butchered. Go along purchasing if you think it
necessary, but you have nothing to fear up there. Here are only Delhi and
Meerut in a state of uproar - all other places quiet I hear, and when once
we get at the Moofsids in Delhi all will be quiet. The King I believe is
not implicated. He is not fit for anything. His sons are, and I hope they
will hang them all. I am very busy getting supplies ready. ...'

26 May 1857   Colonel [? J.] Nuthall, Calcutta, to
                              James Graham, Landour,
Mic. 305 Vol. 2
                              giving him commissariat instructions during
                              the early phase of the mutiny.

'The post has become so uncertain and irregular that every com[mis]sariat
official must act in [the] emergency on his own judgement in concurrence
with his commanding officer. You must be particularly careful to have a
good supply of slaughter cattle available. The malt liquor at Meerut has
been destroyed. What you may require you must get from Umbala if the road
be open. In short everything that you cannot get from Meerut you must
obtain elsewhere. I trust all will be settled in a week and our communications all open again. If you have not received the usual means of
obtaining cash for commissariat purposes you must apply to the civil
treasurer for an advance if necessary, and duly report your proceedings for
approval. Please go to Mr [? Maddocks] and enquire after my boys.

Simpson and all his family escaped, but his office was destroyed and a vast
deal of gov[ernmen]t property.'

7 May 1858   Major C. M. FitzGerald, Lucknow, to
                              James Graham, Faizabad. [This letter
Mic. 305 Vol. 2   is bound out of chronological order].

                              'From the 1st ins[tan]t all your force comes

under me, and I keep accounts of it. Dickens ignores you altogether.
Strike out his name (he is a major now) and address acc[ount]s to me -
I'll approve and confirm so as to put you all right and then send on for
sanction to stifle Newbolt. I don't wish to worry you or to ask for
returns *etc.*, which a temperature of 115°f. is adverse to, but *when* you do
get a cool day in a hut or under a tree, try and give me a roll of the
elephants and camels employed with your force. If you can't manage
reg[imenta]l rolls *i.e.* in detail - one general roll of the cattle as they
stood on the 1st May.

I hope you and Hogg will get the kudos you deserve. I have included you
both in a roll of officers deserving honorable mention for service before
Lucknow, but I am afraid you are both too small as indeed am I - being a
subaltern, for any reward like Macbean and Dickens have earned
(b[reve]t majorities). ...'

8 February 1858   Major C. M. FitzGerald, Camp Kanpur,
                         to James Graham, [Kanpur?].
Mic.305 Vol. 2

                         'Yours of the 6th has just reached [me] -
                         you have done quite right in everything. I
should like to have more of your kidney.

It is impossible to say when we march - but you must prepare without a
moments delay - send your indents to Christopher and complete everything
even to gallon measures *etc. etc.*

One point is of importance and I hope you will see to it. Make your bazar
and all reg[imenta]l bazars fill up thirty days if possible before you come
in. Get them carriage and do this before you come in. I am buying up the
Cawnpore market. The bazar won't like doing this but do you persuade them.'

6 August 1858   Major C. M. Fitzgerald, Lucknow, to
                         James Graham, Faizabad.
Mic. 305 Vol. 2

                         'I have just rec[eive]d yours of the 4th
                         ins[tan]t and am very sorry to hear that the
bread agents are not doing well. Your note has been translated to Kissen
Jahail and I have ordered him off to Fyzabad to put all things right there.
I have given him ninety-six mules and thirty-five tattoos which will be
laden with soojee and chukees and started tonight. They ought to reach
Fyzabad in three days, whereas carts will take ten in the present state of
the roads.

Carts laden with soojee shall also be started at once. The worst of
keeping up supplies of *soojee* is that in this weather it goes bad in a few
days.

Advance Mohun Lall funds to buy wheat and make him set up a chukkee go-down.
He can debit Kissen Jahail and you can too with the advance and expenses.
Kissen Jahail in his [? urgie] has begged that Mohun Lall might get advances
for bread.

Send in an official requisition for writers and establishments of all kinds, which you may require for yourself or Graeme and I'll not stint you, but give you all you require. At the end of the month Dickens will be discharging a number of hands.

Graeme had better look still to you and report, because your position is his proper base. If the force arrives from Sultanpore towards this he can report to me when within postal range. ...'

9 August 1858

Mic. 305 Vol. 2

Major C. M. FitzGerald, Lucknow, to James Graham, Faizabad,

informing Graham of arrangements he has made to secure grain and bread supplies for Graham at Faizabad. He discusses the various problems which he faces supplying the troops in Oudh with bread, and he hopes that the native bread agents he has sent to help Graham at Faizabad will be successful in their work.

'... The supply of bread to so large a force as we have in Oude scattered about without easy means of communication, and the country not yet well organized under our rule - is no easy matter. Bakers are scarce [and] soojee stored at this season goes bad. ...'

FitzGerald also makes the point that '... under your supervision at Fyzabad nothing unfortunate will happen ...', and that he will assist Graham to the utmost with supplies of essentials and equipment.

11 August 1858

Mic. 305 Vol. 2

Major C. M. FitzGerald, Lucknow, to James Graham, Faizabad,

informing Graham that supplies of grain and flour had been despatched to Faizabad.

FitzGerald gives Graham instructions for the sale of these commodities to Sikh troops serving at Faizabad, and for their sale in the bazar. He also informs Graham that he can obtain supplies of hospital clothing if he makes application for them.

20 August 1858

Mic. 305 Vol. 2

Major C. M. FitzGerald, Lucknow, to James Graham, Faizabad,

informing Graham that a convoy of carts has started for Faizabad with '... two months supplies for 1,000 men ...'. FitzGerald also comments that Graham '... need not look out for river steamers. They have not left Calcutta and won't reach you before Xmas if then ...'.

FitzGerald ends discussing commissariat appointments and he states that Graham's '... proper place is Fyzabad ...'.

13 November 1858

Mic. 305 Vol. 2

Major C. M. FitzGerald, 'Camp Oodeypore', to James Graham, Faizabad,

discussing troop movements and related commissariat problems. FitzGerald also discusses Graham's promotion and his own failure to effect another commissariat officer's advancement. He feels it will prove impossible to get this decision reversed as the '... gov[ernmen]t will not undo their own act ...'. The letter ends with FitzGerald stating that he will support any commissariat decisions Graham makes at Faizabad.

'... Do everything to secure efficiency and appeal to me if you are attacked - I'll accept the responsibility. ...'

19 November 1858

Mic. 305 Vol. 2

Major C. M. FitzGerald, Bareilly, to James Graham, Faizabad,

warning Graham of the imminent arrival at Faizabad of a column under the command of General Sir J. Hope Grant.

'Gen[era]l Grant will be at Fyzabad tomorrow and the day after probably cross the bridge.

The chief-of-staff desires that the columns operating trans-Gogra shall be most efficiently equipped in camel carriage, and sanctions the diversion of the whole of your transport (Fyzabad cattle) for this purpose.

The dak is just going out. I will communicate officially tomorrow. In the meanwhile act of course upon this.

Call upon Leven for the transport you want. I have just sent instructions to Cawnpore for the despatch from it to Lucknow of very large numbers of cattle, and Leven shall also be told to comply with your wants.

Provide *throughly* for the trans-Gogra troops ...'.

FitzGerald ends giving Graham instructions concerning the amount of supplies he is to furnish to the troops crossing the River Gogra. Basically the various columns were to be supplied with one month's provisions. FitzGerald also makes it clear that Graham is to be the superior of any commissariat officer serving with Hope Grant's column. This he hopes will prevent any disputes over rank and seniority, when the columns reach Faizabad.

30 November 1858

Mic. 305 Vol. 2

Major C. M. FitzGerald, Camp Lucknow, to James Graham, Faizabad,

giving Graham further commissariat instructions.

'... Use your own discretion on all points and rely on my backing you through everything. Just received yours of the 23rd ins[tan]t and another

without date but apparently of a later date ... . You have done quite
right. You are of more use at Fyzabad than with the force, but not being
on the spot I could come to no decision. Fear nothing - I'll accept your
acts as my own. ...

Eight hundred camels have been sent out to you, also soojee, and I hope you
will have plenty. Let me know how much (how many days supply) the troops
across the river have on your receipt of this. ...'

20 December 1858

Mic. 305 Vol. 2

Major C. M. FitzGerald, 'Camp
Baraitch', Bahraich, to James Graham,
Faizabad,

keeping him informed on commissariat affairs,
and arrangements to improve the supply of
wheat. FitzGerald inquires about failures in the supply of '... slaughter
cattle ...' and he asks Graham to '... send out one of your butchers on
this side of the Gogra to bring all on to Baraitch - and send all
consignments which may reach you. ...'

The letter continues with FitzGerald assuring Graham that he has the ability
to administer commissariat affairs at Faizabad. FitzGerald also makes the
point that Graham has the confidence of his superiors and this will maintain
him at Faizabad when the present military campaign in that area is over.

'... Fyzabad even with the force you detail for it will not be by any means
too large a charge for a man who ranks so high in general estimation as
yourself. In ten days I think the whole business will be over and then
something definite may be looked for in our respect. ...'

FitzGerald ends discussing the limited chances of promotion which he sees
within the commissariat.

APPENDICES

APPENDIX A

ULSTER ATTITUDES TO THE INDIAN MUTINY

The reports of mutiny battles and military campaigns printed by
Ulster's newspapers were basically similar and were probably syndicated. To
obtain an insight into the attitudes of the various sections of the local
community an examination o f editorials and articles on the topic of the
mutiny is necessary. Four of the most prominent Ulster newspapers were, the
Belfast Daily Mercury, the *Belfast Newsletter*, the *Ulsterman* and the
Northern Whig. Ulster's politics at this time were complicated, due to the
political ramifications of the province's religious divisions, which gave
British political groupings certain idiosyncratic local features.

The *Belfast Daily Mercury* was the paper of conservatively minded
Protestant Liberals. It advocated carefully considered reform, wishing to
see the Irish establishment (which included the Anglican Church of Ireland)
modified but not overthrown. It was the most pragmatic of the Ulster
papers, examining political and social problems less from the viewpoint of
party or factional interest than from the standpoint of the public good.
The *Mercury* stood for compromise and generally abjured simple partisanship,
both political and religous. It viewed the mutiny as a temporary setback
for British rule, which once overcome would pave the way for reform of the
structure of Indian government.

> 'Never since the British flag was planted on the soil of India did
> such disastrous tidings reach this country as what the last mail had
> brought. ... It is no doubt very bad; but after all, it has no
> substance in it. The might of British power has been surprised, and
> the poor miserable revolters have been seduced into a momentary belief
> in their own omnipotence. They have had a jubilee of crime - they
> have massacred and plundered, and set up a mock king in the insane
> hope of restoring old Delhi to its past glories; but there is a wall
> of fire gathering around them ... there are marching deadly
> battalions to begirt them, and terrible will be the vengeance that
> will speedily overtake them. ...
>
> But while we may say this, we must, at the same time express a hope
> that the present calamitous occurrence will lead to a total change
> in the Government of India. It is one of the monstrous absurdities
> of the age to have an empire, greater than all the other possessions
> of England together, governed in a second-hand fashion, through the
> intervention of a company of retired merchants and their military
> dependants who have used, and still use the Government as a means of
> individual advantage and jobbery, and only value it as it conduces
> to that end. ...'

This article ends lamenting the low standard of officers recruited
into the East India Company forces through nepotism and corruption. Such
officers, it asserted, were arrogant and unsympathetic to the sepoy and his
religious sensibilities, and were unable to cope with the problem of the
greased cartridges.

> '... We may think this is a silly prejudice, but we have just as
> silly amongst ourselves; but let that pass. The troops refused to
> use the cartridges; and had there been a wise and benevolent military
> authority, the whole affair could have been easily quieted. But we
> had British officers who damned the natives and their prejudices, and

took no pains to undeceive them, then the deadly feelings of religion came into play - feelings which when excited are the most absorbing and truculent that can sway either civilized or savage - and out of that small matter the terrible revolt ... originated.'[1]

In view of the severe sectarian riots that afflicted Belfast in July and and September 1857, these comments on religious prejudice were poignant indeed.

The *Mercury* continued the theme of nepotism and jobbery in the inefficient Indian administration, and its obituary for John Nicholson, after singing fulsome praises for this glorious son of Ulster, makes the following telling comment;

'John Nicholson ... obtained from his uncle a direct appointment to India early in 1839 ... and however glad we may be to see the East India Civil Service thrown open to public competition, we must do Sir James Hogg the justice to say that his nepotism in this instance was fully justified in its results. ...'[2]

The *Mercury* also attacked 'Irish sepoy patriots', who used the example of the mutiny in an attempt to stir up disaffection in the south and west of the island. It reprinted proclamations and manifestoes posted in these areas calling on all 'true Irishmen' to rise against their English oppressors. The *Mercury* was concerned that such proclamations could lead to violent outbursts against British rule. It dropped its usual impartiality and urged the government to take firm action against persons issuing seditious proclamations, which could, find sympathy with a '... large portion of the Celtic population ...'.[3] These proclamations had little effect (except to antagonise Protestants) as Ireland was relatively passive in 1857, and in no mood for widespread revolt. It is worth quoting from a couple of these proclamations for they are examples of the interaction of nationalist development in Ireland and India. Irish and Indian nationalisms were both opposed to British rule, and throughout their development to national independence gained from the example of each other.

'Men of Carlow. The time of England's downfall is at hand.
Ireland awake.
Will you be up?
Long live Nena [*sic*] Sahib. Down with England.
Hurrah for liberty.
God save the people ...

Men of Cavan - Glorious news! Our Tyrants are in
deep mourning - wailing is heard in every corner -
thirteen thousand of our oppressors killed by the sepoys.
Three cheers for the gallant sepoys.
Men of Cavan, now is the time to strike; strike for your
country and nationality. ...'[4]

1.   *B.D.M.* 30 June 1857.

2.   *B.D.M.* 14 November 1857.

3.   *B.D.M.* 2 November 1857.

4.   *Ibid.*

In the mid 1880s the process was reversed and the correspondence (on deposit in P.R.O.N.I.) between the then Viceroy of India, Lord Dufferin, and the various Secretaries of State for India during this period, contain references to the growth of Indian nationalism, stimulated by the Irish Home Rule movement's example.[5]

The *Ulsterman* was the newspaper of the Roman Catholics of Ulster. Its politics reflected the dilemma of the Roman Catholic population in the province. Being in the minority in many areas and, constituting a disproportionately large section of the lower orders of society, it had little political influence (especially with a property based franchise), except during close election contests. The Roman Catholic vote went invariably to the Liberal candidates, as, despite occasional threats of abstention, Roman Catholics generally felt that Liberals were more favourably disposed to Irish reforms. The *Ulsterman* therefore with neither power nor responsibility pursued a rather negative inconsistent editorial course, attacking with equal ardour both Liberal and Conservative between elections. Conservatives were branded by it as inveterate enemies of Roman Catholic and Irish aspirations, whilst Liberals were scorned as traitors who, once in power with the help of Roman Catholic votes failed to effect promised reforms. The *Ulsterman* executed many a *volte-face* at election time, when, after years spent berating Liberals, it had to advise its enfranchised readers to vote for a Liberal candidate and keep the Conservatives out. The *Ulsterman* saw the Indian upheaval as an illustration of the oppression it ascribed to English rule both in Ireland and throughout England's empire. By portraying the mutiny as a justified rising against English misrule, the *Ulsterman* gave vent to the Ulster Roman Catholics' frustration at their continued impotence under the English supported Protestant establishment in Ireland.

'It is not wonderful that great alarm and uneasiness should be excited among the authorities in England by the news from India. Six regiments in open mutiny - a native King proclaimed - and all the English officers, and all the British inhabitants of one city slaughtered. This is such intelligence as people do not look for every day. ...

Of one thing there is no doubt, that the Indian troops are infamously treated by their British officers. Of one other thing there is as little doubt: that the natives of that gorgeous land are subjected to tyranny and oppression unparalleled under the sway of Britain. Public testimony has shown that the English in India treat the natives as dogs; even dogs will turn and bite when they are too cruelly used. ...

Hindoos, Buddhists, Mussulmen all alike, they have chosen a Mahometan for their King.

Now this last fact is singular. The antagonism between the native Hindoo population and their former Mahometan conquerors is very great, for the bitterness of religious difference is strong everywhere. May we not conclude then, that the hatred which the natives bear to their English rulers must be of the most virulent kind, when men so antagonistic in religious feeling unite under a Mahometan leader to battle against a common tyrant. ...

5. *P.R.O.N.I. D.1071H/M 1-4.*

The mutiny will be crushed of course ... but the slaughter of the mutineers will not eradicate disaffection and discontent. The fire of insurrection will be instantly breaking out here and there; and, if it be finally crushed, England will achieve that result only at a frightful cost of blood and slaughter. ...'[6]

This article reflects the oft-repeated hope, held by Irish nationalists, that all Irishmen, regardless of creed, would one day unite against English domination. Another article uses the example of the mutiny to comfort its readers that English rule cannot last forever in India (or Ireland).

'... They [the sepoys] and all who join them in the mutiny will be drowned in a tide of blood. But when that ensanguined deluge shall have flowed back again, the old landmarks will be laid bare, the old monuments of oppression and wrong will be revealed to the burning and revengeful eye of India. The cry of revenge will again ring from a million lips. The avenging arm will be again raised to strike its death-dealing blow. Through blood and slaughter England may, from year to year, uphold her sway in the East, and master the struggling nations; but, through slaughter and blood, the struggle will, from year to year, go on, wave after wave of revolution dashing against the citadel of foreign rule, till at last the empire of Britain in that historic land shall have melted away as the winter snow melts from the hillside in the sunlight, leaving no stain, even of its bloody deeds, on the green future.

For as there is crime, and oppression and wrong, as surely is there also retribution.'[7]

The ultra-Protestant Orangemen of Ireland put an entirely different construction on the events of the mutiny. They stated that they saw little evidence of Roman Catholic sympathy for the British victims of the mutiny and indeed, they viewed Roman Catholic reaction to the mutiny as another example of 'popish' disloyalty when Britain was endangered by foreign war. They placed it in the context of a chain of development which stretched back to the French Revolutionary period.

'... Years have gone by since our institution was founded [1795]. Revolutionary politicians, at home and abroad, then contemplated a system of government which would utterly subvert religion and law; and they proposed for adoption by mankind their extraordinary creed - "Deny God and dethrone the King." Leaguing, for their own purposes, with these men, the votaries of Rome took up arms [the 1798 Rebellion], and conspired against the British Constitution; not more from a desire to substitute liscentiousness for liberty, than to elevate the Church of Rome, on the ruins of Protestantism. Crime and outrage accordingly prevailed. The blood that had flowed, by revolutionary tribunals in a neighbouring state, had excited in the minds of certain of our countrymen that desire for sanguinary results, which the unjust and violent deaths of innocent victims seldom fail to create, whether these victims die on the scaffold, by the hand of the executioner, or in the streets of Indian cities, by the atrocity of the sepoy. ...

6.   *Ulsterman 1 July 1857.*

7.   *Ulsterman 15 July 1857.*

Idolatrous and disloyal popery has been too long encouraged and fostered by the British Government, at home; as the idolatrous and disloyal religions of the Hindoo and Mohammedan have been, in India. The tribute paid to the pagoda, and the honour done to Moslem festivals, in India, averted not, nay rather, brought on, the cruel dishonour of women, and slaughter of babes at Delhi and Cawnpore.

Many of the caressed and subsidized Romanists of Ireland, instead of mourning for deeds that disgraced humanity, openly expressed sympathy with the murderous and revolted legions, whose ferocity had done such foul dishonour to the name and rights of England; the Irish sepoy press exulted over butchery and slaughter; while placards were audaciously posted calling upon the Papists of Ireland to imitate the example of Indian Rebels. ...'[8]

The *Belfast Newsletter*, which was the organ of the Conservative Protestant section of the Ulster population, came to conclusions similar to those of the Orange Order, though it expressed its views of alleged Roman Catholic disloyalty during Britain's period of crisis in a more restrained manner. It used the device of reprinting from the London press anti-Roman Catholic articles on the topic rather than presenting its readership with homespun editorials or articles. Obviously the *Newsletter* hoped to avoid the charge of pursuing a narrow-minded provincial sectarian attack upon Ulster's Roman Catholics by repeating mainstream British views. Its choice of reprinted articles shows an attempt to place the subject in the context of the wider struggle between Protestantism and Roman Catholicism. This, of course, was the age when the Protestant Churches viewed themselves as under increasing threat from Roman Catholic expansion. Ultramontanism, 'papal aggression' and, in Britain, the Oxford Movement and Anglican conversions to Rome, were the background to the *Newsletter's* handling of the mutiny. There are a number of references to the 'uncharitable and disloyal' pastorals of various members of the Roman Catholic hierarchy in Britain and Ireland including Nicholas Wiseman, Cardinal Archbishop of Westminister, and Paul Cullen, Archbishop of Dublin, and Papal Legate in Ireland.[9] The early *Newsletter* mutiny articles were full of imperialist confidence in Britain's ability to control India and to bring the mutineers to justice. The following quotations reflect the *Newsletter's* attitudes.

'... The victory of Plassey was the vengeance which English justice wreaked upon the butcher of the horrible "Black Hole", and whilst celebrating in England, a hundred years after the victory ... news comes to us of a massacre, the extent of which we do not yet know,

8.   *P.R.O.N.I. D.2966/16/1. Report of the proceedings of the Grand Orange Lodge of Ireland at the half yearly meeting held at Newry [Co. Down] 26-27 May 1858: Appendix No 1: Address of the Grand Lodge of Ireland pp.17-23, 26 May 1858, printed at Downpatrick by the Downshire Protestant press.*

9.   *Both Wiseman (an Anglican 'high church' convert) and Cullen issued pastorals advising Roman Catholics not to subscribe to the Indian Relief Fund, which was set up to help the victims of the mutiny. The Ulsterman, 11 October 1857, reported that Cullen had asked for an assurance from the organizers of the fund that it would not indulge in Protestant prostylizing among the widows and orphans of Roman Catholic soldiers. Cullen, the paper stated had received no such undertaking and it advised its readers to abstain from the fund.*

save that it has not spared old men, or women, or children. ...
But England is never startled for terror. It is in a crisis her
strong character is fairly tried. In a crisis she has not yet been
found wanting. For this emergency, also, she will be found prepared.
Swift, vigorous, retributive as fate itself must be her action and
her justice now. The mutiny at Delhi must be read in history as the
prelude to another Plassey. ...'[10]

'"THE ROMAN CATHOLICS AND THE CALAMITIES IN INDIA *(from the Times)*

It is no small consolation for our Indian calamity that it has proved
the happy occasion for an almost unprecedented national reunion. All
parties, all classes, all schools: Liberals, Conservatives, and
Radicals; men of war, and men of peace; they who had much to expect
from Government, and they who had nothing; Churchmen and dissenters,
have all forgotten their differences under the influences of a common
humanity, and on an appeal of the most touching and universal
character. Here and there comes out a slight difference of opinion
as to the causes of the misfortune, the persons answerable, and the
degree of prescience, promptitude, or skill displayed by those whose
business it was to prevent or arrest the catastrophe. But no opinions
on these points have been suffered to mar the national unanimity of
feeling and purpose, to qualify sympathy or divert the flow of
benevolence. ...

Why do we mention all this that everybody knows? Who denies it? It
is not denied. But there is one lamentable exception; only one. It
is forced upon us. Gladly would we shut our eyes and ears to it, but
it is obtruded and dinned into us. The Roman Catholics are resolved
that they shall stand out in odious relief as the only people in
these islands who in this solemn hour have no heart for the fate of
their countrymen, the distresses of the survivors, and the disaster
of the country. They are determined to show themselves wholly
exempt from British smypathies and regards. Whether they fulminate
a "pastoral" or write a "leader", or send a private letter to their
co-religionists at home, or ispire an Ultramontane journal abroad, or
show themselves at a public meeting it is always the same story.
They carefully repudiate every national weakness, and proclaim themselves the un-English, un-insular, cosmopolitan Papists, taking not
even a dispassionate view of the country. Whatever the view, the
result is that they deliberately and most unnecessarily inform the
public that they don't mean to subscribe a farthing to the relief of
vulgar, temporal distress, to mere worldly widowhood, to secular
orphanage, to profane want of food, clothing, and other creature
comforts. Perhaps we might have guessed this without their telling
us. ..."'[11]

10.   *B.N.L.* 29 *June 1857.*

11.   *B.N.L.* 16 *October 1857.*

147

Appendix A

'"ROMISH DISLOYALTY *(from the Record)*

'"... is there not a **general** wide-spread feeling of triumph in the
Roman Catholic mind that England's time of test and trial has arrived?
The *Univers* of Paris, the *Civilia Cattolica* of Geneva, the *Armonia* of
Turin, the *Nation* and the *Telegraph* in Ireland, are all alike
celebrating an ovation of triumph over England's day of affliction.
These are no small or insignificant powers in the European press.
They carry weight in their own circles, and leave their sting behind
them in many a heart at home and abroad. The Irish "Sepoy Journals"
openly dissuade the peasantry from enlistment, and even throw out
suggestive hints to mutiny in the hearing of the Irish regiments.
The Belfast rioters have been detected in the very act of sowing
the seed of disaffection in the mind of the Irish soldiery. The
walls of the Irish cities and towns have been placarded by fiery
phillippics *[sic]* against England and English rule. ...

And yet, what means all the vapouring and extravagant attempt after
loyalty of which we once heard so much, when Rome sought emancipation?
Whither have fled all those mild, loyal, peaceful, and oft-repeated
assurances once made on oath before the House of Lords by popish
Bishops, and others of high station and influence? What has become
of all the pledges of attachment to the British Crown and Constitution,
the promises of non-interference with the established religion, and the
indignant repudiation of all indication of disturbing it? Compare all
these with our experience of the past, and with the present facts of
the case; Rome's aggressive, illegal, insolent and disloyal attitude
in this country! Is there nothing here to create regret for the past,
and well grounded alarm for the future? ... it turns out that, in
this eventful juncture England's worst enemies are those that she
has "emancipated", patronized, pensioned, endowed, petted, pampered,
and almost bribed to keep them loyal, quiet and peacable. ..."'[12]

**The Newsletter also quoted from an article in the *Dublin Evening
Packet* which reflects the besieged mentality of Protestants in the South of
Ireland, surrounded by a large Roman Catholic majority.**

'"NANAISM *(from the Dublin Evening Packet)*

In the lurid phraseology of disloyalty the *Nation*[13] glares more
fiercely than the basest of its brethren. The writers of that
journal have not exhaused their treasury of seditious language.
Encouraged by certain dignitaries of the Papal Church, who are still
doing their little best to render Ireland infamous in the eyes of
foreigners by manifestations of sepoyism, they are producing weekly
fresh exhortations to uncharitableness and rancour - new outrage-
suggesting harangues eminently fitted to excite dangerous animosities
in the minds of the ignorant peasantry towards the "Protestant
landlord" which term is the synonym for "Saxon". ..."'[14]

12. *B.N.L. 17 October 1857.*

13. *The* Nation *was a Dublin journal of strong Irish nationalist sympathies.*

14. *B.N.L. 14 November 1857.*

148

The *Northern Whig* which was the paper read by the majority of Liberals took up a stance on the mutiny similar to that of the *Mercury*, advocating abolition of the East India Company structure of Indian government, which the close examination of Indian affairs caused by the mutiny, made inevitable. Such reform the *Whig* viewed as both a utilitarian, and, a moral necessity. The articles of early 1858 when proposals for reorganizing Indian government were before Parliament, also reflect the paper's attitude to the issue of punishment of the mutineers. The *Whig* took the view that the guilty sepoys should be given no mercy. It maintained this attitude even when other newspapers and individuals, who had originally called for wholesale revenge to be taken on Indians - whether innocent or stained with British blood - had began to advocate moderation as a penance for their former bloodthirstiness. The *Whig* made a special point of criticizing Lord Shaftesbury (the noted social reformer and philanthropist) on this score. It like the *Newsletter* and the *Mercury,* attacked the supposed disloyalty of Irish Roman Catholics during the mutiny; but it is its attitude on the punishment of mutineers that deserves quotation.

> '... When the Indian mutiny broke out, ... We [the British people] were ready to believe anything evil of a people who could rise against us; and we heard more than enough of the horrible atrocities committed upon our women and children, and upon men, taken by the rebels. Such stories poured in thick and fast; we took for granted that the Sepoys were fiends; and the cry for vengeance - for unsparing and indiscriminate slaughter - was fierce. ... Letters came home from officers and privates, gloating over incidents in which they had sabred or bayoneted crowds of crushed Sepoys; and our tenderest wives and daughters were not shocked, - regarding these reprisals as bare justice. ... Our blood was up, and we were not inclined to stop short in the due punishment of miscreants of whom it was forbidden to us to think that they could be human.
>
> All this was un-English, as the phrase goes, and could not last. The reaction has come, and we are expected to plunge into the opposite extreme of commiserating belief as to the sepoy. All the stories of the atrocities are now boldly denied, *en masse;* so boldly indeed that Lord Shaftesbury, who almost indecently particularised the alleged horrors, in several highly-applauded speeches which he made before Christmas, apologises, being challenged for proofs, can only submit that he had heard so-and-so. ...
>
> We are a fair people; and apprehending that we have been unjust to the Sepoys, we should, probably, get angry if there were any more pellmell massacring, or any new experiment in blowing chance taken deserters from the mouths of big guns.
>
> Now at some risk of being thought brutal, we really cannot see that in this war the question raised as to "dishonour" and "mutilation" should effect the political or the judicial course, consequent upon these military events. The Sepoys have betrayed, and turned against, their masters and pampered Sepoyism should be done away with, at once and forever. Hideous, wholesale, murders were committed at Meerut, at Futtyghur, at Delhi, and at Cawnpore; and the murderers should be traced, taken, and straight away hung by the neck until they are dead. Hundreds were concerned in those murders, from Nana Sahib downwards,

and not one murderer should be spared. It is a consolation to think
that the atrocities were, in some respects, exaggerated; but, when
we know that women and children by the dozen were shot, or cut to
pieces, and then thrown into wells and ditches, surely infamy enough
remains to demand that British power shall make a terrible example in
India. We never joined with this journal in the mad cry for blind
vengeance, and we beg to keep clear, now, of the sentimental, reaction.
The Oude Sepoy seems to us, on a candid examination of the evidences
about him, to be the most loathsome personage of modern history, and
we hope that *strict* justice will be served out to him.'[15]

**The *Whig*, despite an ostensibly radical tinge, expressed rather
bigoted views of the Indian national character and culture. Today we would
regard such expressions as being blatantly chauvinistic. In the 1850s,
however, even the Whig's 'progressive' readership would have accepted them
simply as statements of the natural superiority of Western Christian
civilization over the decadent 'barbarism' of the East.**

'... In the history of the world there is not a parallel for the
Government of India. One hundred and fifty millions of people,
professing a mysterious faith, which an European can hardly comprehend;
with habits of life nearly all of which are religious observances
utterly repugnant to Western ideas; with subtle intellects and
desperate fanaticism; a large proportion of them warlike, and all
suspicious, restless, intriguing, treacherous, instinctive with Oriental
vices, consistent only in their bad faith, were handed over to the
rule, not of statesmen who had made the art of government the business
of their lives, but of a successful body of traders and of parliamentary
personages combined. ... The persons who profess to forsee danger to
national independence in the possession of Indian patronage by the
advisors of the Crown, subject to Parliamentary *surveillance* forget
the age in which they live. Somewhere the nominations to Indian
cadetships, judgeships, and commissionerships must lie; and, surely
they are as safe in the hands of a functionary having a seat in the
House of Commons or the House of Lords, and responsible for all his
acts, as in those of the Company, who, as a corporation having neither
body, soul, nor heart, can set public opinion at defiance. ...

The vice of circumlocution was brought to elaborate perfection by the
joint efforts of the Board of Control and the Court of Directors. ...

It is, evident however, that we must get rid of the present complicated
system, by which action is paralysed. ...'[16]

**The above quotation shows how the reforming philosophy of mid 19th
century 'liberal democracy' was imbued with a strong tinge of arrogant
cultural imperialism. Democracy at home meant the expansion of political
power to the middle class heirs of industrialization. Radicalism in the
empire meant the destruction of traditional cultures and the establishment
of 'enlightened despotisms' to spread British civilization.**

15. *N.W.* 6 February 1858.

16. *N.W.* 15 February 1858.

APPENDIX B

Parliamentary Papers, **Accounts and papers, 1859, (48, 2nd Session, XXV,p. 331.) Letter from R. Temple, secretary to the chief commissioner of the Punjab, to G. F. Edmonstone, secretary to the governor general, 28 April 1858, outlining Sir John Lawrence's viewpoint of the causation of the mutiny and Bahadur Shah's role in the rebellion. In the** *Parliamentary Papers* **this document is misleadingly entitled,** *Letter of the Chief Commissioner of the Punjab, forwarding to the Governor General of India the proceedings on the trial of the King of Delhi.*

'... It is Sir John Lawrence's very decided impression that this mutiny had its origin in the army itself; that it is not attributable to any external or any antecedent conspiracy whatever, although it was afterwards taken advantage of by disaffected persons to compass their own ends; and that its proximate cause was the cartridge affair, and nothing else. ...

... It may be that discontented sepoys worked upon the minds of their less guileless comrades, and persuaded them that a sinister but systematic attempt was about to be made on their ceremonial religion; and that in many regiments the majority were misled by designing individuals. But as a body, the native army did really believe that the universal introduction of cartridges destructive of their caste was a matter only of time. ...

... the first feelings of disaffection, arose among the high caste Hindoos, Brahmins and Rajpoots of both the infantry and the cavalry; this disaffection then spread to the Mahomedans of the same regiments. With them also the feeling was at first a desire to resist the infringement of their caste and religion. Then, when they saw that the mutiny, which had now settled deep in the minds and hearts of the Hindoos, might be expanded into a political movement calculated to subserve Mussalman interests, they sedulously fanned the flame ... the Hindoos and Mahomedans of the line had united to mutiny ... .

... But although stories against the British were fabricated and circulated by persons with ulterior designs; although individual intrigues were rife within and without the army; though the Mahomedans very frequently breathed a spirit of fanatic ferocity against the British, yet all their influences could not have drawn our native army from its allegiance, if it had not been already penetrated by that unfortunate belief about the cartridges. Nor would such an ill feeling have so speedily arisen, nor would it have produced such a desperate disaffection, if the army had not been in an unsound and unsatisfactory state for some years past ... .

... in the Chief Commissioner's belief, there was not any conspiracy in the army irrespective of the cartridge affair, and no really organized conspiracy even in respect of that. The sepoys had corresponded in order to unite in refusing the cartridges; ... they had probably engaged to stand by one another in resistance to the supposed oppression; and being a fraternity with hopes, fears, prejudices, feelings all in common, they all felt that such an engagement would be acted up to by the whole body. No doubt the course of affairs at Meerut precipitated the outbreak, and it is vain to speculate as to what could have been designed if that outbreak had been postponed. But it seems that no regular rising had up to that time been planned. ...

It was when the native army at large saw the immense success of the Meerut and Delhi mutineers, and the disasters of the British in the first instance, that they resolved to convert what had been a combination against supposed oppression into a struggle for empire and for a general military domination. ...

Next I am to state that Sir John Lawrence does not believe that there was any previous conspiracy, Mahomedan or other, extending first through the influential classes in the country, then to the native army. If there were such a thing, how comes it that no trace has been discovered in this part of India, the very quarter where any such conspiracy must have been hatched? How can it reasonably be explained, why none of those who have adhered to our cause were acquainted with such a conspiracy? The number of those who were with us in Hindoostan may have been small, as compared with the number of those who were against us; but still the number of our adherents was considerable. Of these many remained true to us under all trials; others again died fighting on our side, yet not one of these has ever been able to speak of any general conspiracy previous to the outbreak. Again none of the mutineers and rebels who paid for their guilt the forfeit of their lives ever confessed in their last moments a knowledge of any such conspiracy, though they knew that any revelations on this subject would have saved them from death. ...

... Furthermore the Chief Commissioner considers that the conduct of the people generally negatives the supposition of a general conspiracy. If the people had conspired with the army, why was not the first outbreak immediately followed by a general insurrection?   If there was concert and premeditation then why did not the population obey the first signals of revolt, such remarkable and encouraging signals as they were? Why did not all Hindoostan rebel directly that Delhi had fallen to the mutineers, when the English there had been massacred, ... when the King's sons, courtiers, and retainers had joined, and when the King himself had consented to head the movement? Why had not the population everywhere taken advantage immediately of our weakness? ...

... The fact that afterwards in many districts the people threw off or ignored our authority, and that many individuals, and some classes openly rose against us, will by no means prove a preconcerted conspiracy, but on the contrary, will admit of much explanation. In no case did popular tumult precede the military outbreak; but invariably where it occurred at all, it ensued upon a mutiny, like cause following effect. The population generally were passive at first. Then as it appeared that the British were being swept off the face of the land, every village began to follow its own course. In most districts there was of course more or less of misconduct. But through the whole time the people, even in the worst districts, never embarrassed us half as much as they would have done had they been rebels at heart. Large masses of people were coerced by the mutineers into insurrection, if insurrection it could be called; where, again, the mutineers were beaten and expelled, the country rapidly settled down to peace and order. Wherever our officers were able to hold their own, the people remained wholly or partially tranquil; when British rule ceased, utter disorder necessarily followed. ...

Appendix B

... When the influential classes, whom our policy had provoked,
found that the native army was ripe for revolt, they added fuel to
a rising fire; and when the crisis arrived, mutiny was immediately
followed by insurrection. ...'

N

APPENDIX C

Times **report of Dr Graham's death, 31 August 1857, p. 6, col. 1.**

'... But at Sealkote a terrible tragedy has been enacted. There, on
the morning of the 9th [of July], the wing of the 9th light cavalry
and the 46th native infantry rose in mutiny. Brigadier Brind,
commanding the station was shot while riding out of his compound.
Captain Bishop, of the 46th, was waylaid by a trooper, who brought him
from the saddle by a shot from his carbine, and, then reloading, fired
again and killed him as he lay wounded on the ground. Most of the
other officers, though repeatedly fired at, gained the fort in safety.
Dr Graham was driving his daughter thither in his gig, when a
trooper rode up to him and shot him dead. His daughter seized the
reins, and drove screaming into the nearest compound with her father's
body in her lap. I think it fitting that you should know something
in England of what your countrymen have been going through, or I
should shrink from making public this poor young lady's sorrow. She
escaped, however, as did the family with whom she took refuge, though
exposed for hours to the most imminent danger of sudden and violent
death. Their hiding place was good, and was discovered by one only
of the mutineers, who met a fitting fate from the barrel of a revolver.
The rebels having sacked the station, rushed off, and three days
afterwards crossed the river Ravee by a ford. There they were
attacked by Brigadier Nicholson with his flying column ... with
considerable loss of life and the capture of the camp and plunder. ...'[1]

Dr Graham's memorial at Sialkot

1. Cited, S. Patton, *Reflections on the Indian Mutiny 1857: An Ulster
Perspective,* unpublished undergraduate dissertation, Queen's University
Belfast, 1978, pp. 22-23.

Glossary and Index

155

GLOSSARY OF ANGLO-INDIAN AND INDIAN WORDS

anna: an Indian coin

bagh: garden

bahadur (bahadoor): Indian title of respect, literally meaning gallant

batta: a military bounty or special allowance

bazaar (bazar): market or market-place

bearer: a servant who; carries a load, acts as a personal valet, or who carries messages

bhisti (bheestie): water carrier

brahmin (brahman, brammin): high caste Hindu of priestly status

burdar: a bearer who carries a load

chaprasi (chuprassie): office messenger who often carried an inscribed badge of office

dawk (dak): Indian post, mails carried by relay of runners (**dawk-wallahs**)

dhal (dal): an Indian variety of legume

dhobi(e): washerman

dooli (dhoolie, doolie): canvas bed, litter or stretcher

dour (douar): military campaign composed of a series of fast-moving marches

firinghi (feringhee, feringhi): a European

gharry: carriage or cart

ghat (ghaat, ghaut): river jetty or landing place

ghazi (ghazee): a Muslim warrier fighting in a holy war or jihad - literally a holyman, colloquially a madman

ghee: clarified butter

go-down: warehouse or store

goojur: robber

griffin (griff): a newly arrived European in India, literally a novice or greenhorn

havildar: a non-commissioned officer in a sepoy regiment corresponding to a sergeant in a European regiment

khansamah: cook

khidmutgar (khitmatgar): butler or waiter

kooch (koosh): safe, secure, comfortable etc.

kunkur: roadstone

lac (lak, lakh): a hundred thousand

mahout: elephant driver

maidan: parade ground

maund (mannd): Indian measure of weight

metha: sweeper

moulvi: Muslim teacher of Islamic law and theology

mujawa: pannier

ottali: ground corn with unsifted husks

pice: an Indian coin of small denomination

puggree (puggaree, pugree): light turban or a thin muslin scarf worn around, or at the back of a hat as a protection from the sun

pukka (puka): genuine, correct, permanent - original Hindi meaning for something properly cooked or ripe

punkah: a large fan fixed to a wall or ceiling, and pulled to and fro by a servant **(punkah-wallah)** via a system of cords

purbiah (poorbiah): a high Hindu caste, found especially in Oudh, and recruited for the Bengal East India Company army

rupee: Indian coin

sahib log: the European ruling class in India under the British Raj

soojee: flour made from Indian wheat, or a nutritious food made from the same

sowar: native cavalryman

subahdar: senior native officer in charge of a company of sepoys

suttee: immolation of a Hindu wife on her husband's funeral pyre

syce (sais): groom

tat (tatoo): pony

tathi (tatty): matting of cuscus grass, hung and wetted, which cools and perfumes the air

thermantidote: a cooling fan which combined the features of a 'punkah' and a 'tathi' (see both above)

thuggee: institutionalized robbery and murder (by strangulation), carried out by a sect who worshipped the Hindu goddess Kali

tope: a grove, especially of mango trees

SELECTIVE INDEX

Afghanistan, xiv, xxviii, xxxiii

Agra, *passim*
  panic of Europeans at, 29

Albert, Prince Consort, lvii, 64, 67, 71

Aligarh, *passim*
  defection of 9th native infantry at, 21
  skirmish at, 6

Ambala, *passim*
  loyalty of sepoys at, 61

Amritsar, *passim*
  loyalty of sepoys at, 20, 43

Anglo-Indian society, *passim*
  organisation and nature of, ix-xi, xvi, xxii, xxv, 19
  views of Britain, xi, xii and n.6

Anson, George, commander-in-chief, xxxiv, xxxvi, lvii, 20, 21, 62, 65-67, 70

Army, *see under* East India Company's, and Her Majesty's

Bahadur Shah, xxi, xxiii, xxxiii, lviii, 69, 80, 82, 83, 85, 86, 91, 127,
  135, 142, 144, 151, 152

Bannu, xiv

Barnard, Lieutenant General Sir William Henry, xxxvi, 28, 42, 65, 70

Belfast, 87, 128, 143, 148

Bengal Bank, 46

Blackwood, Frederick Temple Hamilton-Temple-, 1st Marquess of Dufferin and
  Ava, ix and n.1, x and n.5, 144

Bombay Bank, 46

Britain, *passim*
  imperial civilizing mission, xx, xxiii-xxvi
  reaction in, to news of mutiny, xx, lvi, 19, 34, 41
  society at time of mutiny, ixx, xx

Brown Bess musket, ixxx

Campbell, Sir Colin, commander-in-chief (created Baron Clyde in 1858), 8,
  10, 97, 108, 129

Cave-Browne, Rev. J, 27

Chamberlain, Brigadier Neville, xxxiv and n's. 48 & 50, xxxvii, 26, 28, 30,
  32, 34, 36, 38, 40, 42, 43

Ghazni, xiv

Ghurkas, xlv, xlvi, 65, 66, 69, 78, *see also* Jang Bahadur and Nepal

Graham family, *passim*
  Anglo-Indian tradition of, ix-xii
  genealogy of, viii
  origins, ix
  papers of, significance and organisation, xvi-xviii and n.21,
  lvii-lix
  role in mutiny, xv-xvii, lvii-lix

Graham, Dr James, *passim*
  establishment of family's Anglo-Indian tradition, x
  military service, ix n.4, x
  quarrel with son James, xvii, 27, 44, 51
  views on sepoys, xvii, lix, 17, 18, 22, 23, 25, 29, 33-35, 38, 42-44
  death of, xv, xxxv and n.51, 44, 71-73, 76, 87, 111, 154
  will of, 44, 45, 50, 51, 72, 73, 82, 85, 86, 88, 91-93, 98, 99, 102,
    111-113, 116, 120-124
  character of, xvii, 44, 72, 73, 87, 99, 111

Graham, James (1830-c.1905), *passim*
  military service of, x n.4, xvii
  finances during mutiny, 14
  view of Muslim mutiny conspiracy, lviii, 66, 69
  mutiny will of, 92
  retirement of, xvii
  character of, xvii

Graham, James (1831-57), *passim*
  quarrel with father over marriage, xvii, 27, 44, 51
  military service of, x n.4
  suicide of, xvi, xvii, 51-54, 92, 93, 95, 96, 102, 111
  character of, xvii, 51, 92, 96, 111

Graham, Sarah, *passim*
  remains at Sialkot when other Sialkot ladies leave, 23, 27
  view of Sialkot chaplain, lviii, 27, 95
  ill with fever, 34-38, 40-42, 68, 70, 74
  pension from military orphan's fund, 14, 46, 47, 56, 112
  attitude towards her brother James, xvii, 95, 96
  character, xvii, 34

Graham, Sarah Ann (née Riddell), *passim*
  marriage to James Graham, xvii
  death of children during Lucknow siege, 51

Graham, Thomas Chadwick, *passim*
  military service of, x n.4
  illness and wounding of, 54-56, 112, 113, 116, 123
  character of, xvii

Graham, William Stuart, *passim*
  military service of, ix n.4,
  tries to heal breach between his father and brother
  James, 27

efforts to have his father reburied, 87
witnesses executions of mutineers, 33
experiences at Delhi during assault, xvii, 48-50, 80-82, 84, 87
ill with cholera after Delhi campaign, 5, 49, 50, 84-86
romance with Miss Roberts, 46, 50, 51, 60, 85, 86, 88, 93, 95, 97, 99, 102, 106, 110, 111, 113
marriage, 118, 124-127
character of, xvii, 118, 121, 125

Grant, General Sir James Hope, 11, 13, 104-108, 115, 120, 121, 123, 138

Grant, Sir Patrick, commander-in-chief at Madras, 24, 25, 31, 63, 64, 67, 71

greased cartridge, xxi, xxiii, xxviii, ixxx, xxxi, xxxii, xxxix, 3, 65, 142, 151

Great Exhibition, ixx, xx n.24

Greathed, Harvey, lv and n.3, 49

Hanna, Rev. Hugh, 87

Havelock, General Sir Henry, 70, 76

Her Majesty's Army, *passim*

REGIMENTS
8th regiment of foot, 30, 31, 34
9th regiment of lancers, 62
24th regiment of foot, 22, 40-42, 44
27th regiment of foot, 18
37th regiment of foot, 43
38th regiment of foot, 102
52nd regiment of foot, 20, 22, 24
56th regiment of foot, 126
60th rifles, 62
61st regiment of foot, 30, 31
64th regiment of foot, 41
75th regiment of lancers, 62
78th regiment of foot, 41
84th regiment of foot, 35, 41, 43

Hertford, Marquess of, *see under* Seymour-Conway

Hodson, Major William S.R. xl, 11 and n.8, 78

Hodson's Horse, 11 and n.8, 90

Hogg, Sir James Weir, xiii, 143

Ilbert Sir Courtney, xlviii n.72

imperial wars, ixx and n.1

Indian nationalism, xxi and n.27, xxii, xlv, xlix-li, 143, 144

Irish educational system, 111, 112

162

Virgemont, County Dublin, xiii and n.9

'white mutiny', xliv

Wilson, Brigadier Sir Archdale, xxxvi-xxxviii, 23-26, 33

Wiseman, Nicholas, cardinal archbishop of Westminister, 146 and n.9

Printed in Northern Ireland for Her Majesty's Stationery Office
by Brough. Cox and Dunn Ltd. Belfast. Dd.8073793. 1m. 3/80. Gp.55-5272.